D0597675

Captivating
CROCHET™

the Needlecraft Shop™

Publisher: Donna Robertson
Design Director: Fran Rohus
Production Director: Ange Van Arman

EDITORIAL
Senior Editor: Jennifer Simcik McClain
Editor: Sharon Lothrop
Associate Editors: Jana Robertson, Trudy Atteberry

PHOTOGRAPHY
Photographers: Mary Craft, Tammy Cromer-Campbell
Photo Stylist/Coordinator: Ruth Whitaker
Assistant Photo Stylist: Jan Jaynes
Cover Photograph: Tammy Cromer-Campbell

BOOK DESIGN/PRODUCTION
Production Manager: Betty Gibbs

PRODUCT DESIGN
Design Coordinator: Brenda Wendling

BUSINESS
CEO: John Robinson **Vice President / Customer Service:** Karen Pierce
Vice President / Marketing: Greg Deily **Vice President / M.I.S.:** John Trotter

CREDITS
Sincerest thanks to all the designers, manufacturers and other professionals whose
dedication has made this book possible. Special thanks to David Norris and
Kaye Stafford of Quebecor Printing Book Group, Kingsport, TN.

Copyright © 1996 *The Needlecraft Shop, LLC*
All rights reserved. No part of this book may be reproduced in any form or
by any means without the written permission of the publisher, excepting brief
quotations in connection with reviews written specifically for inclusion in
magazines, newspapers and other publications.

Library of Congress Cataloging-in-Publication Data
ISBN: 1-57367-048-0
First Printing: 1996
Library of Congress Catalog Card Number: 95-72040
Published and Distributed by
The Needlecraft Shop, LLC, Big Sandy, Texas 75755
Printed in the United States of America.

Poetry composed by Sharon Lothrop.

Dear Friends,

Each stitch lovingly created by hand, crochet always has and always will be a needlecraft of the heart. Just as our lives are made up of bits and pieces of memories and dreams joined in a continuous circle, so crochet mimics life by joining tiny stitches to form a thing of enduring pleasure and beauty. From timeless, elegant thread work to warm, cozy throws, crochet is truly a captivating art. That's the feeling we kept in mind when choosing all the wonderful products that make up this one-of-a-kind collection. You'll find something for every occasion, every room, every person.

Grace your home with the enchanting ambiance of lacy doilies and filigree ornaments to enhance everyday moments. Add lazy, colorful charm to your bedroom or den with soft, fuzzy afghans that make staying home the top activity on your list. Stitch cute home decor or casual wearables as heartfelt remembrances for friends and loved ones. Regardless of the reason or the season, you're sure to find the perfect pattern among the pages of this unique book, complete with an inspiring original poem to set the mood for each chapter.

Next time you want to show your love and appreciation to someone special, pick up your hook and appeal to their heart with the captivating beauty of crochet.

Pleasant stitching,

Jennifer

CONTENTS

POETIC PLEASURES

ONE GLORIOUS DAY

The days were dark, drizzly, rainy, and gray.
It was cold and lonely as the hours slipped away.

Then I awoke one morning to an enchanting sight.
The sky was blue, beautiful, and bright.

The wind struck a song as it brushed through the trees.
The grass whispered a prayer as it felt the warm breeze.

The birds shouted with glee as they played up above,
and my heart rose with gladness to laughter and love.

Next day, as before, winter returned to the land.
Snow came in a rush like the stroke of a hand.

But my heart still was light as I went on my way,
For God promised hope in one glorious day.

Magical texture stitched in pristine white creates a beautiful piano scarf that would also enhance your dining decor as a table runner. You'll appreciate the lasting elegance of this classic design.

DIAMOND MOTIF PIANO SCARF

DESIGNED BY DOT DRAKE

SIZE
13" x 36".

MATERIALS
Size 10 bedspread cotton — 350 yds. white;
No. 7 steel crochet hook or size needed
to obtain gauge.

GAUGE
Rnds 1-3 of Motif = 1½" across. Each
Motif = 4½" across.

MOTIF NO. 1

Rnd 1: (Ch 3, sc in 3rd ch from hook) 4 times, join with sl st in first ch of first ch-3 to form ring (4 ch sps).

Rnd 2: (Ch 5, sc in ring between next 2 ch sps) 3 times, ch 5, sc in ring between last and first ch sps (4 ch-5 sps).

NOTE: For **picot,** ch 3, sl st in top of last st made.

Rnd 3: Ch 1, (4 sc, picot, 4 sc) in each ch-5 sp around, join with sl st in first sc (32 sc, 4 picots).

Rnd 4: Ch 1, sc in same st, ch 12, skip next 3 sts, skip next picot, skip next 4 sts, (sc in next st, ch 12, skip next 3 sts, skip next picot, skip next 4 sts) around, join (4 ch-12 sps).

Rnd 5: Ch 1, 17 sc in each ch-12 sp around, join (68 sc).

Rnd 6: Ch 1, sc in each of first 2 sts, *[ch 2, skip next st, (dc in next st, ch 2, skip next st) 2 times, tr in next st, (ch 2, tr in next st) 2 times, ch 2, skip next st, (dc in next st, ch 2, skip next st) 2 times], sc in next 4 sts; repeat from * 2 more times; repeat between [ ], sc in each of last 2 sts, join (44 sts, 32 ch-2 sps).

Rnd 7: Sl st in next st, ch 1, sc in same st, *[(2 sc in next ch-2 sp, sc in next st) 3 times, picot, 2 sc in next ch-2 sp, sc in next st, ch 5, drop lp from hook, insert hook in top of last sc made, draw dropped lp through, 10 sc in ch-5 lp just made, sl st in same st on rnd 6, 2 sc in next ch-2 sp, sc in next st, picot, (2 sc in next ch-2 sp, sc in next st) 3 times, skip next 2 sts], sc in next st; repeat from * 2 more times; repeat between [ ], join, fasten off.

MOTIF NO. 2

NOTES: For **joining picot,** ch 1, sc in next picot on corresponding Motif, ch 1.

For **joining ch-5 lp,** ch 5, drop lp from hook, insert hook in top of last sc made, draw dropped lp through, 5 sc in ch-5 lp just made, sc in 5th sc of next ch-5 lp on corresponding Motif, 5 sc in same ch-5 lp on this Motif.

Rnds 1-6: Repeat same rnds of Motif No. 1.

Rnd 7: Sl st in next st, ch 1, sc in same st, (2 sc in next ch-2 sp, sc in next st) 3 times, picot, 2 sc in next ch-2 sp, sc in next st; working on side of Motif No. 1 according to Joining Diagram on page 17, work joining ch-5 lp, sl st in same st on rnd 6, 2 sc in next ch-2 sp, sc in next st, joining picot, (2 sc in next ch-2 sp, sc in next st), 3 times, skip next 2 sts, sc in next st, (2 sc in next ch-2 sp, sc in next st) 3 times, joining picot, 2 sc in next ch-2 sp, sc in next st, joining ch-5 lp, sl st in same st on rnd 6, *[2 sc in next ch-2 sp, sc in next st, picot, (2 sc in next ch-2 sp, sc in next st) 3 times, skip next 2 sts], sc in next st, (2 sc in next ch-2 sp, sc in next st) 3 times, picot, 2 sc in next ch-2 sp, sc in next st, ch 5, drop lp from hook, insert hook in top of last sc made, draw dropped lp through, 10 sc in ch-5 lp just made, sl st in same st on rnd 6; repeat from *; repeat between [ ], join, fasten off.

MOTIFS NO. 3-34

Join Motifs according to Joining Diagram.

Rnds 1-6: Repeat same rnds of Motif No. 1.

Rnd 7: Repeat same rnd of Motif No. 1 using joining picots and joining ch-5 lps when joining Motifs.❖

Surprise a special friend or secret pal with a dainty bookmark stitched in size 30 crochet cotton. What could be more heartfelt than a hand-crafted gift made with affection and love.

LACY BOOKMARKS

DESIGNED BY KIM GOETZ

SIZE
Picot Ribbon Bookmark is 12" long. Heart Bookmark is 10" long.

MATERIALS
Size 30 crochet cotton — 100 yds. white; 12" piece ⅜" satin picot ribbon; No. 10 steel crochet hook or size needed to obtain gauge.

GAUGE
3 sc and 2 ch-3 sps = ½".

NOTE
For **cluster (cl)**, *yo, insert hook in st, yo, draw lp through, yo, draw through 2 lps on hook; repeat from * one time in same st, yo, draw through all 3 lps on hook.

PICOT RIBBON BOOKMARK

Row 1: For **first side,** join with sc in first picot on ribbon, (ch 3, sc in next picot) across, turn.

Row 2: Ch 4, sc in first ch-3 sp, (ch 3, sc in next ch-3 sp) across, ch 1, dc in last sc, turn.

Row 3: Ch 1, sc in first dc, ch 1, cl in next sc, ch 1, sc in next ch-3 sp, *ch 3, sc in next ch-3 sp, ch 1, cl in next sc, ch 1, sc in next ch-3 sp; repeat from * across to last ch-4 sp, ch 3, sc in 3rd ch of last ch-4, turn.

Row 4: Ch 4, sl st in first ch-3 sp, ch 3, sl st in top of next cl, *dc in next ch-3 sp, (ch 1, dc) 4 times in same sp, sl st in top of next cl; repeat from * across, fasten off.

For **2nd side,** working in picots on opposite side of ribbon, work same as first side.

HEART BOOKMARK

Row 1: Ch 25, sc in 2nd ch from hook, (ch 3, skip next 2 chs, sc in next ch) 7 times, ch 1, skip next ch, dc in last ch, turn (8 ch sps).

Rows 2-4: Ch 1, sc in first dc, (ch 3, sc in next ch-3 sp) 7 times, ch 1, dc in last sc, turn.

Row 5: Ch 1, sc in first dc, (ch 3, sc in next ch-3 sp) 3 times, ch 1, cl in next sc, ch 1, sc in next ch sp, (ch 3, sc in next ch sp) 3 times, ch 1, dc in last sc, turn.

Row 6: Ch 1, sc in first dc, (ch 3, sc in next ch-3 sp) 3 times, ch 1, cl in next sc, ch 1, sc in next cl, ch 1, cl in next sc, ch 1, sc in next ch sp, (ch 3, sc in next ch sp) 2 times, ch 1, dc in last sc, turn.

Row 7: Ch 1, sc in first dc, (ch 3, sc in next ch sp) 2 times, (ch 1, cl in next sc, ch 1, sc in next cl) 2 times, ch 1, cl in next sc, ch 1, sc in next ch sp, (ch 3, sc in next ch sp) 2 times, ch 1, dc in last sc, turn.

Row 8: Ch 1, sc in first dc, (ch 3, sc in next ch sp) 2 times, (ch 1, cl in next sc, ch 1, sc in next cl) 3 times, ch 1, cl in next sc, ch 1, sc in next ch sp, ch 3, sc in next ch sp, ch 1, dc in last sc, turn.

Row 9: Ch 1, sc in first dc, ch 3, sc in next ch sp, (ch 1, cl in next sc, ch 1, sc in next cl) 4 times, ch 1, cl in next sc, ch 1, sc in next ch sp, ch 3, sc in next ch sp, ch 1, dc in last sc, turn.

Row 10: Ch 1, sc in first dc, ch 3, sc in next ch sp, ch 3, sc in next cl, (ch 1, cl in next sc, ch 1, sc in next cl) 4 times, ch 3, sc in next ch sp, ch 1, dc in last sc, turn.

Row 11: Ch 1, sc in first dc, ch 3, sc in next ch sp, (ch 3, sc in next cl, ch 1, cl in next sc, ch 1, sc in next cl) 2 times, (ch 3, sc in next ch sp) 2 times, ch 1, dc in last sc, turn.

Row 12: Ch 1, sc in first dc, (ch 3, sc in next ch sp) 2 times, ch 3, sc in next cl, ch 3, sc in next ch sp, ch 3, sc in next cl, (ch 3, sc in next ch sp) 2 times, ch 1, dc in last sc, turn.

Rows 13-14: Repeat row 2.

Rows 15-16: Repeat rows 5 and 6.

Row 17: Ch 1, sc in first dc, (ch 3, sc in next ch sp) 2 times, (ch 3, sc in next cl) 2 times, (ch 3, sc in next ch sp) 3 times, ch 1, dc in last sc, turn.

Row 18: Ch 1, sc in first dc, (ch 3, sc in next ch sp) 2 times, ch 1, cl in next sc, ch 1, sc in next ch sp, (ch 3, sc in next ch sp) 2 times, ch 1, cl in next sc, ch 1, sc in next ch sp, ch 3, sc in next ch sp, ch 1, dc in last sc, turn.

Row 19: Ch 1, sc in first dc, (ch 3, sc in next ch sp, ch 1, cl in next sc, ch 1, sc in next cl, ch 1, cl in next sc, ch 1, sc in next ch sp) 2 times, ch 3, sc in next ch sp, ch 1, dc in last sc, turn.

Row 20: Ch 1, sc in first dc, *ch 3, sc in next ch sp, (ch 3, sc in next cl) 2 times; repeat from *, ch 3, sc in next ch sp, ch 1, dc in last sc, turn.

Rows 21-22: Repeat rows 5 and 6.

Row 23: Repeat row 17.

Rows 24-80: Repeat rows 2-23 consecutively, ending with row 14. At end of last row, fasten off.❖

Purple, teal and pink fashioned into lacy floral motifs, reflect crochet perfection at its finest. The unusual two-piece block in this colorful design lends an interesting kaleidoscope effect.

Starflower Afghan

Designed by Susie Spier Maxfield

SIZE
49" x 65".

MATERIALS
Worsted-weight yarn — 35 oz. purple/teal/pink variegated, 27 oz. teal, 17 oz. purple and 10 oz. pink; tapestry needle; G crochet hook or size needed to obtain gauge.

GAUGE
4 dc = 1"; 2 dc rows = 1". Each Block is 8" square.

BLOCK (make 48)
Top
Rnd 1: With pink, ch 4, sl st in first ch to form ring, ch 1, (sc in ring, ch 8) 8 times, join with sl st in first sc, fasten off (8 sc, 8 ch-8 sps).

Rnd 2: Join teal with sc in any ch sp, ch 10, (sc in next ch sp, ch 10) around, join, fasten off.

Rnd 3: Join teal with sc in any ch sp, ch 12, (sc in next ch sp, ch 12) around, join, fasten off.

Bottom
Rnd 1: With variegated, ch 4, sl st in first ch to form ring, ch 3, 2 dc in ring, ch 3, (3 dc in ring, ch 3) 3 times, join with sl st in top of ch-3 (12 dc, 4 ch sps).

NOTE: For **beginning shell (beg shell),** (ch 3, 2 dc, ch 3, 3 dc) in same ch sp.

For shell, (3 dc, ch 3, 3 dc) in next ch sp.

Rnd 2: Sl st in each of next 2 sts, sl st in next ch sp, beg shell, ch 1, (shell in next ch sp, ch 1) around, join (4 shells, 4 ch-1 sps).

Rnd 3: Sl st in each of next 2 sts, sl st in next ch sp, beg shell, ch 1, 3 dc in next ch-1 sp, ch 1, (shell in ch sp of next shell, ch 1, 3 dc in next ch-1 sp, ch 1) around, join.

Rnds 4-5: Sl st in each of next 2 sts, sl st in next ch sp, beg shell, ch 1, (3 dc in next ch-1 sp, ch 1) across to next shell, *shell in next shell, ch 1, (3 dc in next ch-1 sp, ch 1) across to next shell; repeat from * around, join. At end of last rnd, fasten off.

Rnd 6: Join purple with sl st in any shell, beg shell, dc in each of next 3 sts; holding Top over Bottom and working through both thicknesses, dc in next ch-1 sp on Bottom and any ch-12 sp of Top at the same time, [◊(dc in each of next 3 sts on Bottom, dc in next ch-1 sp) 2 times, dc in each of next 3 sts, *dc in next ch-1 sp on Bottom and next ch-12 sp on Top at same time*, dc in each of next 3 sts on Bottom◊, shell in next shell, dc in each of next 3 sts; repeat between **]; repeat between [ ] 2 more times; repeat between ◊◊, join, fasten off.

Rnd 7: Join teal with sl st in any shell, beg shell, dc in each st around with shell in each shell, join, fasten off (31 dc on each side between corner ch sps).

Holding Blocks wrong sides together, matching sts, with teal, sew together through **back lps** in six rows of eight Blocks each.

BORDER
Rnd 1: Join pink with sc in any corner ch sp, (2 sc, ch 3, 3 sc) in same sp, sc in each st and in each ch sp on each side of seams around with (3 sc, ch 3, 3 sc) in each corner ch sp, join with sl st in first sc (202 sc on each short end between corner ch sps, 268 sc on each long edge between corner ch sps).

Rnd 2: Sl st in each of next 2 sts, sl st in next ch sp, ch 1, (sc, ch 2, dc, sc, ch 2, dc) in same sp, [◊skip next st, *(sc, ch 2, dc) in next st, skip next 2 sts; repeat from * across◊ to next corner ch sp, (sc, ch 2, dc, sc, ch 2, dc) in next corner ch sp]; repeat between [ ] 2 more times; repeat between ◊◊, join, fasten off.❖

A fragile heart stuffed with aromatic potpourri and a dainty cross, both embellished with silk flowers and colorful gemstones, will make wonderful gifts for family or friends any season of the year.

HEART & CROSS

DESIGNED BY JO ANN MAXWELL

SIZE
Heart is 4" x 4" not including hanger.
Cross is 4¾" x 6" not including hanger.

MATERIALS FOR HEART
Size 10 bedspread cotton — 75 yds. ecru; 4 small silk rosebuds; 20" pink ⅛" satin ribbon; small amount gold metallic dried baby's breath flowers; 3 ruby ¼" beads; 2" gold tassel; 5" piece metallic gold cord; 6" pink net fabric circle; ¼ cup potpourri; gold metallic thread; craft glue; liquid fabric stiffener; two 3" plastic hearts; Styrofoam® or blocking board; plastic wrap; beading needle; rustproof pins; No. 7 steel crochet hook or size needed to obtain gauge.

MATERIALS FOR CROSS
Size 10 bedspread cotton — 35 yds. ecru; 3 pink 9-mm satin ribbon roses; 2" lt. green ⅛" satin ribbon; small amount gold glitter dried baby's breath flowers; 1" jewel drop; 4-mm pearl bead; 5-mm pearl bead; invisible thread; craft glue; liquid fabric stiffener; Styrofoam® or blocking board; plastic wrap; beading needle; rustproof pins; No. 7 steel crochet hook or size needed to obtain gauge.

GAUGE
Rnd 1 of Heart = 1" across. Rnd 1 of Cross (excluding loops) = ¾" across.

HEART SIDE (make 2)
Rnd 1: Ch 16, sl st in first ch to form ring, ch 1, sc in same ch, 2 sc in each of next 7 chs, sc in next ch, 2 sc in each of last 7 chs, join with sl st in first sc (30 sc).

NOTE: For **double treble crochet (dtr)**, yo 3 times, insert hook in next st, yo, draw lp through, (yo, draw through 2 lps on hook) 4 times.

Rnd 2: Working this rnd in **back lps** only, ch 6, tr in next st, ch 3, skip next st, (dtr in next st, ch 3, skip next st) 3 times, tr in next st, ch 3, skip next st, (dc in next st, ch 3, skip next st) 2 times; for **bottom point**, (tr, ch 3, tr) in next st; ch 3, skip next st, (dc in next st, ch 3, skip next st) 2 times, tr in next st, ch 3, skip next st, (dtr in next st, ch 3, skip next st) 3 times, tr in last st, ch 3, join with sl st in 3rd ch of ch-6 (17 sts, 17 ch-3 sps).

Rnd 3: Sc in next ch, 3 sc in next ch, sc in next ch, (sl st in next st, sc in next ch, 3 sc in next ch, sc in next ch) around, join with sl st in joining sl st on last rnd (85 sc, 17 sl sts).

NOTE: For ¼"-**love knot (¼"-lk)**, draw up ¼"-long lp on hook, yo, draw lp through, sc in back strand of long lp (see Steps 1-3 of illustration on pg 16).

For **shell**, (2 dc, ch 2, 2 dc) in next st.

Rnd 4: Ch 1, sc in same st, ch 2, *sc in 2nd st of next 3-sc group, (ch 1, ¼"-lk, sc in 2nd st of next 3-sc group) 7 times*, ch 3, shell in 2nd st of next 3-sc group at bottom point, ch 3; repeat between **, ch 2, join with sl st in first sc.

Rnd 5: Ch 1, sc in same st, ch 1, shell in next sc, *ch 3, skip next lk, (shell in next sc, ch 3, skip next lk) 6 times*, dc in next ch-3 sp, dc in each of next 2 dc, shell in next ch-2 sp, dc in each of next 2 dc, dc in next ch-3 sp; repeat between **, shell in next sc, ch 1, join with sl st in first sc, fasten off.

FINISHING
1: Apply liquid fabric stiffener to Heart Sides according to manufacturer's instructions.

2: Shape each Heart Side over one plastic heart, pin to plastic covered blocking board stretching out shells and bottom point of rnd 5. Let dry completely.

3: Place potpourri in center of net circle. Run gathering thread around outer edge of circle, pull tight to form bag; secure ends.

4: With wrong sides held together and potpourri bag between, glue shells of rnd 5 on Hearts together.

5: Cut 2 pieces ribbon each 9" long. With both pieces held together, tie into a bow. Glue bow, 3 rosebuds and small amount of baby's breath to center top of Heart.

6: Glue remaining rosebud and tiny amount of baby's breath to bottom point of Heart. Fold two 1" pieces of ribbon in half, glue ends to each side of rosebud.

7: Thread tassel and ruby beads onto gold metallic thread, tie to bottom of Heart.

8: For **hanger**, glue ends of gold cord to center top between Heart Sides.

CROSS
Rnd 1: Ch 4, sl st in first ch to form ring, ch 3, 3 dc in ring, (ch 20, sl st in first ch, 4 dc in ring) 3 times; for **bottom loop**, ch 34, sl st in first ch, join with sl st in top of ch-3 (3 ch-20 lps, 1 ch-34 lp).

NOTE: For **double ⅜"-love knot (d-⅜"-lk)**, (draw up ⅜"-long lp on hook, yo, draw lp through, sc in back strand of long lp) 2 times (see illustrations on page 16).

Rnd 2: Ch 1, d-⅜"-lk, *sl st in first ch of next ch-20 lp, sc in next ch, (2 sc in next ch, sc in next ch) 4 times, (sc, ch 2, sc) in next ch, sc in next ch, (2 sc in next ch, sc in next ch) 4 times, sl st in opposite side of first ch, ch 1, d-⅜"-lk; repeat from * 2 more times, sl st in first ch of next ch-34 lp, (sc in next ch, 2 sc in next ch) 8 times, (sc, ch 2, sc) in next ch, (2 sc in next ch, sc in next ch) 8 times, sl

Continued on page 16

HEART & CROSS

Continued from page 15

st in opposite side of first ch, **do not** join, **turn.**

NOTE: For **picot,** ch 3, sl st in top of last st made.

Rnd 3: Sl st in each of next 2 sts, **turn;** working this rnd in **back lps** only, ch 1, sc in same st, *ch 2, sc in center sc of next d-⅜"-lk, picot, ch 2, skip next 3 sts on next ch-20 lp, sc in next st, ch 2, skip next 3 sts, shell in next st, ch 2, skip next 3 sts, sc in next st, picot, ch 2, skip next 2 sts, shell in next ch-2 sp, ch 2, skip next 2 sts, sc in next st, picot, ch 2, skip next 3 sts, shell in next st, ch 2, skip next 3 sts, sc in next st; repeat from * 2 more times, ch 2, sc in center sc of next d-⅜"-lk, ch 2, skip next 2 sts on next ch-34 lp, sc in next st, (ch 2, skip next 4 sts, shell in next st, ch 2, skip next 4 sts, sc in next st, picot) 2 times, ch 2, skip next 2 sts, shell in next ch-2 sp, ch 2, skip next 2 sts, (sc in next st, picot, ch 2,

skip next 4 sts, shell in next st, ch 2, skip next 4 sts) 2 times, join with sl st in first sc, fasten off.

FINISHING

1: Apply liquid fabric stiffener to Cross according to manufacturer's instruction.

2: Pin Cross to plastic covered blocking board, stretching out ch lps and shells on points. Let dry completely.

3: Cut ribbon in half, fold each piece in half. Glue ends to center of Cross. Glue 3 roses and small amount of baby's breath around and over ribbon loops.

4: Thread jewel, large pearl and small pearl onto invisible thread. Tie to center bottom of Cross.

5: For **hanger,** tie small piece of invisible thread to center top of Cross.❖

DOUBLE LOVE KNOT ILLUSTRATION

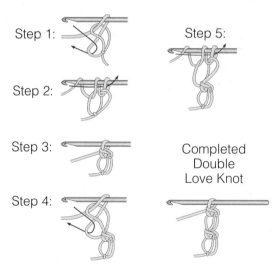

Step 1:
Step 2:
Step 3:
Step 4:
Step 5:
Completed Double Love Knot

PIANO SCARF
Instructions on page 8

JOINING DIAGRAM

Repeat joining sequence in shaded
area 4 times, then work last Motif.

Glowing with the lustrous patina of gently-aged chintz, this elegant burgundy and cream throw, cleverly crafted with a lacy texture and warm worsted-weight yarn, will be the highlight of your favorite room.

❧ BURNISHED MEDALLIONS ❧

DESIGNED BY JENNIFER CHRISTIANSEN McCLAIN

SIZE
49" x 63".

MATERIALS
Worsted-weight yarn — 23 oz. burgundy and 17 oz. off-white; H crochet hook or size needed to obtain gauge.

GAUGE
Rnds 1-3 of Large Motif = 3" across. Each Motif is 7" across.

FIRST ROW
First Large Motif
Rnd 1: With burgundy, ch 5, sl st in first ch to form ring, ch 1, 8 sc in ring, join with sl st in first sc (8 sc).

Rnd 2: Ch 1, sc in first st, ch 3, (sc in next st, ch 3) around, join (8 sc, 8 ch-3 sps).

Rnd 3: Sl st in first ch-3 sp, ch 1, (sc, ch 3, sc) in same sp, ch 1, *(sc, ch 3, sc) in next ch-3 sp, ch 1; repeat from * around, join, fasten off.

NOTE: For **cluster (cl),** *yo, insert hook in ch sp, yo, draw lp through, yo, draw through 2 lps on hook; repeat from * 2 more times in same ch sp, yo, draw through all 4 lps on hook.

Rnd 4: Join off-white with sl st in any ch-3 sp, ch 6, cl in same sp, ch 1, skip next ch-1 sp, *(sl st, ch 6, cl) in next ch-3 sp, ch 1, skip next ch-1 sp; repeat from * around, join with sl st in first sl st, fasten off.

Rnd 5: Join burgundy with sc in any ch-6 lp, ch 3, sc in same lp, (dc, ch 1, dc) in next ch-1 sp, *(sc, ch 3, sc) in next ch-6 lp, (dc, ch 1, dc) in next ch-1 sp; repeat from * around, join with sl st in first sc.

Rnd 6: Sl st in first ch-3 sp, ch 1, (sc, ch 3, sc) in same sp, ch 1, *(sc, ch 3, sc) in next ch-3 or ch-1 sp, ch 1; repeat from * around, join, fasten off.

Rnd 7: Join off-white with sl st in any ch-3 sp, ch 3, sl st in same sp, ch 2, sl st in next ch-1 sp, ch 2, *(sl st, ch 3, sl st) in next ch-3 sp, ch 2, sl st in next ch-1 sp, ch 2; repeat from * around, join with sl st in first sl st, fasten off.

Second Large Motif
Rnds 1-6: Repeat same rnds of First Large Motif.

Rnd 7: Join off-white with sl st in any ch-3 sp, ch 3, sl st in same sp, ch 2, sl st in next ch-1 sp, ch 2, sl st in next ch-3 sp; working on side of last Motif (see Joining Diagram), ch 1, sl st in any ch-3 sp on other Motif, *ch 1, sl st in same ch-3 sp on this Motif, ch 2, sl st in next ch-1 sp, ch 2, sl st in next ch-3 sp, ch 1, sl st in next ch-3 sp on other Motif; repeat from *, ch 1, sl st in same ch-3 sp on this Motif, ch 2, sl st in next ch-1 sp, ch 2, [(sl st, ch 3, sl st) in next ch-3 sp, ch 2, sl st in next ch-1 sp, ch 2]; repeat between [ ] around, join, fasten off.

Repeat Second Large Motif 5 more times for at total of 7 Motifs.

JOINING DIAGRAM

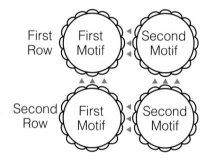

SECOND ROW
First Large Motif
Joining to bottom of First Large Motif on last row, work same as First Row Second Large Motif.

Second Large Motif
Rnds 1-6: Repeat same rnds of First Large Motif.

Rnd 7: Join off-white with sl st in any ch-3 sp, ch 3, sl st in same sp, ch 2, sl st in next ch-1 sp, ch 2, sl st in next ch-3 sp; working on bottom of next Motif on last row, [*ch 1, sl st in corresponding ch-3 sp on other Motif (see diagram), ch 1, sl st in same ch-3 sp on this Motif, ch 2, sl st in next ch-1 sp, ch 2, sl st in next ch-3 sp; repeat from * 2 more times, ch 3, sl st in same ch-3 sp on this Motif, ch 2, sl st in next ch-1 sp, ch 2], sl st in next ch-3 sp; working on side of last Motif on this row, repeat between [ ], ◊(sl st, ch 3, sl st) in next ch-3 sp, ch 2, sl st in next ch-1 sp, ch 2; repeat from ◊ around, join, fasten off.

Repeat Second Large Motif 5 more times for a

Continued on page 23

Fragile as newly fallen snowflakes, these delicate ornaments, made from fine crochet cotton and handsomely embossed with tiny seed pearls, will perfectly enhance your holiday theme.

❧ PEARL ORNAMENTS ❧

DESIGNED BY MELODY MACDUFFEE

SIZE

Bell Ornament is 4" x 4¼". Wreath Ornament is 3¾" across.

MATERIALS

Size 30 crochet cotton — 50 yds.; size 50 crochet cotton — 30 yds.; 1½ yds. white ⅛" ribbon; 77 white 4-mm pearl beads; 2 white

5-mm pearl beads; fabric stiffener; rust proof pins; plastic wrap; Styrofoam® or blocking board; stitch marker; embroidery needle; Nos. 13 and 14 steel crochet hooks or size needed to obtain gauge.

GAUGE

No. 13 hook, 1 dc = ³⁄₁₆" tall.

BELL ORNAMENT

NOTE: With embroidery needle, thread 23 white 4-mm beads onto size 30 crochet cotton. Slide beads back along thread until needed.

Row 1: With No. 13 hook and size 30 cotton, ch 1, pull up one bead, ch 4, sl st in first ch to form ring, ch 3, 5 dc in ring, turn (6 dc).

Row 2: Ch 3, dc in same st, 2 dc in each st across, turn (12). Front of row 2 is right side of work.

Row 3: Ch 5, skip next 2 sts, sl st in next st, ch 5, skip next st, sl st in sp between next 2 sts, (ch 5, skip next 2 sts, sl st in next st) 2 times, turn (4 ch sps).

Row 4: Sl st in each of first 3 chs on next ch-5, (ch 5, sl st in next ch sp) across, turn (3 ch sps).

Row 5: Ch 1, (3 sc, pull up one bead, 3 sc, pull up one bead, 2 sc) in first ch sp, (2 sc, pull up one bead, 3 sc, pull up one bead, 2 sc) in next ch sp, (2 sc, pull up one bead, 3 sc, pull up one bead, 3 sc) in last ch sp, turn (23 sc, 6 beads).

Row 6: (Ch 5, sl st around thread coming from top of next bead) 6 times, ch 5, sl st in last st, turn (7 ch sps).

Row 7: Sl st in each of first 3 chs on next ch-5, 6 dc in each of next 5 ch sps, sl st in last ch sp, turn (30 dc).

Row 8: Ch 1, sc in first 6 dc, (ch 5, skip next 2 sts, sl st in next st, ch 5, skip next 3 sts, sl st in sp between this 6-dc group and next 6-dc group) 2 times, ch 5, skip next 2 sts, sl st in next st, ch 5, skip next 3 sts, sc in last 6 dc, **do not** turn, fasten off (12 sc, 6 ch sps).

Row 9: Join size 30 cotton with sl st in first ch sp, (ch 5, sl st in next ch sp) 5 times, turn (5 ch sps).

Row 10: Sl st in first ch sp, ch 3, 2 dc in same sp, 6 dc in each of next 3 ch sps, 3 dc in last ch sp, turn (24 dc).

Row 11: Ch 5, sl st in sp between this 3-dc group and next 6-dc group, (ch 5, skip next 2 sts, sl st in next st, ch 5, sl st in sp between this 6-dc group and next 6-or 3-dc group) 3 times, ch 5, skip next 2 sts, sl st in last st, turn (8 ch sps).

Row 12: Sl st in each of first 3 chs on next ch-5, (ch 5, sl st in next ch sp) 7 times, turn (7 ch sps).

Row 13: Ch 5, sl st in first ch sp, (ch 5, sl st in next ch sp) 6 times, ch 5, sl st in next sl st on last row, turn (8 ch sps).

Rnd 14: Working in rnds, ch 1, (2 sc, pull up one bead, 3 sc, pull up one bead, 2 sc) in each ch sp across; working in ends of rows, evenly space 30 more sc across to starting ring, sc in ring, mark last sc made, evenly space 30 more sc across ends of rows, join with sl st in first sc, fasten off.

NOTES: For **picot,** ch 3, sl st in 3rd ch from hook.

For **picot ch (p ch),** ch 2, picot, ch 3, picot, ch 2.

Rnd 15: With No. 14 hook and size 50 cotton, join with sl st in marked st, (p ch, skip next 3 sts, sl st in next st) 7 times, p ch, skip next 3 sts, sl st around thread coming from top of next bead, *p ch, skip next bead, sl st around thread coming from top of next bead*; repeat between ** 3 more times, p ch, skip next bead, sl st around thread coming from top of next bead; repeat between ** 3 times; repeat between ( ) 7 times, p ch, join with sl st in first sl st, fasten off.

Rnds 16-17: Join size 30 crochet cotton with sl st in center of any p ch, p ch, (sl st in next p ch, p ch) around, join, fasten off.

NOTE: Thread 24 white 4-mm beads onto size 30 crochet cotton.

Rnd 18: Using No. 13 hook and size 30 crochet cotton, with right side facing you, join with sl st in any p ch, ch 7, (sl st in next p ch, ch 7) around, join.

Rnd 19: Ch 1, (2 sc, picot, 3 dc, pull up one bead, 3 dc, picot, 2 sc) in each ch sp around, join, fasten off.

FINISHING

1: Sew 2 white 5-mm beads to bottom of Bell for clangor.

2: Apply fabric stiffener to Ornament according to manufacturer's instructions; pin to plastic covered blocking board, shaping as shown in photo. Let dry completely.

3: Pull 18" piece of ribbon through ch sps at top of Ornament, tie ends into a bow.

4: Tie 9" piece of ribbon into a bow around st at top of Bell as shown.

WREATH ORNAMENT
Leaf (make 6)

NOTES: With embroidery needle, thread 12 white 4-mm beads onto size 30 crochet cotton. Slide beads back along thread until needed.

For **picot,** ch 3, sl st in 3rd ch from hook.

For **picot ch (p ch),** ch 2, picot, ch 3, picot, ch 2.

With No. 13 hook and size 30 cotton, ch 9, sl st in 2nd ch from hook, sc in next ch, hdc in next ch, picot, sc in each of next 2 chs, hdc in next ch, picot, sc in next ch, sl st in last ch, pull up one bead, ch 1, sl st in same ch, pull up one bead; working on opposite side of ch, sc in each of next 2 chs, hdc in next ch, picot, sc in each of next 2 chs, hdc in next ch, picot, sc in next ch, sl st in last ch, picot, sl st in same ch, fasten off.

Tack two Leaves together at bead ends; repeat with remaining Leaves. Tack tips of Leaf pairs together to form circle as shown in photo.

Continued on page 23

Crochet a lacy edging for a heartwarming wall hanging. Crimson bedspread cotton, worked around a heart-shaped wire form and adorned with pretty flowers, makes a beautiful accent for your wall or door.

≈ HEART WALL DECORATION ≈

DESIGNED BY JUDY TEAGUE TREECE

SIZE
Edging is ¾" wide.

MATERIALS
Size 10 bedspread cotton — 75 yds. dk. red; 6" wire abaca heart; dried statice; silk rose with leaves; invisible thread; craft glue or hot glue gun; sewing needle; No. 7 steel crochet hook or size needed to obtain gauge.

GAUGE
1 dc = ⅜" tall.

EDGING

Rnd 1: Working around wire heart (see illustration), join with sc near center top of heart, sc evenly around heart working in multiples of 6, join with sl st in first sc.

Rnd 2: (Ch 4, dc, ch 2, dc, ch 1, dc) in first st, ch 2, skip next 2 sts, sc in next st, ch 2, skip next 2 sts, *(dc, ch 1, dc, ch 2, dc, ch 1, dc) in next st, ch 2, skip next 2 sts, sc in next st, ch 2, skip next 2 sts; repeat from * around, join with sl st in 3rd ch of ch-4.

Rnd 3: Sl st in next ch-1 sp, sl st in next st, sl st in next ch-2 sp, (ch 4, dc, ch 2, dc, ch 1, dc) in same sp, ch 4, skip next ch-1 sp, sc in next ch-2 sp, ch 3, sc in next ch-2 sp, ch 4, skip next ch-1 sp, *(dc, ch 1, dc, ch 2, dc, ch 1, dc) in next ch-2 sp, ch 4, skip next ch-1 sp, sc in next ch-2 sp, ch 3, sc in next ch-2 sp, ch 4, skip next ch-1 sp; repeat from * around, join as before, fasten off.

Glue dried statice and silk rose to top of heart as shown in photo.

For **hanger,** tack ends of 6" piece of invisible thread to top back of heart.❖

SC OVER WIRE

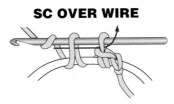

PEARL ORNAMENTS

Continued from page 21

Wreath

Rnd 1: With No. 14 hook and size 50 crochet cotton, join with sl st between 2 picots on outside edge of any Leaf, p ch, sl st in st after next picot, p ch, sl st in st before picot on next Leaf, p ch, (sl st between next 2 picots, p ch, sl st in st after next picot, p ch, sl st in st before picot on next leaf, p ch) around, join with sl st in first sl st, fasten off (18 p chs).

Rnds 2-3: Join size 50 crochet cotton with sl st in center of any p ch, p ch, (sl st in next p ch, p ch) around, join, fasten off.

NOTE: Thread 18 white 4-mm beads onto size 30 crochet cotton.

Rnd 4: With No. 13 hook and size 30 cotton, join with sl st in any p ch, ch 7, (sl st in next p ch, ch 7) around, join.

Rnd 5: Ch 1, (3 sc, picot, 3 sc, picot, 3 sc) in each ch-7 sp around, join with sl st in first sc.

Rnd 6: Sl st in next st, (ch 10, skip next 5 sts, sl st in next 4 sts) 17 times, ch 10, skip next 5 sts, sl st in each of last 2 sts, join with sl st in next sl st.

Rnd 7: Sl st in next sl st, ch 1, (2 sc, 2 hdc, 2 dc, pull up one bead, 2 dc, 2 hdc, 2 sc, ch 2) in each ch-10 sp around, join with sl st in first sc, fasten off.

FINISHING

1: Work steps 2-3 of Bell Ornament Finishing.

2: Tie 9" piece of ribbon into a bow around st at bottom of center opening as shown.❖

BURNISHED MEDALLIONS

Continued from page 18

total of 7 Motifs.

Repeat Second Row 7 more times for a total of 9 rows.

FILLER MOTIF

Rnds 1-2: Repeat same rnds of First Row First Large Motif. At end of last rnd, fasten off.

Rnd 3: Join off-white with sc in any ch-3 sp; working in unworked ch-3 sps and joining ch-3 sps between 4 Large Motifs, *[ch 1, sl st in unworked ch-3 sp on Large Motif, ch 1, sc in same sp on this Motif, ch 1, sc in next ch-3 sp, ch 2, sl st in joining ch-3 sp between Large Motifs, ch 2, sc in same ch-3 sp on this Motif, ch 1], sc in next ch-3 sp; repeat from * 2 more times; repeat between [ ], join, fasten off.

Work one Filler Motif in each space between Large Motifs.❖

SUN-WRAPPED DAYDREAMS

CHILDREN

Yesterday I watched my little boy as he stood and gazed outside.
He reached with his chubby, sturdy hand and drew the drapes aside.

I watched his staunch little back and saw his eyes explore.
I stared as if I'd never seen a child look out before.

If I could snatch this moment and hold it in my heart,
He would stay this small child and we would never be apart.

Time is constant and so swift, it quickly sweeps the years aside.
Youth is just a passing thing, from this we cannot hide.

All too soon our young ones are grown and already out the door.
To college, then to a new life they have only started to explore.

Hold your children close to you and cherish them
every precious day.
Fill your home with laughter and with love,
guide them on their way.

Invite a summer garden into your home with this exhilarating sunflower afghan.
These big bold flowers are so realistic, you can almost see them grow.

⊷ SUNFLOWER AFGHAN ⊷

DESIGNED BY ROSETTA HARSHMAN

SIZE
50" x 68".

MATERIALS
Worsted-weight yarn — 16 oz. each royal blue, dk. green and brown, 14 oz. med. green and 8 oz. yellow; F crochet hook or size needed to obtain gauge.

GAUGE
Rnds 1-3 of Block = 3½" across. Each Block is 9" square.

BLOCK (make 35)
Rnd 1: With brown, ch 5, sl st in first ch to form ring, ch 1, 10 sc in ring, join with sl st in first sc (10 sc).

NOTES: For **beginning popcorn (beg pc)**, ch 3, 4 dc in same st, drop lp from hook, insert hook in top of ch-3, pick up dropped lp, draw lp through ch.

For **popcorn (pc)**, 5 dc in next st, drop lp from hook, insert hook in first st of 5-dc group, pick up dropped lp, draw lp through st.

Rnd 2: Beg pc, ch 2, (pc in next st, ch 2) around, join with sl st in top of beg pc (10 pc, 10 ch-2 sps).

Rnd 3: Sl st in first ch-2 sp, (beg pc, ch 2, pc) in same sp, ch 2, *(pc, ch 2, pc) in next ch-2 sp, ch 2; repeat from * around, join, fasten off (20 pc, 20 ch-2 sps).

Rnd 4: Join yellow with sc in any ch-2 sp, ch 4, (sc in next ch-2 sp, ch 4) around, join with sl st in first sc (20 sc, 20 ch-4 sps).

Rnd 5: Sl st in first ch-4 sp, ch 3, (4 dc, ch 2, 5 dc) in same sp, (5 dc, ch 2, 5 dc) in each ch-4 sp around, join with sl st in top of ch-3, fasten off (200 dc, 20 ch-2 sps).

Rnd 6: Join dk. green with sc in any ch-2 sp, ch 6, (sc in next ch-2 sp, ch 4) 4 times, *sc in next ch-2 sp, ch 6, (sc in next ch-2 sp, ch 4) 4 times; repeat from * around, join with sl st in first sc, fasten off (16 ch-4 sps, 4 ch-6 sps).

Rnd 7: Join royal blue with sl st in any ch-6 sp, ch 3, (4 dc, ch 2, 5 dc) in same sp, ch 1, sc in next ch-4 sp, (ch 4, sc in next ch-4 sp) 3 times, ch 1, *(5 dc, ch 2, 5 dc) in next ch-6 sp, ch 1, sc in next ch-4 sp, (ch 4, sc in next ch-4 sp) 3 times, ch 1; repeat from * around, join with sl st in top of ch-3.

Rnd 8: Ch 3, dc in each dc, in each ch-1 sp and in each sc around with (dc, ch 3, dc) in each corner ch-2 sp and 3 dc in each ch-4 sp, join, fasten off (108 dc, 4 ch-3 sps).

Rnd 9: Join med. green with sc in any ch-3 sp, (sc, ch 2, 2 sc) in same sp, sc in each st around with (2 sc, ch 2, 2 sc) in each ch-3 sp, join with sl st in first sc, fasten off (124 sc, 4 ch-2 sps).

Rnd 10: Join dk. green with sc in any ch-2 sp, sc in same sp, sc in each st around with 2 sc in each ch-2 sp, join, fasten off.

Holding Blocks wrong sides together, matching sts, sew Blocks together through **back lps** in five rows of seven Blocks each.

BORDER
Rnd 1: Working around entire outer edge, join dk. green with sl st in first st of any 2-sc corner, ch 3, (2 dc, ch 2, 2 dc) in next st, dc in each st and in each seam around with (2 dc, ch 2, 2 dc) in 2nd st of each 2-sc corner, join with sl st in top of ch-3, fasten off.

Rnd 2: Join med. green with sl st in any corner ch-2 sp, ch 2, 2 hdc in same sp, hdc in each st around with 3 hdc in each corner ch-2 sp, join with sl st in top of ch-2.

Rnd 3: Ch 4, 2 tr in same st, 3 tr in each st around, join with sl st in top of ch-4, fasten off.

Rnd 4: Join royal blue with sl st in any st, ch 4, tr in each st around, join, fasten off.❖

Let springtime blossom all around you with this unique pillow topper made in the earthy tones of yellow sunshine, sky blues and grass greens. Let this colorful pillow be a sweet reminder of life's renewal.

FLORAL PILLOW

DESIGNED BY KATHERINE ENG

SIZE
Fits 12" square pillow.

MATERIALS
Worsted-weight yarn — 1½ oz. med. blue, 1 oz. each med. green, dk. green, royal blue and yellow; 12" square purchased pillow with 3" ruffle; F crochet hook or size needed to obtain gauge.

GAUGE
Rnds 1-2 = 1½" across.

PILLOW TOP

Rnd 1: With yellow, ch 4, sl st in first ch to form ring, ch 1, 8 sc in ring, join with sl st in first sc (8 sc).

Rnd 2: Working this rnd in **front lps**, ch 3, sl st in same st, ch 3, *(sl st, ch 3, sl st) in next st, ch 3; repeat from * around, join with sl st in joining sl st of last rnd, fasten off (16 ch lps).

Rnd 3: Working in **back lps** of rnd 1, join med. blue with sc in any st, ch 3, (sc in next st, ch 3) around, join with sl st in first sc (8 ch lps).

Rnd 4: Ch 1, sc in first st, (hdc, 3 dc, hdc) in next ch lp, *sc in next st, (hdc, 3 dc, hdc) in next ch lp; repeat from * around, join (48 sts).

Rnd 5: Ch 1, sc in first st, ch 3, skip next 5 sts, (sc in next st, ch 3, skip next 5 sts) around, join, fasten off (8 ch lps).

Rnd 6: Join royal with sc in any st, (hdc, 5 dc, hdc) in next ch lp, *sc in next st, (hdc, 5 dc, hdc) in next ch lp; repeat from * around, join (64 sts).

Rnd 7: Ch 1, sc in first st, ch 4, skip next 7 sts, (sc in next st, ch 4, skip next 7 sts) around, join, fasten off (8 ch lps).

Rnd 8: Join med. green with sl st in any ch lp, ch 2, 3 sc in same lp, *[sc in next st, (3 sc, hdc) in next ch lp; for **corner**, (2 dc, ch 2, 2 dc) in next st], (hdc, 3 sc) in next ch lp; repeat from * 2 more times; repeat between [ ], join with sl st in top of ch-2.

Rnd 9: Ch 1, sc in each st around with (sc, ch 2, sc) in each corner ch-2 sp, join with sl st in first sc, fasten off (15 sc on each side between corner ch sps).

Rnd 10: Join dk. green with sc in any ch-2 sp, ch 2, sc in same sp, ch 1, skip next st, (sc in next st, ch 1, skip next st) across to next ch-2 sp, *(sc, ch 2, sc) in next ch-2 sp, ch 1, skip next st, (sc in next st, ch 1, skip next st) across to next ch-2 sp; repeat from * around, join.

Rnd 11: Ch 1, sc in each st and in each ch-1 sp around with (sc, ch 2, sc) in each corner ch-2 sp, join, fasten off (19 sc on each side between corner ch sps).

Row 12: For **first triangle,** working in rows, join med. blue with sc in any ch-2 sp, sc in each st across to next ch-2 sp, sc in next ch-2 sp leaving remaining sts unworked, **turn** (21).

Rows 13-21: Ch 1, sc first 2 sts tog, sc in each st across to last 2 sts, sc last 2 sts tog, **turn,** ending with 3 sts in last row.

Row 22: Ch 1, sc in first st, ch 1, skip next st, sc in last st, fasten off.

Row 12: For **2nd triangle,** join med. blue with sc in last worked ch-2 sp on rnd 11, sc in each st across to next ch-2 sp, sc in next ch-2 sp leaving remaining sts unworked, **turn** (21).

Rows 13-22: Repeat same rows of first triangle.

For **3rd and 4th triangles,** work same as 2nd triangle.

Rnd 23: Working around outer edge, with right side facing you, join med. blue with sc in any corner ch-1 sp, ch 2, sc in same sp, *[evenly space 15 sc across ends of rows of first triangle, dc in next ch-2 sp on rnd 11 between triangles, evenly space 15 sc across ends of rows on next triangle], (sc, ch 2, sc) in next corner ch-1 sp; repeat from * 2 more times; repeat between [ ], join with sl st in first sc, **do not** turn, fasten off (33 sts on each side between corner ch sps).

Rnds 24-25: With royal blue, repeat rnds 10 and 11. At end of last rnd, **do not** fasten off.

Rnd 26: Ch 1, sc in each st around with (sc, ch 2, sc) in each ch-2 sp, join, fasten off.

Rnds 27-28: With med. green, repeat rnds 10 and 11.

Rnd 29: Join dk. green with sl st in any ch-2 sp, ch 3, (dc, ch 2, 2 dc) in same sp, dc in each st around with (2 dc, ch 2, 2 dc) in each ch-2 sp, join with sl st in top of ch-3, fasten off.

Rnd 30: Join med. blue with sc in any ch-2 sp, ch

Continued on page 39

Keep your little one comfy and warm in this delightful baby ensemble designed in cascades of rainbow pastels. Gently accented with soft white birds, this adorable outfit is worth a pot of gold.

❧ Rainbow Baby Set ❧

Designed by Alma Shields

SIZE
Afghan is 30½" x 41". Instructions given for Sweater and Cap are for small(3-6 mos.). Changes for medium (6-9 mos.) and large (9-12 mos.) are in [ ].

MATERIALS
Worsted-weight yarn — 9 oz. lt. blue, 4 oz. each pink, peach, yellow, lt. green and lavender, 2 oz. white; 5 white ½" buttons; 2½" square piece of cardboard; tapestry needle; E, H and I crochet hooks or size needed to obtain gauge.

GAUGE
I hook, 3 extended sc = 1"; 5 extended sc rows = 2".

AFGHAN

NOTES: Use I hook throughout unless otherwise stated.

For **extended single crochet (esc),** insert hook in next ch or st, yo, draw lp through, yo, draw through one lp on hook, yo, draw through both lps on hook.

For **esc color change,** insert hook in next st, yo, draw lp through, yo, draw through one lp on hook, drop first color, with next color, yo, draw through both lps on hook.

Each square on graph equals one esc.

When changing colors, always drop yarn to wrong side of work. Use a separate skein of yarn for each color section. Do not carry yarn across from one section to another. Fasten off colors at end of each color section.

Work odd-numbered rows from right to left and even numbered rows from left to right.

Row 1: With pink, ch 81, esc in 2nd ch from hook, esc in each ch across, turn (80 esc). Front of row 1 is right side of work.

Rows 2-90: Changing colors according to Afghan Graph on page 33, ch 1, esc in each st across, turn. At end of last row, fasten off.

Row 91: With right side facing you, working in ends of rows across one side of Afghan, join pink with sc in row 1; changing colors to match ends of rows, sc in each row across, fasten off.

Row 92: Working in ends of rows across other side of Afghan, join lavender with sc in row 90; changing colors to match ends of rows, sc in each row across, fasten off.

Border

Rnd 1: Working around entire outer edge of Afghan, join lt. blue with esc in any st, esc in each st around with 3 esc in each corner, join with sl st in first esc, **turn.**

Rnds 2-5: Ch 1, esc in each st around with 3 esc in each center corner st, join, **turn.** At end of last rnd, **do not** turn.

Rnd 6: Ch 1; working from left to right, **reverse sc** (see page 159) in each st around, join with sl st in first sc, fasten off.

Bird (make 3)

Rnd 1: With white, ch 18, sl st in 2nd ch from hook, sc in next ch, (hdc in next ch, 2 dc in next ch, 2 tr in next ch, 2 dc in next ch, hdc in next ch), sl st in next ch, skip next ch, sl st in next ch; repeat between ( ), sc in next ch, sl st in last ch, ch 3, sl st in 3rd ch from hook; working on opposite side of starting ch, sc in next 8 chs, (2 sc, ch 1, 2 sc) in next ch, sc in next 8 chs, ch 3, sl st in 3rd ch from hook, **do not** join.

NOTE: Sl st is used and counted as a st.

Row 2: Sc in first 5 sts, 2 sc in each of next 2 sts, sc in next 4 sts, skip next sl st, sc in each of next 3 sts, 2 sc in each of next 2 sts, sc in next 4 sts, sl st in next st leaving remaining sts unworked, fasten off.

Sew Birds to Afghan as shown in photo.

CAP

NOTES: Use I hook throughout.

For **esc next 2 sts tog,** (insert hook in next st, yo, draw lp through, yo, draw through one lp on hook) 2 times, yo, draw through both lps on hook.

Rnd 1: With lt. blue, ch 52 [54, 56], sl st in first ch to form ring, ch 1, esc in each ch around, join with sl st in first esc, **turn** (52 esc) [54 esc, 56 esc].

Rnds 2-3: Ch 1, esc in each st around, join, **turn.** At end of last rnd, fasten off.

Rnd 4: Join pink with esc in first st, esc in each st around, join, **turn.**

Rnd 5: Ch 1, esc in each st around, join, **turn,** fasten off.

Continued on page 32

RAINBOW BABY SET

Continued from page 30

Rnds 6-7: With peach, repeat rnds 4 and 5.

Rnd 8: With yellow, repeat rnd 4.

Rnd 9: Ch 1, esc in first 11 [13, 12] sts, esc next 2 sts tog, (esc in next 11 [11, 12] sts, esc next 2 sts tog) around, join, **turn,** fasten off (48) [50, 52].

Rnd 10: Join lt. green with esc in first st, esc in next 9 [11, 10] sts, esc next 2 sts tog, (esc in next 10 [10, 11] sts, esc next 2 sts tog) around, join, **turn** (44) [46, 48].

Rnd 11: Ch 1, esc in first 9 [11, 10] sts, esc next 2 sts tog, (esc in next 9 [9, 10] sts, esc next 2 sts tog) around, join, **turn,** fasten off (40) [42, 44].

Rnd 12: Join lt. blue with esc in first st, esc in next 7 [9, 8] sts, esc next 2 sts tog, (esc in next 8 [8, 9] sts, esc next 2 sts tog) around, join, **turn** (36) [38, 40].

Rnd 13: Ch 1, esc in first 7 [9, 8] sts, esc next 2 sts tog, (esc in next 7 [7, 8] sts, esc next 2 sts tog) around, join, **turn,** fasten off (32) [34, 36].

Rnd 14: Join lavender with esc in first st, esc in next 5 [7, 6] sts, esc next 2 sts tog, (esc in next 6 [6, 7] sts, esc next 2 sts tog) around, join, **turn** (28) [30, 32].

Rnd 15: Ch 1, esc in first 5 [7, 6] sts, esc next 2 sts tog, (esc in next 5 [5, 6] sts, esc next 2 sts tog) around, join, **turn** (24) [26, 28].

Rnd 16: Ch 1, (esc next 2 sts tog) around, join, fasten off leaving long end for gathering.

Weave end through sts on last rnd, pull tight to gather; secure.

Ribbing

Rnd 1: Working in starting ch on opposite side of rnd 1, join lt. blue with sl st in first ch, ch 2, hdc in each ch around, join with sl st in top of ch-2, **turn.**

NOTES: For **front post stitch (fp)** (see page 159), yo, insert hook from front to back around post of next st, yo, draw lp through, (yo, draw through 2 lps on hook) 2 times.

For **back post stitch (bp),** yo, insert hook from back to front around post of next st, yo, draw lp through, (yo, draw through 2 lps on hook) 2 times.

Rnd 2: Ch 2, fp around next st, (bp around next st, fp around next st) around, join, **turn.**

Rnd 3: Ch 2, bp around next st, (fp around next st, bp around next st) around, join, fasten off.

Turn Ribbing up.

Pom-pom

Wrap white around cardboard 75 times. Slide loops off cardboard, tie separate strand white tightly around center of all loops. Cut loops and trim ends to 1".

Sew to top of Cap.

SWEATER
Body

NOTES: Use I hook unless otherwise stated.

For color change information, read Notes for Afghan on page 30.

Row 1: With pink, ch 59 [63, 67], esc in 2nd ch from hook, esc in each ch across, turn (58 esc) [62 esc, 66 esc].

Rows 2-16 [2-16, 2-18]: Changing colors according to Sweater Graph for size you are making (see page 34), ch 1, esc in each st across, turn.

Row 17 [17, 19]: For **right front,** changing colors according to Sweater Graph, ch 1, esc in first 12 [13, 14] sts leaving remaining sts unworked, turn (12) [13, 14].

Rows 18-20 [18-21, 20-22]: Repeat row 2.

NOTES: For **decrease** at beginning of row, ch 1, esc first 2 sts tog (see Notes for Cap on page 30).

For **decrease** at end of row, esc last 2 sts tog.

Rows 21-28 [22-30, 23-32]: Decreasing and changing colors according to graph, work according to graph, turn, ending with 4 esc in last row. At end of last row, fasten off.

Row 17 [17, 19]: For **first armhole opening,** skip next 6 sts on row 16 [16, 18]; for **back,** join lt. blue with esc in first st; changing colors according to graph, esc in next 21 [23, 25] sts leaving remaining sts unworked, turn (22) [24, 26].

Rows 18-28 [18-30, 20-32]: Repeat row 2. At end of last row, fasten off.

Row 17 [17, 19]: For **second armhole opening,** skip next 6 sts on row 16 [16, 18]; for **left front,** join lt. blue with esc in first st; changing colors according to graph, esc in each st across, turn (12) [13, 14].

Rows 18-28 [18-30, 20-32]: Repeat same rows of right front.

Matching sts, sew shoulder seams.

Bottom Ribbing

Row 1: Working in starting ch on opposite side of row 1, with H hook and lt. blue, join with sl st in first ch, ch 2, hdc in each ch across, turn.

Rows 2-3: Ch 2, fp around next st, (bp around next st, fp around next st) across, turn. At end of last row, fasten off.

Neck Ribbing

Row 1: Working in sts and ends of rows, with H hook and lt. blue, join with sl st in first st on row 20 [21, 22] of right front, ch 2, evenly space 9 [10, 11] esc across to shoulder seam, esc in shoulder seam, esc in each st across back, esc in shoulder seam, evenly space 10 [11, 12] esc across to row 20 [21, 22] on left front, turn.

Rows 2-3: Repeat same rows of Bottom Ribbing.

Button Band

Row 1: Working in ends of rows across left front, join lt. blue with sc in top left corner, evenly space 27 [29, 31] more sc across, turn (28 sc) [30 sc, 32 sc].

Rows 2-3: Ch 1, sc in each st across, turn. At end of last row, **do not** turn.

Row 4: Ch 1, reverse sc in each st across, fasten off.

Buttonhole Band

Row 1: Working in ends of rows across right front, join lt. blue with sc in bottom right corner, evenly space 27 [29, 31] more sc across, turn (28 sc) [30 sc, 32 sc].

Row 2: Ch 1, sc in first 1 [2, 1] st; for **buttonhole,** ch 1, skip next st; (sc in next 5 [5, 6] sts, buttonhole) 4 times, sc in each of last 2 [3, 2] sts, turn (5 buttonholes).

Row 3: Ch 1, sc in each st and in each ch across, **do not** turn.

Row 4: Ch 1, reverse sc in each st across, fasten off. Sew buttons to Button Placket opposite buttonholes.

Sleeve (make 2)

Row 1: With lt. blue, ch 21 [25, 25], esc in 2nd ch from hook, esc in each ch across, turn (20 esc) [24 esc, 24 esc].

Rows 2-5: Ch 1, esc in each st across, turn.

Row 6: Ch 1, 2 esc in first st, esc in each st across with 2 esc in last st, turn (22) [26, 26].

Continued on next page

AFGHAN GRAPH

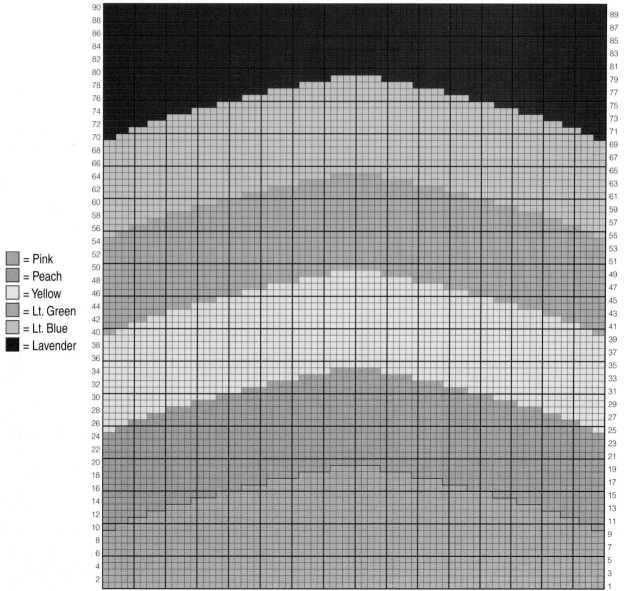

= Pink
= Peach
= Yellow
= Lt. Green
= Lt. Blue
= Lavender

RAINBOW BABY SET

Continued from page 33

Rows 7-16: Repeat rows 2-6 consecutively, ending with 26 [30, 30] sts in last row.

Rows 17-18 [17-20, 17-22]: Repeat row 2. At end of last row, fasten off.

Sleeve Cuffs

Row 1: Working in starting ch on opposite side of row 1, with H hook and lt. blue, join with sl st in first ch, ch 2, hdc in each ch across, turn.

Rows 2-3: Repeat same rows of Bottom Ribbing. Repeat on other Sleeve.

Matching center of last row on Sleeve to shoulder seam, sew Sleeves to armholes.

Sew Sleeve seams.

Bird (make 2)

With E hook and white, ch 9, sl st in 2nd ch from hook, 2 hdc in next ch, sl st in next ch, skip next 2 chs, sl st in next ch, 2 hdc in next ch, sl st in last ch, fasten off. Sew to left front as shown in photo.❖

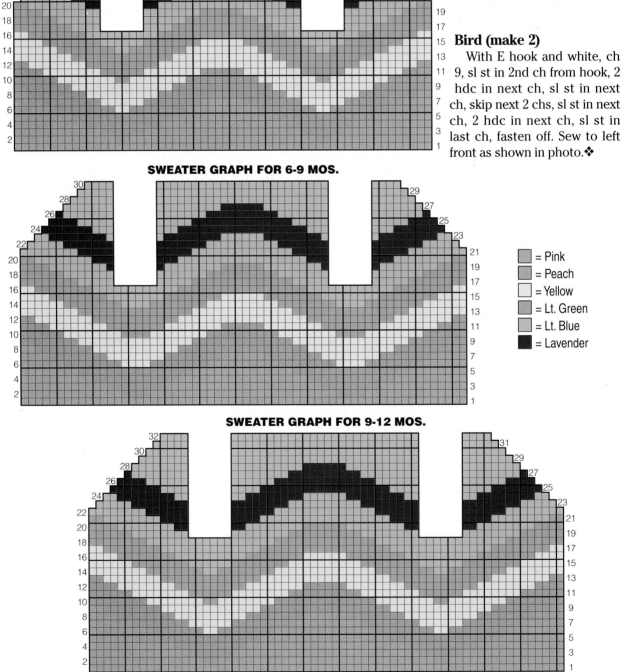

SWEATER GRAPH FOR 3-6 MOS .

SWEATER GRAPH FOR 6-9 MOS.

SWEATER GRAPH FOR 9-12 MOS.

= Pink
= Peach
= Yellow
= Lt. Green
= Lt. Blue
= Lavender

Teens will love this stylish hair accessory suitable for casual or dressy wear.
This single evening project, richly textured in hues of peach, will make a tasteful gift.

PEACH HEADBAND

DESIGNED BY KATHERINE ENG

SIZE
Teen's/adult's one size fits all. 2¾" wide.

MATERIALS
Acrylic sport-weight thread — 1½ oz. dk. peach, small amount each lt. peach and watermelon; B and D crochet hooks or sizes needed to obtain gauges.

GAUGE
With B hook, flower is 1" across. With D hook, 7 sc sts and 6 ch-1 sps = 2"; 11 sc rows = 2".

Continued on page 41

Make this heart motif in a variety of colors to adorn your favorite shirt, sweatshirt or purse. Its lacy beauty would look lovely framed for a dainty picture or placed on a pillow as a topper.

❦ FLOWER HEART MOTIF ❧

DESIGNED BY CAROL SMITH

SIZE
8" x 10".

MATERIALS
Size 10 bedspread cotton — 50 yds. green, 35 yds. each pink and ecru; No. 5 steel crochet hook or size needed to obtain gauge.

GAUGE
5 dc = ½"; 3 dc rows = 1".

FIRST MOTIF
NOTE: This project may ruffle until blocked.

Rnd 1: With pink, ch 4, sl st in first ch to form ring, ch 4, (hdc in ring, ch 2) 7 times, join with sl st in 2nd ch of ch-4 (8 hdc, 8 ch-2 sps).

Rnd 2: Sl st in first ch-2 sp, ch 1, (sc, hdc, dc, hdc, sc) in same sp and in each ch-2 sp around, join with sl st in first sc (8 small petals).

Rnd 3: Working behind last rnd, sl st in first ch-2 sp on rnd 1 between petals, ch 1, sc in same sp, ch 3, (sc in next ch-2 sp on rnd 1 between petals, ch 3) around, join.

Rnd 4: Sl st in first ch-3 sp, ch 1, (sc, hdc, 3 dc, hdc, sc) in same sp and in each ch-3 sp around, join (8 large petals).

Rnd 5: Working behind last rnd, sl st in first ch-3 sp on rnd 3 between petals, ch 1, sc in same sp, ch 4, (sc in next ch-3 sp on rnd 3 between petals, ch 4) around, join, fasten off (8 ch-4 sps).

Rnd 6: Join green with sl st in any ch-4 sp, ch 3, 3 dc in same sp, ch 3, sc in next ch-4 sp, ch 3, *4 dc in next ch-4 sp, ch 3, sc in next ch-4 sp, ch 3; repeat from * around, join with sl st in top of ch-3 (16 dc, 8 ch-3 sps, 4 sc).

Rnd 7: Ch 3, dc in same st, *[dc in each of next 2 dc, 2 dc in next dc, ch 5, sc in next sc, ch 5], 2 dc in next dc; repeat from * 2 more times; repeat between [ ], join (24 dc, 8 ch-5 sps, 4 sc).

Rnd 8: Ch 2, dc in next dc, (dc next 2 dc tog) 2 times, ch 10, tr in next sc, ch 10, *(dc next 2 dc tog) 3 times, ch 10, tr in next sc, ch 10; repeat from * around, join with sl st in top of first dc (12 dc, 8 ch-10 lps, 4 tr).

Rnd 9: Ch 2, dc next 2 dc tog, *[ch 10, sl st in top of last st made, ch 5, (sc, ch 5, sc) in next ch-10 lp, ch 5, sc in next tr, ch 5, (sc, ch 5, sc) in next ch-10 lp, ch 5], dc next 3 dc tog; repeat from * 2 more times; repeat between [ ], join as before, fasten off.

SECOND MOTIF
NOTES: For **joining ch-10 lp,** ch 5, sc in corresponding ch-10 lp on other Motif, ch 5, sl st in top of last st made on rnd you are working.

For **joining ch-5 sp,** ch 2, sc in corresponding ch-5 sp on other Motif, ch 2.

Rnds 1-8: Repeat same rnds of First Motif.

Rnd 9: Ch 2, dc next 2 dc tog; joining to bottom of First Motif, joining ch-10 lp, ch 5, (sc, joining ch-5 sp, sc) in next ch-10 lp, ch 5, sc in next tr, ch 5, (sc, joining ch-5 sp, sc) in next ch-10 lp, ch 5, dc next 3 sts tog, joining ch-10 lp, *ch 5, (sc, ch 5, sc) in next ch-10 lp, ch 5, sc in next tr, ch 5, (sc, ch 5, sc) in next ch-10 lp, ch 5, dc next 3 sts tog, ch 10, sl st in top of last st made on rnd you are working; repeat from *; repeat between [ ], join with sl st in top of first dc, fasten off.

THIRD MOTIF
Joining to side of Second Motif, work same as Second Motif.

EDGING
Working around entire outer edge of Motifs, join ecru with sl st in any corner ch-10 lp, ch 2, 11 hdc in same lp, 5 hdc in each ch-5 sp, 6 hdc in ch-5 sp on each side of ch-10 joining and 12 hdc in each corner ch-10 lp around, join with sl st in top of ch-2, fasten off.❖

Slide your water bottle into this handy carrier for a fun day in the sun. A quick-as-a-wink project made with easy shells, it's the perfect gift for a sports enthusiast.

WATER BOTTLE

DESIGNED BY GINGER SMITH

SIZE
Holds 32-oz. plastic bottle measuring 11" around.

MATERIALS
Acrylic sport-weight yarn — 3½ oz. white;

B crochet hook or size needed to obtain gauge.

GAUGE
Rnds 1-5 = 1¾" across.

CARRIER

NOTE: Do not join rnds unless otherwise stated. Mark first st of each rnd.

Rnd 1: Starting at bottom, ch 2, 8 sc in 2nd ch from hook (8 sc).

Rnd 2: 2 sc in each st around (16).

Rnd 3: (Sc in next st, 2 sc in next st) around (24).

Rnd 4: (Sc in each of next 2 sts, 2 sc in next st) around (32).

Rnd 5: (Sc in each of next 3 sts, 2 sc in next st) around (40).

Rnd 6: (Sc in next 4 sts, 2 sc in next st) around (48).

Rnd 7: (Sc in next 5 sts, 2 sc in next st) around (56).

Rnd 8: (Sc in next 6 sts, 2 sc in next st) around (64).

Rnd 9: (Sc in next 7 sts, 2 sc in next st) around (72).

Rnd 10: Sc in each st around, join with sl st in first sc.

Rnd 11: Working this rnd in **back lps** only, ch 1, sc in each st around, join.

NOTES: For shell, 5 dc in next st.

For **reverse shell**, (yo, insert hook in next st, yo, draw lp through, yo, draw through 2 lps on hook) 5 times, yo, draw through all 6 lps on hook.

Rnd 12: Ch 1, sc in first st, skip next 2 sts, shell in next st, skip next 2 sts, (sc in next st, skip next 2 sts, shell in next st, skip next 2 sts) around, join with sl st in first sc (12 shells, 12 sc).

Rnd 13: Sl st in each of next 3 sts, ch 1, sc in same st, ch 2, reverse shell, ch 2, (sc in next st, ch 2, reverse shell, ch 2) around, join with sl st in first sc (24 ch-2 sps, 12 reverse shells, 12 sc).

NOTE: For beginning shell (beg shell), ch 3, 4 dc in same st.

Rnd 14: Beg shell, skip next ch-2 sp, sc in top of next reverse shell, skip next ch-2 sp, (shell in next sc, skip next ch-2 sp, sc in top of next reverse shell, skip next ch-2 sp) around, join with sl st in top of ch-3 (12 shells, 12 sc).

Rnds 15-16: Repeat rnds 13 and 14.

Rnd 17: Ch 1, sc in first st, sc in each dc of each shell and in each sc around, join with sl st in first sc (72 sc).

NOTES: For decrease (dec), *yo 2 times, insert hook in next st, yo, draw lp through, (yo, draw through 2 lps on hook) 2 times*, skip next 4 sts or chs; repeat between **, yo, draw through all 3 lps on hook.

(Ch 4, skip next 4 sts or chs, tr in next st) counts as first decrease.

Rnd 18: Ch 4, skip next 4 sts or chs, tr in next st, ch 4, tr in same st, (dec, ch 4, tr in same st) around, join with sl st in top of ch-4, **turn** (12 dec, 12 tr, 12 ch-4 sps).

Rnd 19: Sl st in next tr, ch 4, skip next 4 chs, tr in next dec, ch 4, tr in same st, (dec, ch 4, tr in same st) around, join, **turn.**

Rnd 20: Sl st in next tr, repeat rnd 18.

Rnds 21-23: Repeat rnds 19 and 20 alternately, ending with rnd 19.

Rnd 24: Ch 1, sc in each tr and in top of each dec around with 4 sc in each ch-4 sp, join with sl st in first sc, **do not** turn (72 sc).

Rnd 25: Beg shell, skip next 2 sts, sc in next st, skip next 2 sts, (shell in next st, skip next 2 sts, sc in next st, skip next 2 sts) around, join with sl st in top of ch-3 (12 shells, 12 sc).

Rnd 26: Working this rnd in **front lps** only, sl st in each st around, join with sl st in first sl st.

Row 27: Working in rows in **back lps** of rnd 25, sl st in each of next 3 sts, ch 1, sc in same st, (ch 2, reverse shell, ch 2, sc in next st) 2 times leaving remaining sts unworked, **turn** (4 ch-2 sps, 3 sc, 2 reverse shells).

Row 28: Ch 3, 2 dc in same st, skip next ch-2 sp, sc in top of next reverse shell, skip next ch-2 sp, shell in next sc, skip next ch-2 sp, sc in top of next reverse shell, skip next ch-2 sp, 3 dc in last sc, **turn** (6 dc, 2 sc, 1 shell).

Row 29: Ch 1, sc in first st, ch 2, reverse shell, ch 2, sc in next st, ch 2, reverse shell, ch 2, sc in last st, **turn** (4 ch-2 sps, 3 sc, 2 reverse shells).

Rows 30-108: Repeat rows 28 and 29 alternately, ending with row 28. At end of last row, leaving 10" for sewing, fasten off.

Sew sts on last row to corresponding sts of rnd 25 on opposite side of Carrier.❖

FLORAL PILLOW

Continued from page 29

2, sc in same sp, sc in each st around with (sc, ch 2, sc) in each ch-2 sp, join with sl st in first sc.

Rnd 31: Repeat rnd 26.

Rnd 32: With yellow, repeat rnd 10.

Rnd 33: Sl st in first ch-2 sp, (ch 4, sl st, ch 5, sl st, ch 4, sl st) in same sp, ch 4, (sl st in next ch-1 sp, ch 4) around to next ch-2 sp, *(sl st, ch 4, sl st, ch 5, sl st, ch 4, sl st) in next ch-2 sp, ch 4, (sl st in next ch-1 sp, ch 4) around to next ch-2 sp; repeat from * around, join with sl st in first sl st, fasten off.

Sew rnd 31 to outer edge of pillow.❖

CAPTIVATING CROCHET

A medley of fall colors wind their way around this delightful doily. Delicate chain loops create an interesting texture on this charming design which lends a feeling of warmth and comfort.

∽ AUTUMN ROUNDS DOILY ∽

DESIGNED BY ZELDA WORKMAN

SIZE
11" across.

MATERIALS
Size 8 pearl cotton or size 20 crochet cotton — 28 yds. green, 10 yds. each coral and yellow variegated, 3 yds. yellow and small amount brown; No. 10 steel crochet hook or size needed to obtain gauge.

GAUGE
Rnds 1-3 = 2¾" across.

DOILY
NOTES: For **double treble crochet (dtr),** yo 3 times, insert hook in next st, yo, draw lp through, (yo, draw through 2 lps on hook) 4 times.

This project may ruffle until blocked.

Rnd 1: With brown, ch 5, 19 tr in 5th ch from hook, join with sl st in top of ch-4, fasten off (20 tr).

Rnd 2: Join yellow with sl st in first st, ch 8, (dtr in next st, ch 3) around, join with sl st in 5th ch of ch-8 (20 dtr, 20 ch-3 sps).

NOTES: For **beginning cluster (beg cl),** ch 4, dtr in same sp.

For **cluster (cl),** *yo 3 times, insert hook in next ch sp, yo, draw lp through, (yo, draw through 2 lps on hook) 3 times; repeat from * one more time in same sp, yo, draw through all 3 lps on hook.

Rnd 3: Sl st in first ch-3 sp, beg cl, ch 6, (cl in next ch-3 sp, ch 6) around, join with sl st in top of beg cl, fasten off (20 cls, 20 ch-6 lps).

Rnd 4: Join coral with sc in any ch-6 lp, (ch 8, sc in next ch-6 lp) around; to **join,** ch 4, dtr in first sc (20 ch-8 lps).

Rnds 5-6: Ch 1, sc around joining dtr, (ch 9, sc in next ch lp) around; to **join,** ch 5, dtr in first sc (20 ch-9 lps).

Rnd 7: Beg cl around joining dtr, ch 6, *(cl, ch 6, cl) in next ch lp, ch 6; repeat from * around, cl in joining ch-5 sp on last rnd, ch 6, join with sl st in top of beg cl, fasten off (40 cls, 40 ch-6 lps).

Rnd 8: Join green with sc in any ch lp, (ch 9, sc in next ch lp) around; to **join,** ch 5, dtr in first sc (40 ch lps).

Rnds 9-11: Repeat rnds 5-7, ending with 80 cls and 80 ch-6 lps in last rnd.

Rnd 12: Join yellow variegated with sc in any ch lp, (ch 8, sc in next ch lp) around; to **join,** ch 4, dtr in first sc.

Rnd 13: Ch 1, sc around joining dtr, ch 8, (sc in next ch lp, ch 8) around, join with sl st in first sc, fasten off.❖

PEACH HEADBAND

Continued from page 35

HEADBAND
Row 1: With D hook and dk. peach, ch 18, sc in 2nd ch from hook, (ch 1, skip next ch, sc in next ch) across, turn (9 sc, 8 ch-1 sps).

Row 2: Ch 3, sc in first st, (ch 1, skip next ch sp, sc in next st) across, turn (9 sc, 8 ch-1 sps, 1 ch-3).

Rows 3-95: Ch 3, sc in first st, (ch 1, skip next ch sp, sc in next st) across leaving last ch-3 unworked, turn. At end of last row, leaving 8" for sewing, fasten off.

Sew first and last rows together.

CENTER TIE
Row 1: With D hook and lt. peach, ch 18, sc in 2nd ch from hook, sc in each ch across, turn (17 sc).

Rows 2-6: Ch 1, sc in each st across, turn.

Row 7: Ch 3, skip first 2 sts, sl st in next st, (ch 3, skip next st, sl st in next st) across, fasten off.

Row 8: Working in starting ch on opposite side of row 1, with right side facing you, join lt. peach with sl st in first ch, (ch 3, skip next ch, sl st in next ch) across, leaving 8" for sewing, fasten off.

Wrap Center Tie around seam of Headband; sew ends of rows together.

For **flower,** with B hook and watermelon, ch 6, sl st in first ch to form ring, ch 3, dc in ring, ch 3, (sl st, ch 3, dc, ch 3) 4 times in ring, join with sl st in first ch of first ch-3, leaving 8" for sewing, fasten off.

Sew over Center Tie.❖

GRANDMA'S PANTRY

GRANDMA'S HOUSE

There was something almost magic in my Grandma's home.
Everything was warm and cozy and you never felt alone.

Morning was at daybreak and the old stove glowed
While Grandma fixed more food than our tummies could hold.

The air was filled with spices and the house was always clean.
There was always someone laughing and no one acted mean.

I just loved Grandma's fancy handkerchiefs
she had neatly packed away.
We pretended they were dolls and played throughout the day.

People loved to come to Grandma's house to join in on the fun.
They would join us at the table and stay till night was done.

Now I smile with sweet remembrances and thank the Lord above,
For now I know that Grandma's house was another name for love.

Invite Daisy Maid into your home to help with the chores. She is always helpful as you work around the house and she never causes a fuss because she's as quiet as a mouse.

DAISY MAID VACUUM COVER

DESIGNED BY CINDY HARRIS

SIZE
50" tall. Fits over upright vacuum cleaner.

MATERIALS
Worsted-weight yarn — 58 oz. black, 14 oz. white, 9 oz. peach and 7 oz. brown; 2 black ⅝" shank buttons; black sewing thread; polyester fiberfill; sewing and tapestry needles; G and K crochet hooks or sizes needed to obtain gauges.

GAUGES
G hook, 4 sc = 1"; 9 sc rows = 2". K hook, with 2 strands held together, 9 dc = 4"; 4 dc rows = 3".

HEAD & BODY
NOTE: Do not join rnds unless otherwise stated. Mark first st of each rnd.

Rnd 1: For **inner Head & Body,** with G hook and one strand peach, ch 3, sl st in first ch to form ring, ch 1, 2 sc in each ch around (6 sc).

Rnd 2: 2 sc in each st around (12).

Rnd 3: (Sc in next st, 2 sc in next st) around (18).

Rnd 4: (Sc in each of next 2 sts, 2 sc in next st) around (24).

Rnd 5: (Sc in each of next 3 sts, 2 sc in next st) around (30).

Rnds 6-7: Sc in each st around.

Rnd 8: (Sc in next 4 sts, 2 sc in next st) around (36).

Rnds 9-17: Sc in each st around. At end of last rnd, join with sl st in first sc, fasten off.

Rnd 18: Working this rnd in **front lps** only, with black and G hook, join with sc in first st, sc in each st around.

Rnds 19-42: Sc in each st around. At end of last rnd, join with sl st in first sc, fasten off. Turn work so right side of last rnd is on inside of tube.

Rnd 43: With K hook and 2 strands black, working this rnd in **back lps** only, join with sc in first st, sc in next st, 2 sc in next st, (sc in each of next 2 sts, 2 sc in next st) around, join (48).

Rnds 44-47: Sc in each st around. At end of last rnd, join with sl st in first sc.

Rnd 48: For **outer Body,** working this rnd in **back lps** only, ch 1, sc in each st around.

Rnds 49-56: Sc in each st around.

Rnd 57: Sc in next 20 sts; for **front,** 2 sc in next 12 sts; sc in last 16 sts (60).

Rnds 58-65: Sc in each st around.

Rnd 66: Sc in next 21 sts, (sc next 2 sts tog) 12 times, sc in last 15 sts (48).

Rnd 67: Sc in each st around.

Rnd 68: (Sc in next 6 sts, sc next 2 sts tog) around (42).

Rnd 69: Sc in each st around.

Rnd 70: (Sc in next 5 sts, sc next 2 sts tog) around (36).

Rnds 71-73: Sc in each st around. At end of last rnd, join with sl st in first sc, fasten off.

Rnd 74: For **outer Head,** with K hook and 2 strands of peach, working in **back lps** of rnd 73 and **remaining lps** of rnd 17, join with sc at center back, sc in each st around, stuffing before closing.

Rnds 75-76: Sc in each st around.

Rnd 77: Sc in next 15 sts; for **front of Head,** 2 sc in next 6 sts; sc in last 15 sts (42).

Rnds 78-83: Sc in each st around.

Rnd 84: Sc in first 7 sts, *2 sc in next st, (sc in next st, 2 sc in next st) 3 times*, sc in next 16 sts; repeat between **, sc in last 5 sts (50).

Rnd 85: (Sc in next 8 sts, sc next 2 sts tog) around (45).

Rnd 86: (Sc in next 7 sts, sc next 2 sts tog) around (40).

Rnd 87: (Sc in next 6 sts, sc next 2 sts tog) around (35).

Rnd 88: (Sc in next 5 sts, sc next 2 sts tog) around (30). Stuff. Continue stuffing as you work.

Rnd 89: (Sc in each of next 3 sts, sc next 2 sts tog) around (24).

Rnd 90: (Sc in each of next 2 sts, sc next 2 sts tog) around (18).

Rnd 91: (Sc in next st, sc next 2 sts tog) around (12).

Rnds 92-93: (Sl st in next st, skip next st) around. At end of last rnd, join with sl st in first sl st, fasten off.

SKIRT
Rnd 1: Working in **front lps** of rnd 47 on outer Body, with K hook and 2 strands black held tog, join with sl st at center back, ch 3, dc in each of next 2

Continued on next page

DAISY MAID VACUUM COVER

Continued from page 45

sts, 2 dc in next st, (dc in each of next 3 sts, 2 dc in next st) around, join with sl st in top of ch-3 (60 dc).

Rnd 2: Ch 3, dc in next 8 sts, 2 dc in next st, (dc in next 9 sts, 2 dc in next st) around, join (66).

Rnd 3: Ch 3, dc in next 9 sts, 2 dc in next st, (dc in next 10 sts, 2 dc in next st) around, join (72).

Rnd 4: Ch 3, dc in next 10 sts, 2 dc in next st, (dc in next 11 sts, 2 dc in next st) around, join (78).

Rnd 5: Ch 3, dc in next 11 sts, 2 dc in next st, (dc in next 12 sts, 2 dc in next st) around, join (84).

Rnd 6: Ch 3, dc in next 12 sts, 2 dc in next st, (dc in next 13 sts, 2 dc in next st) around, join (90).

Rnd 7: Ch 3, dc in next 13 sts, 2 dc in next st, (dc in next 14 sts, 2 dc in next st) around, join (96).

Rnd 8: Ch 3, dc in next 14 sts, 2 dc in next st, (dc in next 15 sts, 2 dc in next st) around, join (102).

Rnd 9: Ch 3, dc in next 15 sts, 2 dc in next st, (dc in next 16 sts, 2 dc in next st) around, join (108).

Rnd 10: Ch 3, dc in next 16 sts, 2 dc in next st, (dc in next 17 sts, 2 dc in next st) around, join (114).

Rnd 11: Ch 3, dc in next 17 sts, 2 dc in next st, (dc in next 18 sts, 2 dc in next st) around, join (120).

Rnd 12: Ch 3, dc in next 18 sts, 2 dc in next st, (dc in next 19 sts, 2 dc in next st) around, join (126).

Rnd 13: Ch 3, dc in next 19 sts, 2 dc in next st, (dc in next 20 sts, 2 dc in next st) around, join (132).

Rnd 14: Ch 3, dc in next 20 sts, 2 dc in next st, (dc in next 21 sts, 2 dc in next st) around, join (138).

Rnds 15-35: Ch 3, dc in each st around, join.

Rnd 36: Ch 1; working left to right, **reverse sc** (see page 159) in each st around, join with sl st in first sc, fasten off.

ARM (make 2)
Hand & Forearm

Rnd 1: Starting at Hand, with K hook and 2 strands peach held tog, ch 3, sl st in first ch to form ring, ch 1, 2 sc in each ch around (6 sc).

Rnd 2: 2 sc in each st around (12).

Rnds 3-11: Sc in each st around. At end of last rnd, join with sl st in first sc, fasten off.

Rnd 12: For **Forearm,** with K hook and 2 strands black held tog, join with sc in first st, sc in each st around.

Rnd 13: (Sc in next 5 sts, 2 sc in next st) 2 times (14).

Rnds 14-15: Sc in each st around.

Rnd 16: (Sc in next 6 sts, 2 sc in next st) 2 times (16).

Rnds 17-22: Sc in each st around. At end of last rnd, join with sl st in first sc, fasten off. Stuff.

Upper Arm

Rnds 1-2: With 2 strands black, repeat same rnds of Hand & Forearm.

Rnd 3: (Sc in next st, 2 sc in next st) around (18).

Rnds 4-21: Sc in each st around.

Rnd 22: (Sc in next st, sc next 2 sts tog) around (12). Stuff.

Rnd 23: (Sc next 2 sts tog) around (6).

Rnd 24: (Sl st in next st, skip next st) around, join with sl st in first sl st, fasten off.

Sew last rnd of Forearm to side of Upper Arm over rnds 19-24.

Thumb

Rnd 1: With K hook and 2 strands peach held tog, ch 3, sl st in first ch to form ring, ch 1, 2 sc in each ch around (6 sc).

Rnds 2-3: Sc in each st around. At end of last rnd, join with sl st in first sc, fasten off.

Sew to top of Hand over rnds 8 and 9 as shown in photo.

HAND STRAP (make 2)

Row 1: With K hook and 2 strands peach held tog, ch 3, sc in 2nd ch from hook, sc in each ch across, turn (3 sc).

Rows 2-5: Ch 1, sc in each st across, turn. At end of last row, fasten off.

Sew one end of one Strap to rnd 4 on palm of Hand and other end to rnd 10. Repeat on other Hand.

CUFF (make 2)

Row 1: With K hook and 2 strands black held tog, ch 21, sc in 2nd ch from hook, sc in each ch across, turn (20 sc).

Rows 2-3: Ch 1, sc in each st across, turn. At end of last row, fasten off.

Wrap Cuff around wrist on Arm, with ends on bottom of Arm. Working through both thicknesses, sew Cuff together, ¾" from ends.

Sew one button to outside end of each Cuff.

With Thumbs pointing forward, sew rnds 3-11 of Arms to each side of Body as shown in photo.

COLLAR

Row 1: With K hook and 2 strands black held tog, ch 37, sc in 2nd ch from hook, sc in each ch across, turn (36 sc).

Row 2: Ch 3, dc in same st, 2 dc in next st, 2 hdc in next st, sc in each st across to last 3 sts, 2 hdc in next st, 2 dc in next st, (dc, ch 3, sl st) in last st, fasten off.

Place around neck with ends in front, sew ends of starting ch together.

EAR (make 2)
Rnd 1: With G hook and one strand peach, ch 2, 6 sc in 2nd ch from hook (6 sc).

Rnd 2: 2 sc in each st around (12).

Rnd 3: (Sc in next st, 2 sc in next st) around, join with sl st in first sc, fasten off (18).

Row 4: Fold Ear in half wrong sides together. Matching sts and working through both thicknesses, join with sc in first st on curved edge, sc in each st across, fasten off.

Sew straight edge of each Ear to each side of Head.

NOSE
Row 1: With K hook and 2 strands peach held tog, ch 2, 2 sc in 2nd ch from hook, turn (2 sc).

Row 2: Ch 1, sc in each st across, turn.

Row 3: Ch 1, 2 sc in first st, sc in last st, turn (3).

Rnd 4: Ch 1, sc in each st and in ends of each row around with 3 sc in each corner and in point, join with sl st in first sc, fasten off.

Puckering Nose slightly, sew to center front of Head as shown, stuffing lightly before closing.

HAIR
For each section of Hair, cut three strands of brown each 30" long. Holding all three strands together, draw one end of strands through row or st using crochet hook. Pull ends even.

Make sections of Hair around face and back of Head.

Pull strands of Hair to top of Head and secure with separate strand of brown.

CAP
Rnd 1: With K hook and 2 strands white held tog, ch 4, sl st in first ch to form ring, ch 3, 11 dc in ring, join with sl st in top of ch-3 (12 dc).

Rnd 2: Ch 3, dc in same st, 2 dc in each st around, join (24).

Rnd 3: Ch 3, 2 dc in next st, (dc in next st, 2 dc in next st) around, join (36).

Rnd 4: Ch 3, dc in next st, 2 dc in next st, (dc in each of next 2 sts, 2 dc in next st) around, join (48).

Rnd 5: Ch 3, dc in each st around, join.

Rnd 6: Ch 1, (sc next 2 sts tog) around, join with sl st in first sc (24 sc).

Rnd 7: Ch 1, sc in each st around, join.

Rnd 8: Ch 3, 2 dc in same st, sc in next st, (3 dc in next st, sc in next st) around, join with sl st in top of ch-3, fasten off.

Roll Hair into a bun and tuck inside Cap. Sew rnd 7 of Cap to top of Head.

For **tie,** with K hook and one strand black, ch 76,

sl st in 2nd ch from hook, sl st in each ch across, fasten off. Tie around Cap into a bow at front.

EYE (make 2)
With G hook and one strand black, ch 3, sl st in first ch to form ring, ch 1, 2 sc in each ch around, join with sl st in first sc, fasten off. Sew Eyes to front of Head centered over nose 1¾" apart.

FINISHING
With brown, using Straight Stitch (see page 158), embroider eyebrows above Eyes; with black, embroider mouth below Nose as shown.

APRON
Skirt
Row 1: With K hook and 2 strands white held tog, ch 22, dc in 4th ch from hook, dc in each ch across, turn (20 dc).

Rows 2-4: Ch 3, dc in each st across, turn.

Row 5: Ch 3, dc in same st, dc in each st across with 2 dc in last st, turn (22).

Rows 6-7: Ch 3, dc in each st across, turn.

Rows 8-25: Repeat rows 5-7 consecutively, ending with 34 dc in last row. At end of last row, fasten off.

Bib
Row 1: With K hook and 2 strands white held tog, working in starting ch on opposite side of row 1 on Skirt, join with sl st in first ch, ch 1, sc same ch and next ch tog, (sc next 2 chs tog) across, turn (10 sc).

Row 2: Ch 1, sc in each st across, turn.

Row 3: Ch 3, dc in same st, dc in each st across with 2 dc in last st, turn (12 dc).

Row 4: Ch 3, dc in each st across, turn.

Rows 5-8: Repeat rows 3 and 4 alternately, ending with 16 dc in last row.

Row 9: Ch 3, dc in each st across, turn.

Row 10: For **first strap,** ch 3, dc in each of next 2 sts leaving remaining sts unworked, turn (3).

Rows 11-27: Ch 3, dc in each st across, turn. At end of last row, fasten off.

Row 10: For **second strap,** skip next 10 sts on row 9, join with sl st in next st, ch 3, dc in each of last 2 sts, turn.

Rows 11-27: Ch 3, dc in each st across, turn. At end of last row, fasten off.

For **edging,** working in sts and in ends of rows around Apron, with K hook and 2 strands white held tog, join with sc in end of last row on right strap, sc in same row, 2 sc in each of next 8 rows, (2 hdc, 3 dc) in next row, 6 dc in each of next 7 rows, (3 dc, 2 hdc) in next row, 2 sc in next 7 rows, sc in each of next 2 rows, 2 sc in each row and sc in each st around Apron Skirt, sc in each of next 2 rows, 2 sc in each of next 7 rows, (2 hdc, 3 dc) in next row,

Continued on page 61

Functional practicality and understated elegance come to your kitchen with this rose and white toaster and detergent bottle cover. A kitchen set all will admire!

KITCHEN SET

DESIGNED BY VIDA SUNDERMAN

SIZE
Toaster Cover fits 2-slice toaster measuring 4½" x 6" x 8½". Detergent Apron fits 22-oz. detergent bottle.

MATERIALS
Acrylic sport-weight thread — 4½ oz. rose and 2 oz. white; F crochet hook or size needed to obtain gauge.

GAUGE
5 hdc sts = 1"; 4 hdc rows = 1".

TOASTER COVER
NOTE: Ch-2 at beginning of each row counts as first hdc.

Row 1: Starting at top, with rose, ch 23, hdc in 3rd ch from hook, hdc in each ch across, turn (22 hdc).

Rows 2-33: Ch 2, hdc in each st across, turn.

Rnd 34: For **sides,** working in rnds, ch 1, sc in each st across; *working in ends of rows, 2 sc in first row, (sc in next row, 2 sc in next row) across*; working in starting ch on opposite side of row 1, sc in each ch across; repeat between **, join with sl st in first sc (144 sc).

Rnd 35: Working this rnd in **back lps,** ch 3, dc in each st around with 2 dc in 2 sts at each corner, join with sl st in top of ch-3 (152 dc).

Rnd 36: Join white with sc in first st, ch 4, skip next st, sc in next st, *(ch 4, skip next 3 sts, sc in next st) 5 times, (ch 4, skip next st, sc in next st) 2 times, (ch 4, skip next 3 sts, sc in next st) 12 times*, (ch 4, skip next st, sc in next st) 2 times; repeat between **, ch 4, skip last st, join with sl st in first sc (42 ch lps).

Rnd 37: Sl st in first ch lp, ch 1, sc in same lp, ch 4, (sc in next ch lp, ch 4) around, join, fasten off.

Rnd 38: Join rose with sl st in first ch lp, ch 3, 3 dc in same lp, ch 1, (4 dc in next ch lp, ch 1) around, join with sl st in top of ch-3, fasten off.

Rnd 39: Join white with sl st in last ch-1 sp made on last rnd, ch 4, (sc in next ch-1 sp, ch 4) around, join with sl st in first sc.

Rnd 40: Sl st in first ch lp, ch 1, sc in same lp, ch 4, (sc in next ch lp, ch 4) around, join, fasten off.

Rnds 41-57: Repeat rnds 38-40 consecutively, ending with rnd 39.

Rnd 58: Sl st in first ch lp, ch 1, (sc, dc, ch 3, dc, sc) in same lp and in each ch lp around, join, fasten off.

For **edging,** working in **front lps** of rnd 34, join white with sc in any corner st, dc in same st, *ch 3, (dc, sc) in next st, (sc in next st, dc in next st, ch 3, dc in next st, sc in next st) 5 times, (sc, dc) in next st, ch 3, (dc, sc) in next st, (sc in next st, dc in next st, ch 3, dc in next st, sc in next st) 12 times*, (sc, dc) in next st; repeat between **, join with sl st in first sc, fasten off.

DETERGENT APRON
Rnd 1: Starting at waist, with rose, ch 72, sl st in first ch to form ring, ch 4, skip next ch, (dc in next ch, ch 1, skip next ch) around, join with sl st in 3rd ch of ch-4, fasten off (36 dc, 36 ch-1 sps).

Rnd 2: Join white with sc in first dc, (ch 4, skip next 2 ch-1 sps and 1 dc, sc in next dc) around to last 2 ch-1 sps and 1 dc; to **join,** ch 2, hdc in first sc (18 ch lps).

Rnd 3: Ch 1, sc around joining hdc, ch 4, (sc in next ch lp, ch 4) around, join with sl st in first sc, fasten off.

Rnd 4: Join rose with sl st in first ch lp, ch 3, 3 dc in same lp, ch 1, (4 dc in next ch lp, ch 1) around, join with sl st in top of ch-3, fasten off.

Rnd 5: Join white with sl st in last ch-1 sp made on last rnd, ch 1, sc in same sp, (ch 4, sc in next ch-1 sp) around; to **join,** ch 2, hdc in first sc.

Rnds 6-16: Repeat rnds 3-5 consecutively, ending with rnd 4.

Rnd 17: Join white with sl st in last ch-1 sp made on last rnd, ch 1, sc in same sp, ch 4, (sc in next ch-1 sp, ch 4) around, join with sl st in first sc.

Rnd 18: Sl st in first ch lp, ch 1, (sc, dc, ch 3, dc, sc) in same lp and in each ch lp around, join, fasten off.

Bib
Row 1: Working in starting ch on opposite side of rnd 1, join rose with sl st in any ch-1 sp, ch 2, hdc in same sp, 2 hdc in each of next 5 ch-1 sps leaving remaining sts unworked, turn (12 hdc).

Rows 2-8: Ch 2, hdc in each st across, turn.

For **neck band,** ch 26, sl st in opposite corner of row 8, fasten off.

For **edging,** join white with sc in same ch-1 sp on Apron as first st on row 1; working in ends of rows, *(sc, dc) in next row, ch 3, (dc, sc) in next row*; repeat between ** 2 times, sc in next row, (dc, ch 3, dc) in next st; working across row 8, sc in each of next 2 sts, (dc in next st, ch 3, dc in next st, sc in each of next 2 sts) 2 times, (dc, ch 3, dc) in next st; working in ends of rows, sc in next row; repeat between ** 3 more times, sc in same ch-1 sp on Apron as last st on row 1, fasten off.

For **tie,** holding 2 strands yarn tog, make 24" long chain, fasten off.

Starting at center back, weave tie between dc sts on row 1 of Apron, tie into a bow.❖

Spring is bursting out all over these fanciful kitchen accessories scattered generously with pretty periwinkles and lacy ruffles. This handy wall caddy and pot holder will add fresh appeal to your country kitchen.

KITCHEN CADDY

DESIGNED BY JANE PEARSON

SIZE
Wall Caddy is 5" x 8¼". Pot Holder is 7¼" across.

MATERIALS
Worsted-weight yarn — 3 oz. white, 2 oz. lt. blue, small each amount dk. blue, green and yellow; dish cloth; hand towel; 2 small cup hooks; 4 plastic 1" rings; ⅜" thick x 1½" wide x 7½" long piece wood; craft glue; tapestry needle; G crochet hook or size needed to obtain gauge.

GAUGE
4 sts = 1"; 4 sc rows = 1".

WALL CADDY
Top
Row 1: With white, ch 18, sc in 2nd ch from hook, (dc in next ch, sc in next ch) across, turn (17 sts).

Rows 2-25: Ch 1, sc in each sc and dc in each dc across, turn.

Row 26: Fold last row in half; working through both thicknesses, ch 1, sc in each st across, fasten off.

Fold row 1 in half; working in starting ch on opposite side of row 1 through both thicknesses, join white with sc in first ch at fold, sc in each ch across, insert wood into crocheted piece; working through both thicknesses, sc in end of each row across, fasten off.

Towel Loop
Row 1: With white, ch 12, sc in 2nd ch from hook, (dc in next ch, sc in next ch) across, turn (11 sts).

Rows 2-16: Ch 1, sc in each sc and dc in each dc across, turn.

Row 17: Hold first and last rows tog, matching sts; working through both thicknesses, ch 1, sc in each st across, fasten off.

Sew or glue seam of Towel Loop to center bottom of Caddy.

Flower (make 3 each lt. blue and dk. blue)
Ch 4, sl st in first ch to form ring, (ch 2, 2 dc, ch 2, sl st) 6 times in ring, join with sl st in first ch of first ch-2, fasten off.

With yellow, make one large French Knot (see page 159) in center of each Flower.

Leaf (make 6)
Ch 4, sl st in 2nd ch from hook, sc in next ch, 2 dc in last ch, fasten off.

Glue Fowers and Leaves to front of Caddy Top as shown in photo. Screw one cup hook into wood through bottom of Caddy on each end. Sew 3 rings evenly spaced to back of Caddy. Insert hand towel through Towel Loop.

POT HOLDER
Front
NOTE: Do not join rnds unless otherwise stated. Mark first st of each rnd.

Work in **back lps** unless otherwise indicated.

Rnd 1: With lt. blue, ch 4, sl st in first ch to form ring, ch 1, 7 sc in ring (7 sc).

Rnds 2-3: 2 sc in each st around (14, 28).

Rnd 4: (Sc in next st, 2 sc in next st) around (42).

Rnds 5-6: Sc in each st around.

Rnd 7: (Sc in each of next 2 sts, 2 sc in next st) around (56).

Rnd 8: (Sc in each of next 3 sts, 2 sc in next st) around (70).

Rnds 9-10: Sc in each st around.

Rnd 11: (Sc in next 4 sts, 2 sc in next st) around, join with sl st in first sc (84).

Rnd 12: Working this rnd in **front lps,** ch 1, (sc in next st, ch 4) around, join with sl st in first sc, fasten off.

For **ruffle,** working in **front lps** of rnd 8, join white with sc in first st, ch 4, (sc in next st, ch 4) around, join, fasten off.

Repeat ruffle using lt. blue in **front lps** of rnd 9 and white in **front lps** of rnd 10.

Flower (make 3 each lt. blue and dk. blue and one white)
Work same as Caddy's Flower. Glue Flowers to center of Pot Holder Front as shown in photo.

Back
NOTE: Work in **both lps** unless otherwise stated.

Continued on page 57

Enhance your dining decor with lovely dinner napkins embellished with a delicate edging of crochet cotton. A lacy motif is carefully added to a corner cutout to further complement these stunning napkins.

❧ VICTORIAN NAPKIN ❧

DESIGNED BY JUDY TEAGUE TREECE

SIZE
19" square.

MATERIALS
Size 10 bedspread cotton — 218 yds. pink; 17" square burgundy cloth napkin; burgundy sewing thread; pencil; 2 bobby pins; sewing needle; No. 6 steel crochet hook or size needed to obtain gauge.

GAUGE
Rnds 1-3 of Motif = 1¾"; Rnds 2-5 of Border Edging = 1" wide.

MOTIF
Rnd 1: Ch 5, sl st in first ch to form ring, ch 3, 14 dc in ring, join with sl st in top of ch-3 (15 dc).

Rnd 2: Ch 5, (dc in next st, ch 2) around, join with sl st in 3rd ch of ch-5 (15 dc, 15 ch-2 sps).

Rnd 3: Sl st in first ch-2 sp, ch 3, dc in same sp, ch 1, (2 dc in next ch-2 sp, ch 1) around, join with sl st in top of ch-3 (30 dc, 15 ch-1 sps).

Rnd 4: Ch 3, dc in same st, ch 2, 2 dc in next st, skip next ch-1 sp, *2 dc in next st, ch 2, 2 dc in next st, skip next ch-1 sp; repeat from * around, join (15 ch-2 sps).

Rnd 5: Sl st in next st, sl st in first ch-2 sp, ch 3, (2 dc, ch 2, 3 dc) in same sp, (3 dc, ch 2, 3 dc) in each ch-2 sp around, join.

Rnd 6: Sl st in each of next 2 sts, sl st in first ch-2 sp, ch 3, (dc, ch 2, 2 dc) in same sp, ch 2, *(2 dc, ch 2, 2 dc) in next ch-2 sp, ch 2; repeat from * around, join, fasten off.

NAPKIN PREPARATION
1: Using bobby pins, mark 1st and 15th ch-2 sps of rnd 6 on Motif. Place Motif over one corner of napkin having marked ch-2 sps at edge of napkin on each side. Trace around curved edge of Motif onto napkin with a pencil. Cut out curved corner of napkin, adding ¼" seam allowance.

2: With sewing needle and thread, hem curved raw edge, folding under twice to form ⅛" seam.

3: Using pink bedspread cotton, place slip knot on hook; working around outer edge of napkin, insert hook through fabric, yo, draw lp through, yo, draw through 2 lps on hook (first sc made), ch 1, (sc, ch 1) evenly around napkin with approximately 6 sc per inch and 4 sc in each corner, join with sl st in first sc, fasten off.

BORDER EDGING
Row 1: To **join Motif to napkin,** matching curved edges and working through both thicknesses, with Motif facing you, join with sc in first marked ch-2 sp, (ch 1, skip next st or ch sp, sc in next st or ch sp) across to opposite marked ch-2 sp, **turn.**

NOTE: Each sc or ch-1 around napkin counts as one st each.

Rnd 2: Working around outer edge of Motif and napkin, ch 3, dc in next ch-2 sp on Motif, ch 3, (dc in next ch-2 sp, ch 3, skip next dc, dc in next dc, ch 3, skip next ch-2 sp, dc in next dc, ch 3) 3 times, (dc, ch 3, dc, ch 3, dc) in next ch-2 sp, ch 3, skip next dc, dc in next dc, ch 3, skip next ch-2 sp, dc in next dc, (ch 3, dc in next ch-2 sp, ch 3, skip next dc, dc in next dc, ch 3, skip next ch-2 sp, dc in next dc) 3 times, ch 3, dc in same ch-2 sp as joining; working around napkin, ch 3, skip next 3 sts, (dc in next st, ch 3, skip next 3 sts) around with (dc, ch 3, dc) in each corner st, join with sl st in top of ch-3.

Rnd 3: Sl st in next st, sl st in first ch-3 sp, ch 4, dc in same sp, (ch 1, dc) 4 times in same sp, ch 3, skip next ch-3 sp, sc in next ch-3 sp, ch 3, skip next ch-3 sp, *dc in next ch-3 sp, (ch 1, dc) 5 times in same sp, ch 3, skip next ch-3 sp, sc in next ch-3 sp, ch 3, skip next ch-3 sp; repeat from * around easing to fit if necessary at corners by not skipping ch-3 sps before and after 6-dc groups, join with sl st in 3rd ch of ch-4.

Rnd 4: Ch 4, dc in next dc, (ch 1, dc in next dc) 4 times, ch 2, (sc in next ch-3 sp, ch 2) 2 times, *dc in next dc, (ch 1, dc in next dc) 5 times, ch 2, (sc in next ch-3 sp, ch 2) 2 times; repeat from * around, join.

Rnd 4: Sl st in first ch-1 sp, ch 1, (sc, ch 2, sc) in same sp, (sc, ch 2, sc) in each of next 4 ch-1 sps, ch 2, (sc in next ch-2 sp, ch 2) 3 times, *(sc, ch 2, sc) in each of next 5 ch-1 sps, ch 2, (sc in next ch-2 sp, ch 2) 3 times; repeat from * around, join with sl st in first sc, fasten off.❖

Miss Pig is quite sociable and likes to go calling with her pretty clothes on show. Miss Crow likes to tend to her garden and see how many flowers she can grow. These country cousins will make unique doorstops.

❦ COUNTRY COZY DOLLS ❦

DESIGNED BY ESTELLA WHITFORD

SIZE
Pig is 15" tall not including hat. Crow is 13½" tall not including hat.

MATERIALS FOR PIG
Worsted-weight yarn — 6 oz. peach, 3 oz. pink, 1 oz. green and small amount black; 2 black 12-mm animal eyes with washers; ¼ yd. navy print fabric; 18" square piece white fabric; 1¼ yds. ecru 1¾" gathered cluny lace; 1½ yds. jute; 12" sinamay hat; small bunch of silk flowers; 2¾" square doll glasses; 2 liter plastic soda bottle; blue sewing thread; polyester fiberfill; craft glue or hot glue gun; sewing and tapestry needles; H crochet hook or size needed to obtain gauge.

MATERIALS FOR CROW
Worsted-weight yarn — 7 oz. black, small amount each orange, white, gold, brown and red; 5 white buttons in assorted sizes; one brown 5⁄16" button; 2 black 15-mm animal eyes with washers; 2" square piece white felt; ¼ yd. patterned print fabric; ¼ yd. muslin; 4" x 45" piece coordinating check or print fabric; 3¾" x 4" piece green fabric; 10" straw hat; 2 floral picks; 3¼" clay pot; floral foam to fit pot; natural excelsior; 2 liter plastic soda bottle; polyester fiberfill; sewing thread to match fabric; craft glue or hot glue gun; sewing and tapestry needles; H crochet hook or size needed to obtain gauge.

GAUGE
7 sc = 2"; 7 sc rnds = 2".

PIG

HEAD & BODY
NOTE: Do not join rnds unless otherwise stated; mark first st of each rnd.

Rnd 1: With peach, ch 2, 6 sc in 2nd ch from hook (6 sc).

Rnd 2: 2 sc in each st around (12).

Rnd 3: (Sc in next st, 2 sc in next st) around (18).

Rnd 4: (Sc in each of next 2 sts, 2 sc in next st) around (24).

Rnd 5: (Sc in each of next 3 sts, 2 sc in next st) around (30).

Rnd 6: (Sc in next 4 sts, 2 sc in next st) around (36).

Rnd 7: (Sc in next 5 sts, 2 sc in next st) around (42).

Rnd 8: (Sc in next 6 sts, 2 sc in next st) around (48).

Rnd 9: (Sc in next 7 sts, 2 sc in next st) around (54).

Rnds 10-19: Sc in each st around.

Rnd 20: (Sc next 2 sts tog) around (27). Attach eyes with washers between rnds 10 and 11 of head ½" apart.

Rnds 21-22: Sc in each st around. Stuff Head.

Rnd 23: Repeat rnd 2 (54).

Rnds 24-52: Sc in each st around. At end of last rnd, join with sl st in first sc, fasten off.

ARM (make 2)
Rnds 1-3: Repeat same rnds of Head & Body.

Rnds 4-25: Sc in each st around. At end of last rnd, join with sl st in first sc, fasten off. Stuff.

Flatten last rnd; sew to each side of Body over rnds 25 and 26.

EAR (make 2)
Row 1: With peach, ch 6, sc in 2nd ch from hook, sc in each ch across, turn (5 sc).

Row 2: Ch 1, 2 sc in first st, sc in each st across with 2 sc in last st, turn (7).

Row 3: Ch 1, sc in each st across, turn.

Row 4: Ch 1, sc first 2 sts tog, sc in each st across to last 2 sts, sc last 2 sts tog, turn (5).

Row 5: Ch 1, sc first 2 sts tog, sc in next st, sc last 2 sts tog, turn (3).

Row 6: Ch 1, sc next 3 sts tog, turn (1).

Rnd 7: Working around outer edge, ch 1, 3 sc in next st, sc in ends of each row and in each st around, join with sl st in first sc, fasten off.

Sew Ears to each side of Head over rnds 4-9.

SNOUT
Rnds 1-3: Repeat same rnds of Head & Body.

Rnd 4: Working this rnd in **back lps** only, sc in each st around.

Rnd 5: Sc in each st around, join with sl st in

Continued on page 56
Continued on page 56

Continued from page 54

first sc, fasten off.

Stuff; sew to Head centered below eyes over rnds 12-18.

FINISHING

1: With black, using French Knot (see page 159), embroider nostrils to center of Snout spaced ¼" apart.

2: Place Body over plastic bottle.

WATERMELON
Side (make 6)

Row 1: With pink, ch 13, sc in 2nd ch from hook, sc in each ch across, turn (12 sc).

Row 2: Ch 1, sc first 2 sts tog, sc in each st across to last 2 sts, sc last 2 sts tog, turn (10).

Row 3: Ch 1, sc in each st across, turn.

Rows 4-8: Repeat rows 2 and 3 alternately, ending with row 2 and 4 sts. At end of last row, fasten off.

Row 9: For **edging,** working in ends of rows and in sts, join green with sc in first row, sc in same row, sc in each row across, 3 sc in first st, sc in each of next 2 sts, 3 sc in last st, sc in each row across with 2 sc in last row, fasten off.

For each Watermelon (make 3), hold two sides wrong sides together, matchng sts; with green, sew row 9 together through **back lps.**

Finishing

With black, using French Knot, embroider five seeds randomly across front of each Watermelon.

Leaving 4" end, weave jute through sts on first row on back Side of each Watermelon. Secure ends of jute to each Arm on Pig as shown in photo.

DRESS

1: Allowing ½" for seam, sew short edges of navy fabric right sides together.

2: For top of Dress, turn under 1" on one raw edge. Press. Baste ¾" from folded edge, pull ends to gather around Body of Pig. Secure.

3: Turn under ¼" twice on bottom edge. Press. Holding bound edge of lace to wrong side of fold, machine zigzag or hand stitch together. Sew ends of lace together.

Finishing

1: Glue top of Dress to Body of Pig.

2: Fold white fabric in half to form triangle, tie ends into knot around neck of Pig.

3: Cut Ear holes in Hat. Pull Ears through holes.

4: Fold brim of hat down in front of left Ear, glue in place. Glue flowers over folded-down brim.

5: Place glasses on Pig.

CROW
HEAD & BODY

NOTES: Cut two pieces of felt each 1⁄16" larger than eyes. Push shank of eyes through felt pieces.

When attaching eyes, place side-by-side betweenrnds 10 and 11.

With black, work same as Pig's Head & Body.

BEAK

NOTE: Do not join rnds unless otherwise stated; mark first st of each rnd.

Rnd 1: With orange, ch 2, 6 sc in 2nd ch from hook (6 sc).

Rnd 2: (Sc in next st, 2 sc in next st) around (9).

Rnd 3: (Sc in each of next 2 sts, 2 sc in next st) around (12).

Rnd 4: Repeat rnd 2 (18).

Rnds 5-7: Sc in each st around.

Rnd 8: Repeat rnd 3 (24).

Rnd 9: Sc in each st around, join with sl st in first sc, fasten off.

Flatten last rnd; with sides curved down slightly, sew to Head over rnds 12-17 below eyes.

WING (make 2)
Side (make 2)

Row 1: With black, ch 15, sc in 2nd ch from hook, sc in each ch across, turn (14 sc).

Rows 2-6: Ch 1, sc in each st across, turn.

Row 7: Ch 1, sc first 2 sts tog, sc in each st across, turn (13).

Row 8: Repeat row 2.

Row 9: Repeat row 7 (12).

Row 10: Ch 1, sc in each st across to last 2 sts, sc last 2 sts tog, turn (11).

Row 11: Repeat row 7 (10),

Row 12: Repeat row 2.

Row 13: Ch 3, sc in 2nd ch from hook, sc in next ch, sc in each st across, turn (12).

Row 14: Repeat row 2.

Row 15: Repeat row 7 (11).

Rows 16-19: Repeat row 2.

Row 20: Repeat row 10 (10).

Row 21: Repeat row 2.

Row 22: Repeat row 10 (9).

Row 23: Repeat row 13 (11).

Row 24: Ch 1, sc first 2 sts tog, sc in each st

across to last 2 sts, sc last 2 sts tog, turn (9).

Row 25: Repeat row 2.

Rows 26-27: Repeat row 24 (7, 5).

Row 28: Repeat row 2.

Row 29: Ch 1, sc first 2 sts tog, sc in next st, sc last 2 sts tog, turn (3).

Row 30: Ch 1, sc first 2 sts tog, sc in last st, fasten off.

Holding Sides together, matching shaping, with white, sew long edges and last row together approximately ⅜" from edge.

Sew first row of each Wing to each side of Body as shown in photo.

Place Body over plastic bottle.

APRON & SCARF

1: From muslin, cut 9" x 14½" piece for apron and 1½" x 24" strip for ties. From patterned print, cut 4¼" x 14½" piece for pockets.

2: With right side of pocket piece and wrong sides of apron piece together, match bottom edge of pocket piece to one long edge of apron piece; using ¼" seam, sew together across bottom edge.

3: Press under ¼" on top edge of pocket piece, topstitch in place. Fold pocket piece up over apron; press along bottom seam. Sew across pocket piece every 4½" to form 4 pockets.

4: Press under ¼" on each side edge of apron; press under ¼" again and topstitch in place.

5: Run a gathering thread along top of apron, ½" from edge. Pull to gather until top is 7" wide; secure.

6: Fold ties piece in half lengthwise with right sides together. Allowing ½" for seam, sew along open long edge and ends leaving 8" open at center. Clip corners, turn right side out. Press, turning edges on opening inside.

7: Slip tie piece over gathered edge at top of Apron; top stitch across open edge of tie piece to secure.

8: Place Apron on Crow. Tie coordinating check or print around Head and tie ends into a bow. Place straw hat on Head.

FLOWER POT

LARGE FLOWER

Front

Rnds 1-6: With brown, repeat same rnds of Pig's Head & Body. At end of last rnd, join with sl st in first sc. Leaving long end for weaving, fasten off.

Weave end through sts on last rnd, pull to gather, secure.

Back

Rnds 1-5: With gold, repeat same rnds of Pig's Head & Body.

Rnd 6: Ch 1, sc in first st, ch 4, skip next st, (sc in next st, ch 4, skip next st) around, join with sl st in first sc, fasten off.

Sew Front to center of Back.

SMALL FLOWER

Front

Rnd 1: With gold, ch 2, 6 sc in 2nd ch from hook (6 sc).

Rnd 2: 2 sc in each st around, join with sl st in first sc, fasten off.

Back

Rnds 1-3: With red, repeat same rnds of Pig's Head & Body. At end of last rnd, join with sl st in first sc.

Rnd 4: Ch 4, (sl st in next st, ch 4) around, join with sl st in joining sl st of last rnd, fasten off.

Sew Front to center of Back.

FINISHING

1: Glue white buttons randomly to center of Large Flower.

2: Glue brown button to center of Small Flower.

3: Insert flower pick through back of each Flower, glue in place.

4: Cut four 1¼" x 4" pieces from green fabric. Tie two pieces around floral pick on Large Flower and one piece around floral pick on Small Flower.

5: Place floral foam in clay pot. Insert Flowers in foam. Arrange excelsior on top of pot.❖

KITCHEN CADDY

Continued from page 51

Rnds 1-11: Repeat same rnds of Front.

To **join**, holding Back and Front wrong sides together, matching sts of last rnds, working through both thicknesses, join lt. blue with sl st in any st, sl st in each st around, join with sl st in first sl st, fasten off.

For **hanger**, sew one ring to back of Pot Holder. Hang Pot Holder on one cup hook on Caddy. Loop dish cloth onto opposite cup hook.❖

CAPTIVATING CROCHET

This interesting edging made with a creative twist stitch is suitable for any decor. A versatile design, it exudes county charm as a shelf edging or becomes quite elegant when sewn to crisp linens.

LACE EDGING

DESIGNED BY KIM GOETZ

SIZE

Edging made with size 10 bedspread cotton is 2" wide. Edging made with size 30 crochet cotton is 1½" wide.

MATERIALS

Size 10 bedspread cotton — 5 yds. per inch; size 30 crochet cotton — 3 yds. per inch; No. 11 and No. 9 steel crochet hooks or sizes needed to obtain gauges.

GAUGES

No. 11 steel hook and size 30 crochet cotton, 14 sts = 1"; 4 pattern rows and 3 sc rows = 1". No. 9 steel hook and size 10 bedspread cotton, 10 sts = 1"; 3 pattern rows and 2 sc rows = 1".

EDGING

Row 1: Ch 15, sc in 2nd ch from hook, sc in each ch across, turn (14 sc).

NOTE: For **pattern stitch (pat st)**, yo, (insert hook in next st, yo, draw lp through) 2 times, yo, draw through 3 lps on hook, yo, draw through 2 lps on hook.

Row 2: Ch 3, (pat st, hdc around last st made) 6 times, dc in last st, turn.

Row 3: Ch 1, sc in each st across, turn (14 sc).

Rows 4-5: Repeat rows 2 and 3.

Row 6: Repeat row 2, **do not** turn; for **scallop**, tr in end of next sc row, (ch 1, tr in same row) 5 times, sc in end of next sc row, **turn**, ch 3, dc in last sc made, (sc in next ch-1 sp, ch 3, dc in last sc made) 5 times, sc in next dc, sc in each st across, turn (14 sc).

NOTES: Always leave scallops and picots at end of rows unworked.

For **picot**, ch 4, dc in 4th ch from hook.

Row 7: Repeat row 2, picot, turn.

Row 8: Ch 1, sc in each st across, turn.

Rows 9-12: Repeat rows 2 and 3 alternately.

Next Rows: Repeat rows 6-12 consecutively for desired number of scallops, ending with row 8.

Last Rows: Repeat rows 2 and 3. At end of last row, fasten off.❖

*Brighten up your kitchen with these lively neon and white pot holders. Quick
and easy to make, they will become your favorite gift for special friends.*

SPRINGTIME POT HOLDERS

DESIGNED BY LUCILLE ZETTLER

SIZE
7½" square.

MATERIALS FOR ONE
Worsted-weight yarn — 2 oz. main color (MC) and 1 oz. constrasting color (CC); H crochet hook or size needed to obtain gauge.

GAUGE
2 hdc and 2 sc = 1"; Rows 1-3 = 1".

SIDE (make 2)

NOTE: Ch-2 at beginning of each row counts as first hdc.

Row 1: With MC, ch 29, (sc, hdc) in 3rd ch from hook, *skip next ch, (sc, hdc) in next ch; repeat from * across, turn (15 hdc, 14 sc).

Row 2: Ch 2, *skip next sc, (sc, hdc) in next hdc; repeat from * across, turn, fasten off.

Row 3: Join CC with sc in first hdc, (ch 1, skip next sc, sc in next hdc) across, turn, fasten off.

Row 4: Join MC with sl st in first st, ch 2, *skip next ch-1 sp, (sc, hdc) in next sc; repeat from * across, turn.

Row 5: Ch 2, *skip next sc, (sc, hdc) in next hdc; repeat from * across, turn, fasten off.

Row 6: Join CC with sc in first st, (ch 1, skip next sc, sc in next hdc) across, turn, fasten off.

Rows 7-23: Repeat rows 4-6 consecutively, ending with row 5.

Holding Sides wrong sides together, matching sts, working through both thicknesses, join CC with sc in top left corner, sc in same st; for **hanger,** ch 6; sc in same st, sc in end of each row and 2 sc in each st around with 3 sc in each corner, join with sl st in first sc, fasten off. ❖

DAISY MAID VACUUM COVER
Continued from page 47

6 dc in each of next 7 rows, (3 dc, 2 hdc) in next row, 2 sc in each of next 9 rows; working on opposite side of Straps and around neckline, sc in each st and 2 sc each row around, join with sl st in first sc, fasten off.

For **ties,** with K hook and 2 strands white, join with sl st in st between Apron and Bib, ch 70, fasten off. Repeat on opposite side.

Skirt Pocket (make 2)

Row 1: With K hook and one strand white, ch 7, sc in 2nd ch from hook, sc in each ch across, turn (6).

Rows 2-3: Ch 1, 2 sc in first st, sc in each st across with 2 sc in last st, turn (8, 10).

Rows 4-10: Ch 1, sc in each st across, turn.

Row 11: Repeat row 2, **do not** turn (12).

Row 12: Working in ends of rows, ch 1, sc in first 11 rows; working in starting ch on opposite side of row 1, skip first ch, sc in next 5 chs; working in ends of rows, sc in last 11 rows, **do not** turn, fasten off (27 sc).

Row 13: Working in **back lps** of last row, join with sc in first st, 3 dc in next st, (sc in next st, 3 dc in next st) across, fasten off.

Sew Pockets side-by-side to Skirt over rows 10-15.

Bib Pocket

With one strand white and G hook, work same as Skirt Pocket.

Sew to center front of Bib over rows 5-8.

Place Apron on Daisy, criss-cross straps in back. Insert left tie through end of right strap and right tie through end of left strap. Pull to fit and tie into a bow. ❖

TEATIME CHARMS

PLAYMATES

Two little playmates, dancing in the sun,
Their lives are separate but their hearts are one.

Two little playmates sitting down to tea,
Each with a dolly perched on her knee.

Two little playmates all dressed up,
Laughter and giggles as they sip from their cups.

Two little playmates plotting imaginary games.
Each telling the other of her glory and fame.

Two little playmates shopping side by side.
One wants to be a doctor, the other a bride.

Two little playmates free from strife.
Sisters in blood, but friends for life.

DIAMOND RINGS COVERLET

DESIGNED BY CAROL ALEXANDER & BRENDA STRATTON
FOR MONSANTO'S DESIGNS FOR AMERICA PROGRAM

SIZE
51" x 65".

MATERIALS
3-ply sport yarn — 28 oz. ecru; 8¼ yds. dk. pink ⅜" satin ribbon; 4 dk. pink ½" satin ribbon roses with leaves; dk. pink sewing thread; sewing needle; G crochet hook or size needed to obtain gauge.

GAUGE
Rnd 1 of Motif = 1¼" across. Each Motif is 7¼" across.

MOTIF (make 48)
Rnd 1: Ch 8, sl st in first ch to form ring, ch 1, 30 sc in ring, join with sl st in first sc (30 sc).

NOTES: For **beginning shell (beg shell),** ch 2, (hdc, ch 2, 2 hdc) in same st or sp.

For **shell,** (2 hdc, ch 2, 2 hdc) in next st or ch sp.

Rnd 2: Beg shell, ch 7, skip next 4 sts, (shell, ch 7, skip next 4 sts) around, join with sl st in top of ch-2 (6 shells, 6 ch-7 lps).

Rnd 3: Sl st in next st, sl st in next ch sp, beg shell, ch 7, (shell in ch sp of next shell, ch 7) around, join.

Rnd 4: Sl st in next st, sl st in next ch sp, beg shell, ch 4; working over ch-7 lp on last rnd, sc in next ch-7 lp on rnd before last, ch 4, *shell in next shell, ch 4; working over ch-7 lp on last rnd, sc in next ch-7 lp on rnd before last, ch 4; repeat from * around, join (12 ch-4 sps, 6 shells, 6 sc).

Rnd 5: Sl st in next st, sl st in next ch sp, beg shell; (*for **ring,** ch 10, sl st in 7th ch from hook, ch 2, 13 hdc in ring, join with sl st in top of ch-2; sc in next sc, ch 3*, shell in next shell) 5 times; repeat between **, join (12 ch-3 sps, 6 shells, 6 rings).

Rnd 6: Sl st in next st, sl st in next ch sp, ch 4, (2 tr, ch 2, 3 tr) in same sp, *[ch 4, sc in 7th hdc at center top of next ring, ch 4], (3 tr, ch 2, 3 tr) in next shell; repeat from * around to last ring; repeat between [ ], join with sl st in top of ch-4.

Rnd 7: Sl st in each of next 2 sts, ch 1, sc in same st, *[ch 4, skip next ch-2 sp, skip next tr, sc in next tr, ch 4, skip next tr, (2 sc in next ch-4 sp, ch 4) 2

times, skip next 2 tr], sc in next tr; repeat from * 4 more times; repeat between [ ], join with sl st in first sc (24 ch lps).

Rnd 8: Sl st in first ch-4 sp, ch 1, 5 sc in same sp, *[5 hdc in next ch-4 sp; for **corner,** (4 hdc, 3 dc) in next ch-4 sp, (3 dc, 4 hdc) in next ch-4 sp; 5 hdc in next ch-4 sp], 5 sc in each of next 2 ch-4 sps; repeat from * 2 more times; repeat between [ ], 5 sc in last ch-4 sp, join with sl st in first sc, fasten off.

To **join,** leaving corners free, sew 20 sc and hdc across sides of Motifs together, ending with 6 rows of 8 Motifs each.

BORDER
Rnd 1: Working around entire outer edge of Motifs, join with sl st in sp between 2 corner 7-st groups before one short end, ch 4, (3 tr, ch 3, 4 tr) in same sp; working in sps between sts, ◊*[ch 2, 2 dc in sp before next 5-hdc group, ch 2, (2 hdc in sp between next 2 5-st groups, ch 2) 3 times, 2 dc in sp after next 5-hdc group, ch 2], 4 tr in sp between next 2 corner 7-st groups, ch 3, 4 tr in sp between next 2 corner 7-st groups on next Motif*; repeat between ** 4 more times; repeat between [ ], (4 tr, ch 3, 4 tr) in sp between next 2 corner 7-st groups; repeat between ** 7 more times; repeat between [ ]◊, (4 tr, ch 3, 4 tr) in sp between next 2 corner 7-st groups; repeat between ◊◊, join with sl st in top of ch-4.

Rnd 2: Sl st in next st, ch 2, hdc in each of next 2 sts, 4 hdc in next corner ch-3 sp, hdc in each of next 3 sts, skip next st, ◊*[3 hdc in next ch-2 sp, skip next st, hdc in next st, 3 sc in next ch-2 sp, (skip next st, sc in next st, 3 sc in next ch-2 sp) 3 times, skip next st, hdc in next st, 3 hdc in next ch-2 sp], skip next st, hdc in each of next 3 sts, 4 hdc in next ch-3 sp, skip next st, hdc in each of next 3 sts*; repeat between ** 4 more times; repeat between [ ], •skip next st, hdc in each of next 3 sts, 4 hdc in next corner ch-3 sp, hdc in each of next 3 sts, skip next st•; repeat between ** 7 more times; repeat between [ ]◊; repeat between ••; repeat between ◊◊, join with sl st in top of ch-2 (198 sts across each short end, 264 sts across each long edge).

Continued on page 73

Add feminine grace to her room with this delicate frame made with bedspread cotton and adorned with silk flowers and satin ribbon. Any lady will appreciate its delicate beauty.

Lace Oval Frame

Designed by Margaret Angerstein

SIZE
Frame is 7¼" x 8½"; photo opening is 3¼" x 4".

MATERIALS
Size 10 bedspread cotton — 75 yds. white; 12" each pink and blue ⅛" satin ribbon; 8" white ¹⁄₁₆" satin ribbon; tiny silk flowers in colors to match ribbon; fabric stiffener; Styrofoam® or blocking board; 1" x 12" cardboard strip; plastic wrap; rustproof pins; craft glue or hot glue gun; No. 6 steel crochet hook or size needed to obtain gauge.

GAUGE
One shell = ½".

FRAME

NOTES: For beginning shell (beg shell), (ch 4, dc, ch 1, dc, ch 1, dc) in same ch.

For **shell,** (dc, ch 1, dc, ch 1, dc, ch 1, dc) in next ch.

Rnd 1: Starting at center, ch 132, sl st in first ch to form ring, beg shell, skip next 2 chs, sc in next ch, skip next 2 chs, *shell in next ch, skip next 2 chs, sc in next ch, skip next 2 chs; repeat from * around, join with sl st in 3rd ch of ch-4 (22 shells, 22 sc).

Rnd 2: Sl st in next ch, next st and next ch sp, ch 1, sc in same sp, ch 8, (sc in center ch sp of next shell, ch 8) around, join with sl st in first sc (22 ch-8 lps).

Rnd 3: Ch 1, sc in first st, (ch 5, sc in next ch lp or in next sc) around; to **join,** ch 2, dc in first sc (44 ch-5 lps).

Rnds 4-6: Ch 1, sc around joining dc, (ch 5, sc in next ch lp) around, join as before.

Rnd 7: Ch 1, sc around joining dc, ch 3, skip next sc, (sc in next ch lp or in next sc, ch 3) around, join with sl st in first sc (87 ch-3 sps).

NOTE: For **picot,** ch 3, sl st in top of last sc made.

Rnd 8: Sl st in first ch-3 sp, ch 4, (dc, ch 2, dc, ch 1, dc) in same sp, sc in next ch-3 sp, picot, sc in next ch-3 sp, *(dc, ch 1, dc, ch 2, dc, ch 1, dc) in next ch-3 sp, sc in next ch-3 sp, picot, sc in next ch-3 sp; repeat from * around, join with sl st in 3rd ch of ch-4, fasten off.

PHOTO OPENING

Rnd 1: Working in starting ch on opposite side of rnd 1, join with sc in same ch as first shell was worked, (ch 4, sc in same ch as next shell was worked) around; to **join,** ch 2, hdc in first sc (22 ch-4 sps).

Rnds 2-4: Ch 1, sc around joining hdc, (ch 4, sc in next ch-4 sp) around, join as before.

Rnd 5: Ch 1, sc around joining hdc, ch 4, (sc in next ch-4 sp, ch 4) around, join with sl st in first sc, fasten off.

FINISHING

1: Apply fabric stiffener to Frame according to manufacturer's instructions; pin to plastic covered blocking board.

2: Form a ring with cardboard strip, place inside photo opening overlapping ends of cardboard if necessary. Pin photo opening to cardboard ring. Let dry completely.

3: Form a small bouquet with tiny silk flowers; glue to bottom of Frame slightly to one side. Holding pink and blue ribbons together, tie into a bow. Glue over center of flower bouquet.

4: For **hanging loop,** tie white ribbon around 2 sc on rnd 6 at center top of Frame. ❖

Enjoy the gossamer allure of this mystical doily stitched in fine size 30 crochet cotton. So richly elegant it will be a family treasure to be handed down from generation to generation.

CORONADO DOILY

DESIGNED BY LUELLA L. CARTWRIGHT

SIZE
15" from point to point. This project may ruffle until blocked.

MATERIALS
Size 30 crochet cotton — 250 yds. ecru; No. 6 steel crochet hook or size needed to obtain gauge.

GAUGE
Rnds 1-3 = 2½" across.

DOILY

Rnd 1: Ch 8, (tr in 8th ch from hook, ch 3) 7 times, join with sl st in 4th ch of ch-7 (8 tr, 8 ch-3 sps).

Rnd 2: Sl st in first ch-3 sp, ch 4, 4 tr in same sp, ch 3, (5 tr in next ch-3 sp, ch 3) around, join with sl st in top of ch-4 (40 tr, 8 ch-3 sps).

Rnd 3: Ch 4, tr next 4 sts tog, ch 10, (tr next 5 sts tog, ch 10) around, join.

Rnd 4: Ch 1, sc in same st, ch 14, (sc in top of next st, ch 14) around, join with sl st in first sc (8 ch-14 lps).

Rnd 5: Sl st in first ch-14 lp, ch 3, (6 dc, ch 1, 7 dc) in same lp, (7 dc, ch 1, 7 dc) in each ch-14 lp around, join with sl st in top of ch-3.

Rnd 6: Sl st in next st, ch 3, dc in next 5 sts, (dc, ch 1, dc) in next ch-1 sp, dc in next 6 sts, ch 3, skip next 2 sts, *dc in next 6 sts, (dc, ch 1, dc) in next ch-1 sp, dc in next 6 sts, ch 3, skip next 2 sts; repeat from * around, join.

Rnd 7: Sl st in next st, ch 3, dc in next 5 sts, *[(dc, ch 1, dc) in next ch-1 sp, dc in next 6 sts, ch 6, skip next st, skip next ch-3 sp, skip next st], dc in next 6 sts; repeat from * 6 more times; repeat between [ ], join.

Rnd 8: Sl st in next st, ch 3, dc in next 5 sts, *[(dc, ch 1, dc) in next ch-1 sp, dc in next 6 sts, ch 9, skip next st, skip next ch-6 sp, skip next st], dc in next 6 sts; repeat from * 6 more times; repeat between [ ], join.

Rnd 9: Sl st in next st, ch 3, dc in next 5 sts, *[(dc, ch 1, dc) in next ch-1 sp, dc in next 6 sts, ch 5, skip next st, dc in next ch-9 lp, ch 5, skip next st], dc in next 6 sts; repeat from * 6 more times; repeat between [ ], join.

Rnd 10: Sl st in next st, ch 3, dc in next 5 sts, *[(dc, ch 1, dc) in next ch-1 sp, dc in next 6 sts, ch 5, skip next st, dc in next ch-5 sp, dc in next st, dc in next ch-5 sp, ch 5, skip next st], dc in next 6 sts; repeat from * 6 more times; repeat between [ ], join.

Rnds 11-16: Sl st in next st, ch 3, dc in next 5 sts, *[(dc, ch 1, dc) in next ch-1 sp, dc in next 6 sts, ch 5, skip next st, dc in next ch-5 sp, dc in each st across to next ch-5 sp, dc in next ch-5 sp, ch 5, skip next st], dc in next 6 sts; repeat from * 6 more times; repeat between [ ], join.

Rnd 17: Sl st in next st, ch 3, dc in next 5 sts, *[(dc, ch 1, dc) in next ch-1 sp, dc in next 6 sts, ch 6, skip next st, skip next ch-5 sp, skip next st, dc in next 13 sts, ch 6, skip next st, skip next ch-5 sp, skip next st], dc in next 6 sts; repeat from * 6 more times; repeat between [ ], join.

Rnd 18: Sl st in next st, ch 3, dc in next 5 sts, *[(dc, ch 1, dc) in next ch-1 sp, dc in next 6 sts, ch 7, skip next st, skip next ch-6 sp, skip next st, dc in next 11 sts, ch 7, skip next st, skip next ch-6 sp, skip next st], dc in next 6 sts; repeat from * 6 more times; repeat between [ ], join.

Rnd 19: Sl st in next st, ch 3, dc in next 5 sts, *[(dc, ch 1, dc) in next ch-1 sp, dc in next 6 sts, ch 8, skip next st, skip next ch-7 sp, skip next st, dc in next 9 sts, ch 8, skip next st, skip next ch-7 sp, skip next st], dc in next 6 sts; repeat from * 6 more times; repeat between [ ], join.

Rnd 20: Sl st in next st, ch 3, dc in next 5 sts, *[(dc, ch 1, dc) in next ch-1 sp, dc in next 6 sts, ch 9, skip next st, skip next ch-8 sp, skip next st, dc in next 7 sts, ch 9, skip next st, skip next ch-8 sp, skip next st], dc in next 6 sts; repeat from * 6 more times; repeat between [ ], join.

Rnd 21: Sl st in next st, ch 3, dc in next 5 sts, *[(dc, ch 1, dc) in next ch-1 sp, dc in next 6 sts, ch 11, skip next st, skip next ch-9 sp, skip next st, dc in next 5 sts, ch 11, skip next st, skip next ch-9 sp, skip next st], dc in next 6 sts; repeat from * 6 more times; repeat between [ ], join.

Rnd 22: Sl st in next st, ch 3, dc in next 5 sts, *[(dc, ch 1, dc) in next ch-1 sp, dc in next 6 sts, ch 15, skip next st, skip next ch-11 lp, skip next st, dc in each of next 3 sts, ch 15, skip next st, skip next ch-11 lp, skip next st], dc in next 6 sts; repeat from * 6 more times; repeat between [ ], join.

Rnd 23: Sl st in next st, ch 3, dc in next 5 sts, *[(dc, ch 1, dc) in next ch-1 sp, dc in next 6 sts, ch 18, skip next st, skip next ch-15 lp, skip next st, dc in next st, ch 18, skip next st, skip next ch-15 lp, skip next st], dc in next 6 sts; repeat from * 6 more times; repeat between [ ], join, fasten off. ❖

*Create perfection when you crochet this extra-large centerpiece made with size 10
bedspread cotton in pristine white. It will be the focal point of any room in which it is displayed.*

HARMONY CENTERPIECE

DESIGNED BY DOT DRAKE

SIZE
29" across. This item may ruffle until blocked.

MATERIALS
Size 10 bedspread cotton — 1,125 yds. white;
No. 7 steel crochet hook or size needed to
obtain gauge.

GAUGE
Rnds 1-2 of Motif = 1¼" across. Each Motif
is 5¼" across.

MOTIF NO. 1
Rnd 1: Ch 7, sl st in first ch to form ring, ch 1, 18 sc in ring, join with sl st in first sc (18 sc).

Rnd 2: Ch 3, dc in each of next 2 sts, ch 2, (dc in each of next 3 sts, ch 2) around, join with sl st in top of ch-3 (18 dc, 6 ch-2 sps).

Rnd 3: Ch 1, sc in same st, ch 5, skip next st, sc in next st, 3 sc in next ch-2 sp, *sc in next st, ch 5, skip next st, sc in next st, 3 sc in next ch-2 sp; repeat from * around, join with sl st in first sc (30 sc, 6 ch-5 lps).

Rnd 4: Sl st in first ch lp, ch 3, 6 dc in same lp, ch 2, (7 dc in next ch lp, ch 2) around, join with sl st in top of ch-3 (42 dc, 6 ch-2 sps).

Rnd 5: Ch 3, dc in each of next 2 sts, (dc, ch 2, dc) in next st, dc in each of next 3 sts, ch 3, skip next ch-2 sp, *dc in each of next 3 sts, (dc, ch 2, dc) in next st, dc in each of next 3 sts, ch 3, skip next ch-2 sp; repeat from * around, join (48 dc, 6 ch-3 sps, 6 ch-2 sps).

NOTE: For **picot loop (picot lp)**, ch 5, sl st in 4th ch from hook, ch 1.

Rnd 6: Ch 3, dc in each of next 3 sts, picot lp, skip next ch-2 sp, dc in next 4 sts, ch 4, skip next ch-3 sp, *dc in next 4 sts, picot lp, skip next ch-2 sp, dc in next 4 sts, ch 4, skip next ch-3 sp; repeat from * around, join (48 dc, 6 ch-4 sps, 6 picot lps).

Rnd 7: Ch 1, sc in same st, sc in each of next 3 sts, ch 8, skip next picot lp, sc in next 4 sts, 5 sc in next ch-4 sp, *sc in next 4 sts, ch 8, skip next picot lp, sc in next 4 sts, 5 sc in next ch-4 sp; repeat from * around, join with sl st in first sc (78 sc, 6 ch-8 lps).

NOTES: For **large picot (lg picot)**, ch 4, sl st in top of last st made.

For **small picot (sm picot)**, ch 3, sl st in top of last st made.

Rnd 8: [*Skip next 3 sts, (8 dc, lg picot, 8 dc) in next ch-8 lp, skip next 3 sts, sl st in next st, ch 2, skip next 2 sts, (dc, sm picot, ch 2) 3 times in next st, skip next 2 sts], sl st in next st; repeat from * 4 more times; repeat between [ ] one more time, join with sl st in joining sl st of last rnd, fasten off.

MOTIF NO. 2
NOTES: For **large picot joining**, ch 2, sc in corresponding lg picot on last Motif, ch 2, sl st in top of last st made on this Motif.

For **joining picot lp**, ch 7, sl st in 4th ch from hook, ch 3, (sc in center picot of 3-sm picot group on next Motif, ch 7, sl st in 4th ch from hook, ch 3) 2 times, sl st in top of last dc made on this Motif.

Rnds 1-7: Repeat same rnds of Motif No. 1.

Rnd 8: Skip next 3 sts, 8 dc in next ch-8 lp, large picot joining (see Joining Diagram on page 72), 8 dc in same ch-8 lp as last dc, skip next 3 sts, sl st in next st, ch 2, skip next 2 sts, (dc, sm picot, ch 2) 3 times in next st, skip next 2 sts, sl st in next st; [*skip next 3 sts, (8 dc, lg picot, 8 dc) in next ch-8 lp, skip next 3 sts, sl st in next st, ch 2, skip next 2 sts, (dc, sm picot, ch 2) 3 times in next st, skip next 2 sts], sl st in next st; repeat from * 3 more times; repeat between [ ], join with sl st in joining sl st of last rnd, fasten off.

MOTIF NO. 3
Rnds 1-7: Repeat same rnds of Motif No. 1.

Rnd 8: Skip next 3 sts, 8 dc in next ch-8 lp, large picot joining, 8 dc in same ch-8 lp last last dc, skip next 3 sts, sl st in next st, ch 2, skip next 2 sts, dc in next st, sm picot, dc in same st, joining picot lp, ch 2, dc in same st as last dc, sm picot, ch 2, skip next 2 sts, sl st in next st, 8 dc in next ch-8 lp, large picot joining, 8 dc in same ch-8 lp as last dc, skip next 3 sts, sl st in next st, ch 2, skip next 2 sts, (dc, sm picot, ch 2) 3 times in next st, skip next 2 sts, sl st in next st, [*skip next 3 sts, (8 dc, lg picot, 8 dc) in next ch-8 lp, skip next 3 sts, sl st in next st, ch 2, skip next 2 sts, (dc, sm picot, ch 2) 3 times in next st, skip next 2 sts], sl st in next st; repeat from * 2

Continued on next page

TEATIME CHARMS

71

HARMONY CENTERPIECE
Continued from page 71

more times; repeat between [ ], join with sl st in joining sl st of last rnd, fasten off.

Make 16 more Motifs, joining according to Joining Diagram.

BORDER

Rnd 1: Working around entire outer edge of Motifs, join with sl st in unworked lg picot indicated on diagram, ch 8, dc in 5th ch from hook, (ch 5, dc in 5th ch from hook) 2 times, ◊dc in center picot of next 3-sm picot group, (ch 5, dc in 5th ch from hook) 3 times, dc in next lg picot, (ch 5, dc in 5th ch from hook) 3 times, [ch 7, sl st in 4th ch from hook, ch 3, sc in center picot of next 3-sm picot group, ch 7, sl st in 4th ch from hook, ch 3, sc in center picot of next 3-sm picot group on next Motif, ch 7, sl st in 4th ch from hook, ch 3, sl st in first ch of first ch-7], (ch 5, dc in 5th ch from hook) 3 times, dc in next lg picot, (ch 5, dc in 5th ch from

hook) 3 times, *dc in center picot of next 3-sm picot group, (ch 5, dc in 5th ch from hook) 3 times, dc in next lg picot, (ch 5, dc in 5th ch from hook) 3 times; repeat from * one more time; repeat between [ ] one more time, (ch 5, dc in 5th ch from hook) 3 times•, dc in next lg picot, (ch 5, dc in 5th ch from hook) 3 times; repeat from ◊ around ending last repeat at •, join with sl st in 3rd ch of ch-8 (180 ch-4 lps, 12 joining picot lps).

Rnd 2: Sl st in first ch-4 lp, ch 3, dc in same lp, ch 4, (2 dc in next ch-4 lp, ch 4) 7 times, *[dc next 2 ch-4 lps tog, ch 4, (2 dc in next ch-4 lp, ch 4) 16 times, dc next 2 ch-4 lps tog], ch 4, (2 dc in next ch-4 lp, ch 4) 10 times; repeat from * 4 more times; repeat between [ ], (ch 4, 2 dc in next ch-4 lp) 2 times; to **join,** ch 1, dc in top of ch-3.

Rnd 3: Ch 1, sc around joining dc, ch 5, (sc in next ch lp, ch 5) 7 times, *[dc next 2 ch lps tog, ch 5, (sc in next ch lp, ch 5) 15 times, dc next 2 ch lps

JOINING DIAGRAM

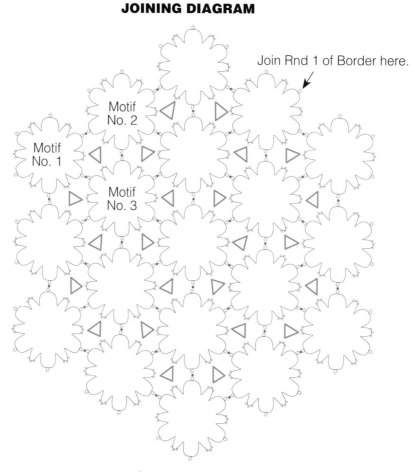

Join Rnd 1 of Border here.

Motif No. 1

Motif No. 2

Motif No. 3

▷ = Joining picot lps
• = Large picot joining

tog, ch 5], (sc in next ch lp, ch 5) 9 times; repeat from * 4 more times; repeat between [ ], sc in last ch lp; to **join,** ch 2, dc in first sc.

Rnd 4: Ch 1, sc around joining dc, sm picot, (ch 5, sc in next ch lp, sm picot) around, join as before.

Rnd 5: Ch 1, sc around joining dc, (ch 6, sc in next ch lp) around; to **join,** ch 3, dc in first sc.

Rnd 6: Ch 1, sc around joining dc, ch 6, (sc in next ch lp, ch 6) around, join with sl st in first sc.

Rnd 7: Sl st in first ch lp, ch 3, 6 dc in same lp, ch 2, sc in next ch lp, ch 2, (7 dc in next ch lp, ch 2, sc in next ch lp, ch 2) around, join with sl st in top of ch-3.

Rnd 8: Ch 3, dc in each of next 2 sts, (dc, ch 2, dc) in next st, dc in each of next 3 sts, ch 3, skip next 2 ch-2 sps, *dc in each of next 3 sts, (dc, ch 2, dc) in next st, dc in each of next 3 sts, ch 3, skip next 2 ch-2 sps; repeat from * around, join.

Rnd 9: Ch 3, dc in each of next 3 sts, picot lp, skip next ch-2 sp, dc in next 4 sts, skip next ch-3 sp, *dc in next 4 sts, picot lp, skip next ch-2 sp, dc in next 4 sts, skip next ch-3 sp; repeat from * around, join.

Rnd 10: Ch 1, sc in first st, sc in each of next 3 sts, ch 7, skip next picot lp, (sc in next 8 sts, ch 7, skip next picot lp) around to last 4 sts, sc in last 4 sts, join with sl st in first sc.

Rnd 11: Skip next 3 sts, *(8 dc, lg picot, 8 dc) in next ch-7 lp, skip next 3 sts, sl st in each of next 2 sts, skip next 3 sts; repeat from * around to last ch-7 lp, (8 dc, lg picot, 8 dc) in last ch-7 lp, skip next 3 sts, sl st in last st, join with sl st in joining sl st of last rnd, fasten off.❖

DIAMOND RINGS COVERLET

Continued from page 64

Rnd 3: Ch 4, skip next st, (dc in next st, ch 1, skip next st) around, join with sl st in 3rd ch of ch-4 (99 ch-1 sps across each short end, 132 ch-1 sps across each long edge).

Rnd 4: Sl st in first ch-1 sp, ch 1, 4 sc in same sp, 4 sc in each of next 3 ch-1 sps, *2 sc in each of next 95 ch-1 sps, 4 sc in each of next 4 ch-1 sps, 2 sc in each of next 128 ch-1 sps*, 4 sc in each of next 4 ch-1 sps; repeat between ** one more time, join with sl st in first sc (206 sc across each short end, 272 sc across each long edge).

Rnd 5: Ch 5, dc in same st, skip next 2 sts, (dc, ch 2, dc) in next st, skip next 2 sts, [(dc, ch 2, 2 dc, ch 2, dc) in next st, skip next st, (dc, ch 2, 2 dc, ch 2, dc) in next st, skip next 2 sts], *(dc, ch 2, dc) in next st, skip next 2 sts*; repeat between ** 66 more times; repeat between [ ]; repeat between ** 89 more times; repeat between [ ]; repeat between ** 67 more times; repeat between [ ]; repeat between ** 87 more times, join with sl st in 3rd ch of ch-5 (328 ch sps).

Rnd 6: Sl st in first ch-2 sp, ch 5, dc in same sp, (dc, ch 2, dc) in each ch-2 sp around, join.

Rnd 7: Sl st in each of next 2 chs, sl st in each of next 2 dc, sl st in next ch-2 sp, ch 1, sc in same sp, *[ch 1, skip next ch-2 sp, tr in next ch-2 sp, (ch 1, tr) 7 times in same sp, ch 1, skip next ch-2 sp], sc in next ch-2 sp; repeat from * around to last 3 ch-2 sps; repeat between [ ], join with sl st in first sc (738 ch-1 sps).

Rnd 8: Ch 3, skip next ch-1 sp, *[sc in next ch-1 sp, (ch 3, sc in next ch-1 sp) 6 times, ch 1, skip next ch-1 sp], hdc in next sc, ch 1, skip next ch-1 sp; repeat from * around to last 8 ch-1 sps; repeat between [ ], join with sl st in 2nd ch of ch-3.

Rnd 9: Sl st in first ch-1 sp, ch 1, sc in same sp, ch 1, ◊*(hdc, ch 1, hdc) in next ch-3 sp, ch 1*; repeat between ** 5 more times, sc in each of next 2 ch-1 sps, ch 1; repeat from ◊ around to last 6 ch-3 sps and one ch-1 sp; repeat between ** 6 more times, sc in last ch-1 sp, join with sl st in first sc, fasten off.

Cut ribbon into 2 pieces each 67" long and 2 pieces each 81" long. Weave 67" pieces through ch-1 sps on rnd 3 of Border on short ends of Coverlet and 81" pieces through long edges, pulling ends even. Tie ends in bow at corners. Tack one rose over center of each bow. ❖

Fill this pretty birdfeeder with a sweetly scented potpourri to freshen a room of your house. Made with size 10 bedspread cotton and accented with ribbons and flowers, it will be a pleasing addition to your decor.

BIRDFEEDER

DESIGNED BY JO ANN MAXWELL

SIZE
4½" tall.

MATERIALS
Size 10 bedspread cotton — 75 yds. white; 24" rose ⅜" satin ribbon; 2" artificial bird; 3 pink silk roses; 2 pink silk rosebuds; small amount baby's breath flowers; 4" tall x 2" across bottom x 3" across top clear plastic disposable cup; potpourri; craft glue or hot glue gun; two 2¼" jar lids; one cotton ball; fabric stiffener; Styrofoam® or blocking board; plastic wrap; rustproof pins; tape; No. 5 steel crochet hook or size needed to obtain gauge.

GAUGE
Rnds 1-2 of Bottom = 1¾" across. 1 tr = ½" tall; 1 dc = ⅜" tall.

TOP

Rnd 1: Ch 3, 15 hdc in 3rd ch from hook, join with sl st in top of ch-3 (16 hdc).

Rnds 2-3: Ch 2, hdc in each st around, join with sl st in top of ch-2.

Rnd 4: Ch 1, sc in first st, skip next st, (sc in next st, skip next st) around, join with sl st in first sc (8 sc).

Rnd 5: Ch 3, 2 dc in same st, 3 dc in each st around, join with sl st in top of ch-3 (24 dc).

Rnd 6: Ch 6, (tr in next st, ch 2) around, join with sl st in 4th ch of ch-6 (24 tr, 24 ch-2 sps).

Rnd 7: Ch 3, dc in each ch and in each st around, join with sl st in top of ch-3 (72 dc).

NOTE: For **picot**, ch 3, sl st in top of last st made.

Rnd 8: Ch 1, sc in same st, picot, ch 4, skip next 2 sts, (sc in next st, picot, ch 4, skip next 2 sts) around, join with sl st in first sc (24 sc, 24 ch-4 sps, 24 picots).

Rnd 9: Sl st in each of first 2 chs on next ch-4 sp, ch 4, tr in next ch, ch 3, skip next sc and picot, (tr in 2nd ch of next ch-4 sp, tr in next ch, ch 3, skip next sc and picot) around, join with sl st in top of ch-4 (48 tr, 24 ch-3 sps).

Rnd 10: Repeat rnd 7 (120 dc).

Rnd 11: Ch 1, sc in same st, picot, ch 4, skip next 3 sts, (sc in next st, picot, ch 4, skip next 3 sts) around, join with sl st in first sc (30 sc, 30 ch-4 sps, 30 picots).

Rnd 12: Sl st in each of first 2 chs on next ch-4 sp, ch 1, sc in same ch sp, ch 6, (sc in next ch-4 sp, ch 6) around, join (30 ch-6 sps).

Rnd 13: (Sc in each of next 2 chs, 2 sc in each of next 2 chs, sc in each of next 2 chs, skip next sc) around, join, fasten off.

BOTTOM

Rnd 1: Ch 4, sl st in first ch to form ring, ch 3, 19 dc in ring, join with sl st in top of ch-3 (20 dc).

Rnd 2: Ch 5, (dc in next st, ch 2) around, join with sl st in 3rd ch of ch-5 (20 dc, 20 ch-2 sps).

Rnd 3: Ch 3, dc in each ch and in each st around, join with sl st in top of ch-3 (60 dc).

Rnd 4: Ch 4, tr in next st, ch 3, skip next st, (tr in each of next 2 sts, ch 3, skip next st) around, join with sl st in top of ch-4 (40 tr, 20 ch-3 sps).

Rnd 5: Repeat rnd 3 (100 dc).

Rnds 6-8: Repeat rnds 11-13 of Top.

FINISHING

1: Stuff rnds 1-3 of Top with cotton ball. Tie separate 4" strand bedspread cotton tightly around rnd 4, secure ends.

2: Cover jar lids with plastic wrap, tape to secure.

3: Apply fabric stiffener to crocheted Top and Bottom according to manufacturer's instructions.

4: With right side up, pin Top to plastic covered blocking board centered over one jar lid. With wrong side up, pin Bottom to blocking board centered over remaining jar lid. Let dry completely.

5: Weave 13" of ribbon through tr sts on rnd 9 of Top, overlapping ends; glue to secure. Weave remaining ribbon through tr sts on rnd 4 of Bottom, overlapping ends; glue to secure.

6: Glue one rose, one rosebud and small amount of baby's breath to one side of Top. Glue bird to opposite side. Glue 2 roses, one rosebud and small amount of baby's breath to right side of Bottom as shown in photo.

7: Fill plastic cup with potpourri; glue top of cup centered to wrong side of crocheted Top. Holding crocheted Bottom right side up, glue bottom of cup centered to crocheted Bottom.❖

Pretty pineapples and shells are combined to create this stunning design. Dress up a sweat shirt or apron bib with this delicate doily.

DAINTY DOILY

DESIGNED BY EUNICE KENNEY THORNBRUGH

SIZE
7¾" across. This project may ruffle until blocked.

MATERIALS
Size 30 crochet cotton — 30 yds. white; No. 11 steel crochet hook or size needed to obtain gauge.

GAUGE
Rnds 1-3 = 1¼" across.

DOILY

Rnd 1: Ch 9, sl st in first ch to form ring, ch 1, 18 sc in ring, join with sl st in first sc (18 sc).

Rnd 2: Ch 10, skip next 2 sts, dc in next st, (ch 7, skip next 2 sts, dc in next st) around to last 2 sts; to **join,** ch 3, skip last 2 sts, tr in 3rd ch of ch-10 (6 dc, 6 ch-7 sps).

Rnd 3: Ch 4, (tr, ch 2, 2 tr) around joining tr, ch 7, *(2 tr, ch 2, 2 tr) in center ch of next ch-7, ch 7; repeat from * around, join with sl st in top of ch-4 (6 ch-7 sps, 6 ch-2 sps).

NOTES: For **beginning shell (beg shell),** ch 4, (2 tr, ch 2, 3 tr) in same sp.

For **shell,** (3 tr, ch 2, 3 tr) in next ch sp.

Rnd 4: Sl st in next st, sl st in next ch sp, beg shell, ch 7, skip next ch-7 sp, (shell in next ch-2 sp, ch 7, skip next ch-7 sp) around, join (6 shells, 6 ch-7 sps).

Rnd 5: Sl st in each of next 2 sts, sl st in next ch sp, beg shell, ch 6; working over last rnd, sc in ch-7 sp on rnd before last, ch 6, (shell in ch sp of next shell, ch 6; working over last rnd, sc in ch-7 sp on rnd before last, ch 6) around, join.

Rnd 6: Sl st in each of next 2 sts, sl st in next ch sp, ch 4, (2 tr, ch 4, 3 tr) in same sp, ch 6, tr in each of next 2 ch-6 sps, ch 6, *(3 tr, ch 4, 3 tr) in next shell, ch 6, tr in each of next 2 ch-6 sps, ch 6; repeat from * around, join.

Rnd 7: Sl st in each of next 2 sts, sl st in next ch sp, ch 4, 6 tr in same sp, (*ch 7, skip next ch-6 sp, tr in next tr, ch 2, tr in next tr, ch 7, skip next ch-6 sp*, 7 tr in next ch-2 sp) 5 times; repeat between **, join, fasten off.

Rnd 8: Join with sl st in any ch-2 sp, beg shell, [*ch 5, skip next ch-7 sp, tr in next tr, (ch 3, tr in next tr) 6 times, ch 5, skip next ch-7 sp], shell in next ch-2 sp; repeat from * 4 more times; repeat between [ ], join.

Rnd 9: Sl st in each of next 2 sts, sl st in next ch sp, beg shell, [*ch 6, skip next ch-5 sp, sc in next ch-3 sp, (ch 6, sc in next ch-3 sp) 5 times, ch 6, skip next ch-5 sp], shell in next shell; repeat from * 4 more times; repeat between [ ], join.

Rnd 10: Sl st in each of next 2 sts, sl st in next ch sp, ch 4, (2 tr, ch 2, 3 tr, ch 2, 3 tr) in same sp, [*ch 6, skip next ch-6 sp, sc in next ch-6 sp, (ch 6, sc in next ch-6 sp) 4 times, ch 6, skip next ch-6 sp], (3 tr, ch 2, 3 tr, ch 2, 3 tr) in next shell; repeat from * 4 more times; repeat between [ ], join.

Rnd 11: Sl st in each of next 2 sts, sl st in next ch sp, beg shell, [*ch 5, shell in next ch-2 sp, ch 6, skip next ch-6 sp, sc in next ch-6 sp, ch 6, sc in next ch-6 sp, 5 tr in next sc, (sc in next ch-6 sp, ch 6) 2 times, skip next ch-6 sp], shell in next ch-2 sp; repeat from * 4 more times; repeat between [ ], join.

Rnd 12: Sl st in each of next 2 sts, sl st in next ch sp, beg shell, (*ch 5, tr in next ch-5 sp, ch 5, shell in next shell, ch 6, skip next ch-6 sp, sc in next ch-6 sp, ch 6, sc in center tr of next 5-tr group, ch 6, sc in next ch-6 sp, ch 6, skip next ch-6 sp*, shell in next shell) 5 times; repeat between **, join.

Rnd 13: Sl st in each of next 2 sts, sl st in next ch sp, beg shell, [*ch 6, (tr in next ch-5 sp, ch 6) 2 times, shell in next shell, ch 6, skip next ch-6 sp, (sc in next ch-6 sp, ch 6) 2 times], shell in next shell; repeat from * 4 more times; repeat between [ ], join, fasten off.

Row 14: For **first point,** working in rows, with wrong side facing you, join with sl st in ch sp of shell before any pineapple, beg shell, ch 5, skip next ch-6 sp, sc in next ch sp, ch 5, skip next ch-6 sp, shell in ch sp of next shell leaving remaining sts unworked, turn.

Row 15: Sl st in each of next 2 sts, sl st in next ch sp, beg shell, ch 5, skip next ch-5 sp, sc in next sc, ch 5, skip next ch-5 sp, shell in last shell, turn.

Row 16: Sl st in each of next 2 sts, sl st in next ch sp, beg shell, ch 1, skip next 2 ch-5 sps, shell in last shell, turn.

Row 17: Sl st in each of next 2 sts, sl st in next ch sp, ch 1, sc in same sp, shell in next ch-1 sp, sc in last shell, turn, fasten off.

For **remaining 5 points,** with wrong side of Doily facing you, join with sl st in ch sp of next unworked shell on rnd 13, repeat rows 14-17 of first point.❖

Experience the pleasure of elegant dining when you grace your table with these distinctive place mats. Simple white motifs join to form a subtle diamond design among the lacy loops.

LACY PLACE MAT

DESIGNED BY ANGELA J. TATE

SIZE
11" x 15". This project may ruffle until blocked.

MATERIALS
Size 10 bedspread cotton — 250 yds. white; Styrofoam® or blocking board; plastic wrap; rust-proof pins; spray starch; No. 7 steel crochet hook or size needed to obtain gauge.

GAUGE
Motif = 2" across.

FIRST ROW
First Motif

Rnd 1: Ch 10, sl st in first ch to form ring, ch 3, dc in ring, (ch 3, 2 dc in ring) 7 times; to **join,** ch 1, hdc in top of ch-3 (16 dc, 8 ch-3 sps).

Rnd 2: Ch 1, sc around joining hdc, ch 7, sc in next ch-3 sp, (ch 5, sc in next ch-3 sp, ch 7, sc in next ch-3 sp) around; to **join,** ch 2, dc in first sc (4 ch-7 sps, 4 ch-5 sps).

NOTE: For **treble shell (tr shell),** (3 tr, ch 3, 3 tr, ch 3, 3 tr) in next ch sp.

Rnd 3: Ch 1, sc around joining dc, ch 3, tr shell in next ch-7 sp, ch 3, *sc in next ch-5 sp, ch 3, tr shell in next ch-7 sp, ch 3; repeat from * around, join with sl st in first sc, fasten off (8 ch-3 sps, 4 tr shells).

Second Motif

Rnds 1-2: Repeat same rnds of First Motif.

NOTES: For **joining ch-3 sp,** ch 1, sl st in corresponding ch-3 sp on other Motif, ch 1.

Rnd 3: Ch 1, sc around joining dc, ch 3, (3 tr, ch 3, 3 tr) in next ch-7 sp, joining to side of last Motif (see Joining Diagram) work joining ch-3 sp, 3 tr in same ch sp on this Motif, ch 3, sc in next ch-5 sp, ch 3, 3 tr in next ch-7 sp, work joining ch-3 sp, (3 tr, ch 3, 3 tr) in same ch sp on this Motif, ch 3, *sc in next ch-5 sp, ch 3, tr shell in next ch-7 sp, ch 3; repeat from *, join with sl st in first sc, fasten off.

Repeat Second Motif 7 more times for a total of 9 Motifs.

SECOND ROW
First Motif

Working on bottom of First Motif on row above,

work same as First Row Second Motif.

Second Motif

Rnds 1-2: Repeat same rnds of First Row First Motif.

Rnd 3: Ch 1, sc around joining dc, ch 3, (3 tr, ch 3, 3 tr) in next ch-7 sp; joining to bottom of next Motif on row above, work joining ch-3 sp, 3 tr in same ch sp on this Motif, ch 3, sc in next ch-5 sp, ch 3, 3 tr in next ch-7 sp, work joining ch-3 sp, 3 tr in same ch sp on this Motif; working on side of last Motif on this row, work joining ch-3 sp, 3 tr in same ch sp on this Motif, ch 3, sc in next ch-5 sp, ch 3, 3 tr in next ch-7 sp, work joining ch-3 sp, (3 tr, ch 3, 3 tr) in same ch sp on this Motif, ch 3, sc in next ch-5 sp, ch 3, tr shell in next ch-7 sp, ch 3, join with sl st in first sc, fasten off.

Repeat Second Motif 7 more times for a total of 9 Motifs.

Repeat Second Row 3 more times for a total of 5 Rows.

JOINING DIAGRAM

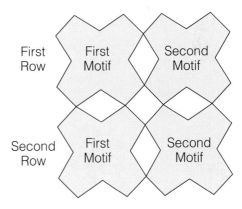

BORDER
Rnd 1: Working around entire outer edge of Motifs, join with sc in first ch-3 sp of corner tr shell before one short edge, *(ch 7, sc in next ch-3 sp) 4 times, ch 7, sc in ch-1 sp of next joining ch-3 sp, ch 3, sc in ch-1 sp of next joining ch-3 sp on next Motif*; repeat between ** 3 more times, [(ch 7, sc in next ch-3 sp) 8 times, ch 7, sc in ch-1 sp of next joining ch-3 sp, ch 3, sc in ch-1 sp of next

Continued on page 81

Your favorite little girl, whether old or young, will giggle with delight when she receives this frilly little basket carefully embellished with lace and flowers for a special surprise.

ROSE POTPOURRI BASKET

DESIGNED BY SUSIE SPIER MAXFIELD

SIZE
5" x 5½".

MATERIALS
Worsted-weight yarn — 2 oz. rose; 26" white ¼" satin ribbon; 1 yd. white ¾" gathered lace; eight 1" silk rosebuds; scrap of white felt; 7-count plastic canvas; white sewing thread; craft glue; polyester fiberfill; H crochet hook or size needed to obtain gauge.

GAUGE
Rnd 1 of Basket = 1¼" across.

BASKET

Rnd 1: Ch 4, 11 dc in 4th ch from hook, join with sl st in top of ch-3 (12 dc).

Rnd 2: Ch 3, dc in same st, 2 dc in each st around, join with sl st in top of ch-3 (24).

Rnd 3: Ch 3, dc in next st, 2 dc in next st, (dc in each of next 2 sts, 2 dc in next st) around, join (32).

Rnd 4: Ch 3, dc in each of next 2 sts, 2 dc in next st, (dc in each of next 3 sts, 2 dc in next st) around, join (40).

Rnds 5-8: Ch 3, dc in each st around, join.

Rnd 9: Repeat rnd 2, fasten off (80).

FINISHING

1: For **form sides,** cut one piece plastic canvas 9 x 57 holes. For **form bottom,** cut one piece according to graph. For **handle,** cut one piece 3 x 47 holes.

2: For **form,** stitch short ends of sides together. Easing to fit, stitch bottom edge of sides to bottom. Using craft glue, cover form and handle completely with felt. Glue 1" on each end of handle to each side of form.

3: Place form inside Basket. Lightly stuff between form and Basket. Tie ribbon in bow tightly around Basket between rnds 8 and 9.

4: Cut two 8" pieces of lace, glue bound edges together. Glue across top of handle as shown in photo.

5: Glue remaining lace around top edge of rnd 9.

6: Glue 4 rosebuds to each side of handle just above Basket.❖

BOTTOM
(cut one)
16 x 17 holes

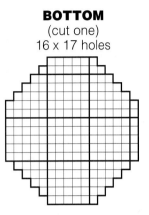

LACY PLACE MAT

Continued from page 79

joining ch-3 sp on next Motif]; repeat between ** 5 more times; repeat between [ ]; repeat between ** 3 more times; repeat between [ ]; repeat between ** 5 more times, ch 7, (sc in next ch-3 sp, ch 7) 3 times, join with sl st in first sc (116 ch-7 sps, 20 ch-3 sps).

NOTE: For beginning treble shell (beg tr shell), (ch 4, 2 tr, ch 3, 3 tr, ch 3, 3 tr) in same ch sp.

Rnd 2: Sl st in first ch-7 sp, beg tr shell, ◊[ch 3, sc in next ch-7 sp, (ch 7, sc in next ch-7 sp) 3 times, 2 dc in next ch-3 sp, sc in next ch-7 sp], *(ch 7, sc in next ch-7 sp) 4 times, 2 dc in next ch-3 sp, sc in next ch-7 sp*; repeat between ** 2 more times, (ch 7, sc in next ch-7 sp) 3 times, ch 3, tr shell in next ch-7 sp; repeat between [ ]; repeat between ** 5 more times, (ch 7, sc in next ch-7 sp) 3 times, ch 3◊, tr shell in next ch-7 sp; repeat between ◊◊, join with sl st in top of ch-4, fasten off.

FINISHING

Spray Place Mat lightly with spray starch; pin to plastic covered blocking board. Press with warm iron using a piece of cloth between to protect crocheted piece.❖

CHEERFUL HAVEN

NEW LIFE

There's a new life stirring and he's growing inside me.
God lead me in the right direction to
make him all that he can be.

There's going to be a child and I want to be his friend.
I want to listen to his dreams and watch him chase the wind.

I want to share his joys and feel his pain when he is sad.
I want to raise my child with love,
whether he's at peace or mad.

I want to be a rock for him when things don't go his way.
I want time to sit and talk with him and hear about his day.

I'm going to love him all his life, this he should always know
And when he's grown I want to be able to simply let him go.

I'm going to be a Mom, that word is music to my ears.
And I am truly blessed for the remainder of my years.

This snuggly little bunny loves to watch over baby as he settles down for sleep. Made of soft worsted-weight yarn with embroidered features, he will be your child's favorite companion.

BABY BUNNY TOY

DESIGNED BY CINDY HARRIS

SIZE
10" long.

MATERIALS
Worsted-weight yarn — 5 oz. white, small amount each black and pink; polyester fiberfill; tapestry needle; G crochet hook or size needed to obtain gauge.

GAUGE
4 sc sts = 1"; 4 sc rnds = 1".

NOTES
Do not join rnds unless otherwise stated. Mark first st of each rnd. Use white unless otherwise stated.

BODY
Rnd 1: Ch 3, sl st in first ch to form ring, ch 1, 6 sc in ring (6 sc).

Rnd 2: 2 sc in each st around (12).

Rnd 3: (Sc in next st, 2 sc in next st) around (18).

Rnd 4: (Sc in each of next 2 sts, 2 sc in next st) around (24).

Rnd 5: (Sc in each of next 3 sts, 2 sc in next st) around (30).

Rnd 6: (Sc in next 4 sts, 2 sc in next st) around (36).

Rnd 7: (Sc in next 5 sts, 2 sc in next st) around (42).

Rnds 8-19: Sc in each st around.

Rnd 20: (Sc in next 5 sts, sc next 2 sts tog) around (36).

Rnd 21: (Sc in next 4 sts, sc next 2 sts tog) around (30).

Rnd 22: (Sc in each of next 3 sts, sc next 2 sts tog) around (24).

Rnd 23: (Sc in each of next 2 sts, sc next 2 sts tog) around, join with sl st in first sc, fasten off (18). Stuff.

HEAD
Rnds 1-6: Repeat same rnds of Body.

Rnds 7-13: Sc in each st around.

Rnd 14: (Sc in next st, sc next 2 sts tog) around (24).

Rnd 15: (Sc in each of next 2 sts, sc next 2 sts tog) around, join with sl st in first sc leaving 12" for sewing, fasten off. Stuff.

Sew last rnd of Head to last rnd of Body.

FRONT LEG (make 2)
Rnds 1-3: Starting at toes, repeat same rnds of Body.

Rnds 4-11: Sc in each st around. Stuff.

Rnd 12: (Sc in next st, sc next 2 sts tog) around (12).

Rnd 13: (Sc next 2 sts tog) around (6).

Rnd 14: (Sl st in next st, skip next st) around; leaving 6" for sewing, fasten off.

Sew sides of Legs to each side of Body as shown in photo.

BACK LEG (make 2)
Rnds 1-3: Starting at toes, repeat same rnds of Body.

Rnds 4-7: Sc in each st around.

Rnd 8: For **top of leg**, 2 sc in each of next 4 sts; sc in each st around (22).

Rnds 9-11: Sc in each st around.

Rnd 12: (Sc next 2 sts tog) 4 times, sc in each st around (18).

Rnds 13-15: Repeat rnds 12-14 of Front Leg.

Sew sides of Legs to each side of Body behind Front Legs.

EAR (make 2)
Rnd 1: Starting at top, ch 3, sl st in first ch to form ring, ch 1, 6 sc in ring (6 sc).

Rnd 2: (Sc in each of next 2 sts, 2 sc in next st) around (8).

Rnd 3: Sc in each st around.

Rnd 4: (Sc in each of next 3 sts, 2 sc in next st) around (10).

Rnd 5: Sc in each st around.

Rnd 6: (Sc in next 4 sts, 2 sc in next st) around (12).

Rnd 7: Sc in each st around.

Rnd 8: (Sc in next 5 sts, 2 sc in next st) around (14).

Rnd 9: Sc in each st around.

Rnd 10: (Sc in next 6 sts, 2 sc in next st) around (16).

Rnds 11-14: Sc in each st around. At end of last rnd, join with sl st in first sc; leaving 12" for sewing, fasten off.

Flatten and sew last rnd closed; tack ends of last rnd together.

Sew Ears to top of Head ¾" apart.

CHEEK (make 2)
Rnds 1-4: Repeat same rnds of Body.

Rnd 5: Sc in each st around.

Rnd 6: (Sc in each of next 2 sts, sc next 2 sts tog) around, join with sl st in first sc; leaving 12" for sewing, fasten off (18).

Sew Cheeks side-by-side over rnds 1-6 on front of Head, stuffing before closing.

TAIL
Rnds 1-6: Working these rnds in **back lps** only, repeat same rnds of Cheek.

For **fuzz**, working in **front lps** of rnds 1-6 on Tail, join with sl st in first st on rnd 1, (ch 3, sl st in next st) around to last st of rnd 6, fasten off.

Sew Tail to back of Body, stuffing before closing.

FINISHING
With 2 strands pink held together, using Satin Stitch (see page 159), embroider **nose** on front of face between Cheeks; with 2 strands black held together, embroider eyes ¾" apart above nose.

For **toes**, with one strand pink, using Straight Stitch (see page 158), embroider 4 long stitches across front of each Leg.❖

Rose and white motifs are artfully combined to create this alluring cover sure to capture the romantic in all of us. Its magical quality will softly enhance your Victorian or contemporary decor.

⫷ PINK & WHITE AFGHAN ⫸

Designed by Carol Nartowicz

SIZE
55" x 68".

MATERIALS
Worsted-weight yarn — 24 oz. white and 16 oz. rose; H crochet hook or size needed to obtain gauge.

GAUGE
Rnd 1 of each Motif= 2¾" across.

FIRST MOTIF
NOTE: For **double treble crochet (dtr),** yo 3 times, insert hook in st or sp, yo, draw lp through, (yo, draw through 2 lps on hook) 4 times.

Rnd 1: With rose, ch 5, sl st in first ch to form ring, ch 5, dtr in ring, ch 3, (2 dtr in ring, ch 3) 7 times, join with sl st in top of ch-5 (16 dtr, 8 ch-3 sps).

Rnd 2: Sl st in next st, sl st in first ch-3 sp, ch 3, (2 dc, ch 4, 3 dc) in same sp, (3 dc, ch 4, 3 dc) in each ch-3 sp around, join with sl st in top of ch-3, fasten off (48 dc, 8 ch-4 sps).

Rnd 3: Join white with sl st in any ch-4 sp, ch 3, 7 dc in same sp, ch 3, (8 dc in next ch-4 sp, ch 3) around, join, fasten off (64 dc, 8 ch-2 sps).

Rnd 4: Join white with sc in any ch-3 sp, 3 sc in same sp, ch 4, sc in 5th dc of next 8-dc group, ch 4, *4 sc in next ch-3 sp, ch 4, sc in 5th dc of next 8-dc group, ch 4; repeat from * around, join with sl st in first sc, fasten off.

NEXT MOTIF (make 47 as instructed; make 32 reversing colors)
NOTES: For **joining sc,** sc in 5th dc of next 8-dc group, drop lp from hook, insert hook in 5th dc of corresponding 8-dc group on next Motif, draw

dropped lp through.

Join Motifs according to Joining Diagram.

Rnds 1-3: Repeat same rnds of First Motif.

NOTE: Work rnd 4 in white for **all** Motifs.

Rnd 4: Repeat same rnd of First Motif, using joining sc to join Motifs.

BORDER
Working around entire outer edge of Motifs, join white with sc in first ch-4 sp after any joining, 4 sc in same sp, ch 6, sl st in 3rd ch from hook, ch 4, *5 sc in each of next 2 ch-4 sps, ch 6, sl st in 3rd ch from hook, ch 4; repeat from * around to last ch-4 sp, 5 sc in last ch-4 sp, join with sl st in first sc, fasten off.❖

JOINING DIAGRAM

Let your mind wander through a field of flowers and enjoy the sweet scent of spring. This glorious afghan sprinkled with gay florals and edged with perky pom-poms is sure to lift your spirits.

⋙ WILDFLOWER AFGHAN ⋙

DESIGNED BY ROSETTA HARSHMAN

SIZE
51" x 72" not including Pom-poms.

MATERIALS
Worsted-weight yarn — 19 oz. med. brown, 9 oz. each white, lt. brown and green, 7 oz. each yellow, lavender, orange and purple; 2" square cardboard; tapestry needle; H crochet hook or size needed to obtain gauge.

GAUGE
7 dc = 2"; Rnd 1 of Motif = 2" across.

MOTIF (make 24 with purple centers, 18 with yellow centers, 15 with orange centers and 15 with lavender centers)

Rnd 1: With center color, ch 5, sl st in first ch to form ring, ch 3, 2 dc in ring, ch 3, (3 dc in ring, ch 3) 5 times, join with sl st in top of ch-3, fasten off (18 dc, 6 ch-3 sps).

Rnd 2: Join green with sl st in any ch sp, ch 4, (2 tr, ch 2, 3 tr) in same ch sp, (3 tr, ch 2, 3 tr) in each ch sp around, join with sl st in top of ch-4, fasten off.

Rnd 3: Join white with sl st in any ch sp, ch 3, (dc, ch 2, 2 dc) in same sp, dc in next 6 sts, *(2 dc, ch 2, 2 dc) in next ch sp, dc in next 6 sts; repeat from * around, join with sl st in top of ch-3, fasten off (60 dc, 6 ch-2 sps).

NOTE: For **cross stitch (cr st)**, skip next st or ch, dc in next st or ch; working over last dc made, dc in skipped st or ch.

Rnd 4: Join lt. brown with sl st in 2nd ch of any ch-2 sp, ch 3; working over ch-3, dc in first ch, cr st around, join, fasten off (36 cr sts).

Rnd 5: Join med. brown with sc in any st, sc in each st around, join with sl st in first sc, fasten off.

Matching corners, sew Motifs together according to Assembly Diagram.

EDGING

Rnd 1: Working around entire outer edge, join white with sc in any st, sc in each st around with sc next 2 sts tog at each indentation and 2 sc in each of 2 sc at each point, join with sl st in first sc, fasten off.

Rnd 2: With med. brown, repeat rnd 1.

POM-POM (make 70)

Wrap med. brown around cardboard 25 times and lt. brown 75 times. Slide loops off cardboard, tie separate strand lt. brown tightly around center of all loops. Cut loops and trim ends to ¾".

Sew one Pom-pom to each point and each indentation on Afghan. ❖

ASSEMBLY DIAGRAM

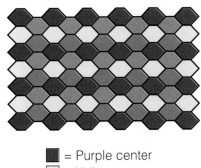

■ = Purple center
□ = Yellow center
■ = Orange center
■ = Lavender center

All the other dolls will turn green with envy when they see your fashion doll all dressed up in this soft and lacy evening ensemble of creamy white peignoir and slippers.

FASHION DOLL LINGERIE

DESIGNED BY PAMELA J. MCKEE

SIZE
Fits 11½" fashion doll.

MATERIALS
Size 20 crochet cotton — 200 yds. white; 12" lavender ⅛" satin ribbon; 5 pearl 4-mm beads; white sewing thread; sewing needle; No. 10 steel crochet hook or size needed to obtain gauge.

GAUGE
10 dc sts = 1"; 4 dc rows = 1".

PEIGNOIR

NOTE: Ch-3 at beginning of each row counts as first dc.

Row 1: Starting at neck, ch 33, dc in 4th ch from hook, (skip next ch, 3 dc in next ch) across to last 3 chs, skip next ch, dc in each of last 2 chs, turn (43 dc).

Row 2: Ch 3, dc in each of next 2 sts, 3 dc in next st, dc in next st, (skip next st, 3 dc in next st, skip next st, dc in next st, 3 dc in next st, dc in next st) across to last 2 sts, dc in each of last 2 sts, turn (57).

Row 3: Ch 3, dc in next st, ch 1, skip next st, (dc in next st, 3 dc in next st, dc in next st, ch 1, skip next st) across to last 2 sts, dc in each of last 2 sts, turn (69 dc, 14 ch-1 sps).

Row 4: Ch 3, dc in next st, dc in next ch-1 sp, (skip next st, dc in next st, 3 dc in next st, dc in next st, skip next st, dc in next ch-1 sp) across to last 2 sts, dc in each of last 2 sts, turn (83 dc).

Row 5: Working this row in **back lps** only, ch 3, dc in next st, 3 dc in next st, (skip next 2 sts, 3 dc in next st) 4 times; for **armhole**, ch 1, skip next 14 sts; 3 dc in next st; repeat between ( ) 8 times; for **armhole**, ch 1, skip next 14 sts; 3 dc in next st; repeat between ( ) 4 times, dc in each of last 2 sts, turn (61 dc, 2 armholes).

Row 6: Skipping ch-1 sps of armholes, ch 3, dc in next st, skip next st, 3 dc in next st, skip next 2 sts, 3 dc in next st, (skip next st, dc in next st, 3 dc in next st, dc in next st, skip next st, 3 dc in next st) 8 times, skip next 2 sts, 3 dc in next st, skip next st, dc in each of last 2 sts, turn (77 dc).

Rows 7-8: Ch 3, dc in next st, skip next st, 3 dc in next st, (skip next 2 sts, 3 dc in next st, skip next 2 sts, dc in next st, 3 dc in next st, dc in next st) 8 times, (skip next 2 sts, 3 dc in next st) 2 times, skip next st, dc in each of last 2 sts, turn.

Row 9: Ch 3, dc in each of next 2 sts, 3 dc in next st, dc in next st, skip next st, (3 dc in next st, skip next 2 sts, dc in next st, 3 dc in next st, dc in next st, skip next 2 sts) 8 times, 3 dc in next st, skip next st, dc in next st, 3 dc in next st, dc in each of last 3 sts, turn (81).

Rows 10-35: Ch 3, dc in next st, skip next st, dc in next st, 3 dc in next st, dc in next st, (skip next 2 sts, 3 dc in next st, skip next 2 sts, dc in next st, 3 dc in next st, dc in next st) 9 times, skip next st, dc in each of last 2 sts, turn.

Row 36: Ch 1, sc in first 4 sts, *(skip next st, sc in next 7 sts) 9 times, skip next st, sc in last 4 sts, turn (71 sc).

Row 37: Ch 4, (dc, ch 1, dc) in same st, *ch 1, dc in next st, ch 1, (dc, ch 1, dc, ch 1, dc) in each of next 2 sts, ch 1; repeat from * across to last st, (dc, ch 1, dc, ch 1, dc) in last st, fasten off.

Sleeve

Rnd 1: Working around armhole in **back lps**, join with sl st in 2nd skipped st of row 4, ch 3, 3 dc in next st, dc in next st, (skip next 2 sts, dc in next st, 3 dc in next st, dc in next st) 2 times, 3 sc in last ch-1 sp, join with sl st in top of ch-3 (15 dc, 3 sc).

Rnds 2-10: Sl st in next st, ch 3, 3 dc in next st, dc in next st, skip next 2 sts, (dc in next st, 3 dc in next st, dc in next st, skip next 2 sts) 2 times, 3 dc in next st, skip last st, join.

Rnd 11: Ch 1, sc in same st, skip next st, (sc in each of next 2 sts, skip next st) 5 times, sc in last st, join with sl st in first sc (12 sc).

Rnd 12: Ch 4, (dc, ch 1, dc) in same st, ch 1, *(dc, ch 1, dc, ch 1, dc) in next st, ch 1; repeat from * around, join with sl st in 3rd ch of ch-4, fasten off.

Repeat on other armhole.

Neck Ruffle

For **buttonholes,** join with sc in end of row 4 on right front, ch 3, sc in same row, (2 sc in end of next row, ch 3) 2 times, sl st in end of row 1; working in starting ch on opposite side of row 1, sl st in first ch, ch 4, (dc, ch 1, dc) in same ch, ch 1, *(dc, ch 1, dc, ch 1, dc) in next ch, ch 1; repeat from * across, dc in end of row 1 on opposite side, fasten off.

Sew three pearls to left front of Peignoir opposite buttonholes.

Bodice Ruffle

Working in **front lps** of row 4, join with sl st in first st, ch 4, (dc, ch 1, dc) in same st, ch 1, (dc, ch 1, dc, ch 1, dc) in next st, *skip next st, (dc, ch 1, dc, ch 1, dc) in each of next 2 sts; repeat from * across, fasten off.

For **belt loop,** join with sl st in top of 23rd st on row 9, ch 5, sl st in top of 23rd st on row 10, fasten off. Repeat in 59th st on rows 9 and 10.

For **belt,** ch 99, sc in 2nd ch from hook, sc in each ch across with 3 sc in end ch; working on opposite side of ch, sc in each ch across with 2 sc in last ch, join with sl st in first sc, fasten off. Pull belt through belt loops.

SLIPPER (make 2)

Rnd 1: Ch 7, 2 sc in 2nd ch from hook, sc in each of next 3 chs, hdc in next ch; for **toe,** 3 hdc in end ch; working on opposite side of ch, hdc in next ch, sc in last 4 chs, join with sl st in first sc (14 sts).

Rnd 2: Ch 1, 3 sc in same st, sc in next 5 sts, 2 sc in next st, 3 sc in next st, 2 sc in next st, sc in last 5 sts, join (20 sc).

Rnd 3: Ch 3, 2 dc in same st, ch 3, skip next 5 sts, dc in next 4 sts, skip next 2 sts, dc in next 4 sts, ch 3, skip last 4 sts, join with sl st in top of ch-3, **turn** (11 dc, 2 ch-3 sps).

Rnd 4: Sl st in each st and in each ch around, join with sl st in first sl st, fasten off.

Sew one pearl to top of toe. Weave 6" piece of ribbon through one st at center back of heel, tie ends into bow around ankle. ❖

You won't keep this treasure hidden! Dainty petals spiral gently out from the center of this delicate doily lending a new twist to an old idea.

STARFISH DOILY

Designed by Emma L. Willey

SIZE
14" across. This project may ruffle until blocked.

MATERIALS
Size 10 bedspread cotton — 300 yds. white; No. 5 steel crochet hook or size needed to obtain gauge.

GAUGE
Rnds 1-4 = 3" across.

DOILY

Rnd 1: Ch 6, sl st in first ch to form ring, ch 3, 15 dc in ring, join with sl st in top of ch-3 (16 dc).

Rnd 2: Ch 4, 2 tr in same st, ch 1, skip next st, (3 tr in next st, ch 1, skip next st) around, join with sl st in top of ch-4 (24 tr).

Rnd 3: Ch 4, tr in same st, tr in next st, 2 tr in next st, ch 1, *2 tr in next st, tr in next st, 2 tr in next st, ch 1; repeat from * around, join (40 tr).

Rnd 4: Ch 4, tr in each of next 3 sts, 2 tr in next st, ch 3, skip next ch-1 sp, *tr in next 4 sts, 2 tr in next st, ch 3, skip next ch-1 sp; repeat from * around, join (48 tr, 8 ch-3 sps).

Rnd 5: Ch 4, tr in next 4 sts, 2 tr in next st, ch 5, skip next ch-3 sp, *tr in next 5 sts, 2 tr in next st, ch 5, skip next ch-3 sp; repeat from * around, join (56 tr, 8 ch-5 sps).

Rnd 6: Sl st in next st, ch 4, tr in next 5 sts, tr in next ch-5 sp, ch 6, skip next st, *tr in next 6 sts, tr in next ch-5 sp, ch 6, skip next st; repeat from * around, join.

Rnd 7: Sl st in next st, ch 4, tr in next 5 sts, tr in next ch-6 sp, ch 5, sc in same sp, ch 5, skip next st, *tr in next 6 sts, tr in next ch-6 sp, ch 5, sc in same sp, ch 5, skip next st; repeat from * around, join.

Rnd 8: Sl st in each of next 2 sts, ch 4, tr in next 4 sts, *[tr in next ch-5 sp, ch 5, sc in same sp, ch 5, sc in next ch-5 sp, ch 5, skip next 2 sts], tr in next 5 sts; repeat from * 6 more times; repeat between [ ], join.

Rnd 9: Sl st in each of next 2 sts, ch 4, tr in each of next 3 sts, *[tr in next ch-5 sp, ch 5, sc in same sp, ch 5, (sc in next ch-5 sp, ch 5) 2 times, skip next 2 sts], tr in next 4 sts; repeat from * 6 more times; repeat between [ ], join.

Rnd 10: Sl st in each of next 2 sts, ch 4, tr in each of next 2 sts, *[tr in next ch-5 sp, ch 5, sc in same sp, ch 5, (sc in next ch-5 sp, ch 5) 3 times, skip next 2 sts], tr in each of next 3 sts; repeat from * 6 more times; repeat between [ ], join.

Rnd 11: Sl st in each of next 2 sts, ch 4, tr in next st, *[tr in next ch-5 sp, ch 5, sc in same sp, ch 5, (sc in next ch-5 sp, ch 5) 4 times, skip next 2 sts], tr in each of next 2 sts; repeat from * 6 more times; repeat between [ ], join.

Rnd 12: Sl st in each of next 2 sts, ch 4, *[tr in next ch-5 sp, ch 5, sc in same sp, ch 5, (sc in next ch-5 sp, ch 5) 5 times, skip next 2 sts], tr in next st; repeat from * 6 more times; repeat between [ ], join.

NOTE: For **double treble crochet (dtr),** yo 3 times, insert hook in next sp, yo, draw lp through, (yo, draw through 2 lps on hook) 4 times.

Joining (ch 2, dc) on next rnd counts as ch-5 sp.

Rnd 13: Sl st in next st, sl st in each of next 3 chs, ch 1, sc in same sp, ch 5, *[dc in next ch-5 sp, ch 5, tr in next ch-5 sp, ch 5, dtr in next ch-5 sp, ch 5, tr in next ch-5 sp, ch 5, dc in next ch-5 sp, ch 5, sc in next ch-5 sp], ch 5, skip next 2 sts, sc in next ch-5 sp, ch 5; repeat from * 6 more times; repeat between [ ]; to **join,** ch 2, skip last 2 sts, dc in first sc (56 ch-5 sps).

Rnd 14: Ch 1, sc around joining dc, ch 5, (dc in next ch-5 sp, ch 5) 6 times, *sc in next ch-5 sp, ch 5, (dc in next ch-5 sp, ch 5) 6 times; repeat from * around, join with sl st in first sc (56 ch sps).

NOTE: For **beginning double crochet shell (beg dc shell),** (ch 3, dc, ch 2, 2 dc) in same ch-5 sp.

For **double crochet shell (dc shell),** (2 dc, ch 2, 2 dc) in next ch-5 sp.

Rnd 15: Sl st in each of next 3 chs, beg dc shell, ch 3, sc in next ch-5 sp, ch 3, (shell in next ch-5 sp, ch 3, sc in next ch-5 sp, ch 3) around, join with sl st in top of ch-3 (28 shells).

Rnd 16: Sl st in next st, sl st in next ch sp, beg dc shell, ch 8, sc in ch-2 sp of next shell, ch 8, *dc shell in ch sp of next shell, ch 8, sc in ch sp of next shell, ch 8; repeat from * around, join.

Rnd 17: Sl st in next st, sl st in next ch sp, beg dc shell, ch 7, (sc in next ch-8 lp, ch 7) 2 times, *dc shell in next shell, ch 7, (sc in next ch-8 lp, ch 7) 2 times; repeat from * around, join.

Rnd 18: Sl st in next st, sl st in next ch sp, beg dc shell, ch 6, (sc in next ch-7 lp, ch 6) 3 times, *dc shell

Continued on page 95

Make this sweet little heart embellished with satin ribbon and silk rose for someone special in your life as a lasting remembrance. It's a geat single evening project.

POTPOURRI HEART

DESIGNED BY ISABELLE WOLTERS

SIZE
3½" x 3½" without hanger.

MATERIALS
100% cotton sport yarn — small amount white; size 10 bedspread cotton — small amount each white and red; 10" red ¼" satin ribbon; ¾" red silk rosebud with leaves; potpourri; polyester fiberfill; craft glue or hot glue gun; No. 0 and No. 5 steel crochet hooks or size needed to obtain gauge.

GAUGE
With No. 0 steel hook and sport yarn, 5 sc sts = 1"; 5 sc rows = 1".

HEART SIDE (make 2)

NOTE: Use No. 0 steel hook and sport yarn unless otherwise stated.

Row 1: Starting at bottom, ch 3, sc in 2nd ch from hook, sc in last ch, turn (2 sc).

Row 2: Ch 1, 2 sc in each st across, turn (4).

Rows 3-4: Ch 1, 2 sc in first st, sc in each st across with 2 sc in last st, turn (6, 8).

Row 5: Ch 1, sc in each of first 3 sts, 2 sc in each of next 2 sts, sc in each of last 3 sts, turn (10).

Row 6: Repeat row 3 (12).

Rows 7-8: Ch 1, sc in each st across, turn.

Row 9: For **first side**, ch 1, sc in first 5 sts leaving remaining sts unworked, turn (5).

Row 10: Ch 1, sc in each of first 3 sts, sc last 2 sts tog, turn (4).

Row 11: Ch 1, sc in each of first 2 sts, sc last 2 sts tog, **do not** turn, fasten off (3).

Row 9: For **2nd side**, skip next 2 sts on row 8, join with sc in next st, sc in last 4 sts, turn (5).

Row 10: Ch 1, sc first 2 sts tog, sc in each st across, turn (4).

Row 11: Ch 1, sc first 2 sts tog, sc in each st across, turn, **do not** fasten off (3).

Rnd 12: For **edging**, working around outer edge, ch 1, sc in each st and in end of each row around to opposite side of row 1, sc in next ch, ch 2, sc in next ch, sc in end of each row and in each st around with sc next 2 skipped sts on row 8 tog at center top, join with sl st in first sc, fasten off (37 sc, 1 ch-2 sp).

FINISHING

Rnd 1: To **join**, holding both Heart Sides wrong sides tog, matching sts, working through both thicknesses in **back lps**, with No. 5 steel hook, join red bedspread cotton with sc in first st after center 3 sts at top of Heart, sc in same st, 2 sc in each st and in each ch around to last 3 sts stuffing with pot-pourri and fiberfill as you work; for **hanger opening**, working through one thickness only, 2 sc in each of last 3 sts, join with sl st in first sc, fasten off (78 sc).

Rnd 2: With No. 5 steel hook, join white bedspread cotton with sl st in first st, ch 3, (2 dc, ch 3, 3 dc) in same st, *skip next 2 sts, (3 dc, ch 3, 3 dc) in next st*; repeat between ** 11 more times, skip next st, (3 dc, ch 3, 3 dc) in next st; repeat between ** 12 more times, skip last 3 sts, join with sl st in top of ch-3, fasten off.

For **hanger**, fold ribbon in half; insert ends into opening at center top of Heart. Sew opening closed, securing ends inside Heart. Glue rosebud to left-hand side of Heart.❖

STARFISH DOILY

Continued from page 92

in next shell, ch 6, (sc in next ch-7 lp, ch 6) 3 times; repeat from * around, join.

Rnd 19: Sl st in next st, sl st in next ch sp, beg dc shell, ch 5, (sc in next ch-6 lp, ch 5) 4 times, *dc shell in next shell, ch 5, (sc in next ch-6 lp, ch 5) 4 times; repeat from * around, join.

NOTE: For **treble crochet shell (tr shell)**, (2 tr, ch 2, 2 tr) in next ch sp.

Rnd 20: Sl st in next st, sl st in next ch sp, ch 1, sc in same sp, *[(ch 5, sc in next ch-5 sp) 2 times, ch 3, tr shell in next ch-5 sp, ch 3, (sc in next ch-5 sp, ch 5) 2 times], sc in next shell; repeat from * 12 more times; repeat between [ ], join with sl st in first sc.

Rnd 21: Sl st in each of next 3 chs, ch 1, sc in same sp, ch 5, sc in next ch-5 sp, ch 5, tr shell in next shell, ch 5, skip next ch-3 sp, *(sc in next ch-5 sp, ch 5) 4 times, tr shell in next shell, ch 5, skip next ch-3 sp; repeat from * around to last 2 ch-5 sps, sc in next ch-5 sp, ch 5, sc in last ch-5 sp; to **join**, ch 2, dc in first sc, **turn.**

Rnd 22: Ch 1, sc around joining dc, ch 5, (sc in next ch-5 sp, ch 5) 2 times, tr shell in next shell, ch 5, *(sc in next ch-5 sp, ch 5) 5 times, tr shell in next shell, ch 5; repeat from * around to last 2 ch-5 sps, (sc in next ch-5 sp, ch 5) 2 times, join with sl st in first sc, **do not** turn.

NOTES: For **beginning treble cluster (beg tr cl)**, ch 4, *yo 2 times, insert hook in same st, yo, draw lp through, (yo, draw through 2 lps on hook) 2 times; repeat from * 3 more times, yo, draw through all 5 lps on hook.

For **treble cluster (tr cl)**, *yo 2 times, insert hook in st, yo, draw lp through, (yo, draw through 2 lps on hook) 2 times; repeat from * 4 times in same st, yo, draw through all 6 lps on hook.

Rnd 23: Beg tr cl, *[(ch 10, skip next ch-5 sp, sc in next ch-5 sp, ch 10, skip next ch-5 sp), tr shell in next shell; repeat between ( )], tr cl in next sc; repeat from * 12 more times; repeat between [ ], join with sl st in top of beg tr cl, fasten off.❖

What a delicious way to start your baby's day, all decked out in this delightful set of sweater, bonnet and booties. Generous sprinkles of popcorns and post stitches add the perfect flavor for any taste.

ORANGE SHERBERT

DESIGNED BY CAROL SMITH

SIZES
Infant's 3 mos., 6 mos. or 12 mos.

MATERIALS
Pompadour baby yarn — 4½ oz. peach for 3 mos., 5 oz. peach for 6 mos. or 5½ oz. peach for 12 mos.; 3⅛ yds. peach ⅛" satin ribbon; D, E or F crochet hook or hook needed to obtain gauge given for size.

GAUGE
For **3 mos.,** using D hook, 4 dc and 4 dc cross sts = 2¼"; 4 pattern rows = 1½".
For **6 mos.,** using E hook, 4 dc and 4 dc c ross sts = 2½"; 3 pattern rows = 1¼".
For **12 mos.,** using F hook, 4 dc and 4 dc cross sts = 2¾"; 4 pattern rows = 1¾".

SWEATER
Body
NOTES: For **double crochet cross stitch (dc cr st),** skip next ch or st, dc in next ch or st; working over dc just made, dc in skipped ch or st.

For **double crochet back post (dc bp,** see page 159), yo, insert hook from back to front around post of next st, complete as dc.

For **double crochet front post (dc fp),** yo, insert hook from front to back around post of next st, complete as dc.

For **popcorn (pc),** 4 dc in next st, drop lp from hook, insert hook in first dc of 4-dc group, draw dropped lp through.

Ch-3 at beginning of rows is used and counted as a st.

Row 1: Starting at waist, ch 101, dc in 4th ch from hook, dc cr st, (dc in next ch, dc cr st) across to last 2 chs, dc in each of last 2 chs, turn (35 dc, 32 dc cr sts). Front of row 1 is right side of work.

Row 2: Ch 3, dc bp, (dc cr st, dc bp) across to last st, dc in last st, turn (33 dc bp, 32 dc cr sts, 2 dc).

Row 3: Ch 3, dc fp, dc cr st, (pc, dc cr st) across to last 2 sts, dc fp, dc in last st, turn (32 dc cr sts, 31 pc, 2 dc fp, 2 dc).

Row 4: Ch 3, dc bp, dc cr st, (dc in next st, dc cr st) across to last 2 sts, dc bp, dc in last st, turn (32

dc cr sts, 33 dc, 2 dc bp).

Row 5: Ch 3, dc fp, (dc cr st, dc fp) across to last st, dc in last st, turn (33 dc fp, 32 dc cr sts, 2 dc).

Row 6: Ch 3, dc bp, (pc, dc cr st) across to last 2 sts, dc bp, dc in last st, turn (32 dc cr sts, 31 pc, 2 dc bp, 2 dc).

Row 7: Ch 3, dc fp, dc cr st, (dc in next st, dc cr st) across to last 2 sts, dc fp, dc in last st, turn.

Row 8: Ch 3, dc bp, (dc cr st, dc bp) across to last st, dc in last st, turn.

Rows 9-14: Repeat rows 3-8 consecutively.

Row 15: Ch 3, dc fp, ch 3, sc in each of next 2 sts, ch 3, (pc, ch 3, sc in each of next 2 sts, ch 3) across to last 2 sts, dc fp, dc in last st, fasten off.

Yoke
Row 1: For **first front,** working in starting ch on opposite side of row 1 on Body, join with sl st in first ch, ch 3, dc fp, (dc cr st, dc fp) 8 times leaving remaining chs unworked, turn (9 dc fp, 8 dc cr sts, 1 dc).

Row 2: Ch 3, (dc cr st, dc bp) across to last st, dc in last st, turn (8 dc cr sts, 8 dc bp, 2 dc).

Row 3: Ch 3, (dc fp, dc cr st) 7 times, dc fp next fp and last dc tog skipping dc cr st in between, turn (8 dc fp, 7 dc cr sts, 1 dc).

Row 4: Repeat row 2.

Row 5: Ch 3, dc fp next 2 fp tog skipping dc cr st in between, dc cr st, (dc fp, dc cr st) 4 times, dc fp next fp and last dc tog skipping dc cr st in between, turn (6 dc fp, 5 dc cr sts, 1 dc).

Row 6: Repeat row 2.

Row 7: Ch 3, dc fp next 2 fp tog skipping dc cr st in between, dc cr st, (dc fp, dc cr st) across to last st, dc in last st, turn (4 dc cr sts, 4 dc fp, 2 dc).

Row 8: Repeat row 2.

Row 9: Repeat row 7 (3 dc cr sts, 3 dc fp, 2 dc).

Row 10: Repeat row 2.

NOTE: For **half double crochet front post (hdc fp),** yo, insert hook from front to back around post of next st, complete as hdc.

For **half double crochet cross stitch (hdc cr st),** skip next st, hdc in next st; working over hdc just made, hdc in skipped st.

Row 11: Ch 3, (dc fp, dc cr st) 2 times, hdc fp, hdc cr st, hdc in last st, **do not** turn, fasten off.

Continued on next page

Orange Sherbert

Continued from page 97

Row 1: For **back,** join with sl st around post of same st as last dc fp made on row 1 of first front; working in starting ch on opposite side of row 1 on Body, ch 3, (dc cr st, dc fp) 16 times leaving remaining chs unworked, turn (17 dc fp, 16 dc cr sts).

Row 2: Ch 3, dc cr st, (dc bp, dc cr st) across to last st, dc in last st, turn (16 dc cr sts, 15 dc bp, 2 dc).

NOTE: (Ch 2, skip next dc cr st, dc fp) counts as dc fp first 2 sts tog.

Row 3: Ch 2, skip next dc cr st, (dc fp, dc cr st) 14 times, dc fp next fp and last dc tog skipping dc cr st in between, turn (15 dc fp, 14 dc cr sts).

Row 4: Repeat row 2.

Row 5: Ch 2, skip next dc cr st, (dc fp, dc cr st) 12 times, dc fp next fp and last dc tog skipping dc cr st in between, turn (12 dc cr sts, 13 dc fp).

Row 6: Repeat row 2.

Row 7: Ch 3, dc cr st, (dc fp, dc cr st) across to last st, dc in last st, turn.

Rows 8-10: Repeat rows 2 and 7 alternately, ending with row 2.

NOTE: For **single crochet front post (sc fp),** insert hook from front to back around post of next st, yo, draw lp through, complete as sc.

Row 11: Ch 2, (hdc cr st, hdc fp) 2 times, dc cr st, dc fp, hdc cr st, hdc fp, sc in each of next 2 sts, (sc fp, sc in each of next 2 sts) 3 times, hdc fp, hdc cr st, dc fp, dc cr st, (hdc fp, hdc cr st) 2 times, hdc in last st, **do not** turn, fasten off.

Row 1: For **2nd front,** join with sl st around post of same st as last dc fp made on row 1 of back; working in starting ch on opposite side of row 1 on Body, ch 3, (dc cr st, dc fp) 8 times, dc in last ch, turn (9 dc fp, 8 dc cr sts, 1 dc).

Row 2: Ch 3, dc bp, (dc cr st, dc bp) across, turn.

Row 3: Ch 2, skip next dc cr st, dc fp, (dc cr st, dc fp) across to last st, dc in last st, turn (8 dc fp, 7 dc cr sts, 1 dc).

Row 4: Repeat row 2.

Row 5: Ch 2, skip next dc cr st, (dc fp, dc cr st) 5 times, dc fp next 2 fp tog skipping dc cr st in between, dc in last st, turn (6 dc fp, 5 dc cr sts, 1 dc).

Row 6: Repeat row 2.

Row 7: Ch 3, dc cr st, (dc fp, dc cr st) 3 times, dc fp next 2 fp tog skipping dc cr st in between, dc in last st, turn (4 dc cr sts, 4 dc fp, 2 dc).

Row 8: Repeat row 2.

Row 9: Ch 3, dc cr st, (dc fp, dc cr st) 2 times, dc

fp next 2 fp tog skipping dc cr st in between, dc in last st, turn (3 dc cr sts, 3 dc fp, 2 dc).

Row 10: Repeat row 2.

Row 11: Ch 2, hdc cr st, hdc fp, hdc cr st, dc fp, dc cr st, dc fp, dc in last st, fasten off.

For **shoulder seams,** matching sts, sew last row of each front to corresponding sts on back.

Sleeve (make 2)

Row 1: For **cuff,** ch 42, dc in 5th ch from hook; working over dc just made, dc in 4th ch from hook (first dc cr st made), (dc in next ch, dc cr st) across to last ch, dc in last ch, turn (14 dc, 13 dc cr sts).

Row 2: Ch 3, dc cr st, (dc bp, dc cr st) across to last st, dc in last st, turn.

Row 3: Ch 3, dc cr st, (pc, dc cr st) across to last st, dc in last st, turn.

Row 4: Ch 3, dc cr st, (dc in next st, dc cr st) across to last st, dc in last st, turn.

Row 5: Ch 3, dc cr st, (dc fp, dc cr st) across to last st, dc in last st, turn.

Rows 6-7: Repeat rows 3 and 4.

Row 8: Repeat row 2.

Row 9: Ch 6, sc in each of next 2 sts, ch 3, (pc, ch 3, sc in each of next 2 sts, ch 3) across to last st, dc in last st, **do not** turn, fasten off.

Row 10: For **Sleeve,** working in starting ch on opposite side of row 1, join with sl st in first ch, ch 3, dc cr st, (dc fp, dc cr st) across to last ch, dc in last ch, turn (13 dc cr sts, 12 dc fp, 2 dc).

Row 11: Ch 3, dc cr st, (dc bp, dc cr st) across to last st, dc in last st, turn.

Row 12: Ch 3, dc cr st, (dc fp, dc cr st) across to last st, dc in last st, turn.

Row 13: Repeat row 11.

NOTES: (Ch 2, dc next 3 sts tog) counts as dc first 4 sts tog.

When working dc next 3 or 4 sts tog, both dc of cr sts count as a st.

Row 14: Ch 2, dc next 3 sts tog, dc cr st, (dc fp, dc cr st) across to last 4 sts, dc last 4 sts tog, turn (11 dc cr sts, 10 dc fp, 2 dc).

Row 15: Ch 2, dc next 3 sts tog, dc cr st, (dc bp, dc cr st) across to last 4 sts, dc last 4 sts tog, turn (9 dc cr sts, 8 dc bp, 2 dc).

Rows 16-18: Repeat rows 14 and 15 alternately, ending with row 14 and 3 dc cr sts, 2 dc fp and 2 dc in last row.

Row 19: Ch 2, dc next 3 sts tog, dc cr st, dc last 4 sts tog, fasten off (2 dc, 1 dc cr st).

For **underarm seam,** sew ends of rows 1-13

together. Easing to fit, sew Sleeve to armhole opening. For **cuff,** fold back between rows 5 and 6, or to desired length.

Repeat on other armhole.

Edging

Row 1: Join with sc in end of row 15 on bottom corner of first front, sc in same row, 2 sc in each row across to shoulder seam, skip seam, sc in each st across back neck edge to next shoulder seam, skip seam, 2 sc in end of each row across to bottom corner on 2nd front, fasten off.

Row 2: With wrong side of Sweater facing you, working this row in **back lps** only, join with sc in st even with first decrease at neck edge, ch 3, pc, ch 3, (sc in each of next 2 sts, ch 3, pc, ch 3) 15 times, sc in next st leaving remaining sts unworked, fasten off.

For **tie** (make 2), cut 20" length of ribbon; tie center of ribbon to sc just below row 2 of Edging.

BONNET

Row 1: Starting at center, ch 66, dc in 5th ch from hook; working over dc just made, dc in 4th ch from hook (first dc cr st made), (dc in next ch, dc cr st) across to last ch, dc in last ch, turn (22 dc, 21 dc cr sts).

Rows 2-9: Repeat same rows of Sleeve.

Row 10: For **back,** working in starting ch on opposite side of row 1, join with sl st in first ch, ch 3, dc cr st, (dc fp, dc cr st) 5 times, dc fp next 2 dc tog skipping dc cr st in between, dc cr st; repeat between ( ) 6 times, dc fp next 2 dc tog skipping dc cr st in between, dc cr st; repeat between ( ) 5 times, dc in last st, turn (19 dc cr sts, 18 dc fp, 2 dc).

Row 11: Ch 3, dc cr st, (dc bp, dc cr st) 5 times, dc bp next 2 fp tog skipping dc cr st in between, dc cr st; repeat between ( ) 4 times, dc bp next 2 fp tog skipping dc cr st in between, dc cr st; repeat between ( ) 5 more times, turn (17 dc cr sts, 16 dc bp, 2 dc).

Row 12: Ch 3, dc cr st, (dc fp, dc cr st) 5 times, dc fp next 2 fp tog skipping dc cr st in between, (dc fp, dc cr st) 2 times, dc fp next 2 bp tog skipping dc cr st in between, dc cr st, (dc fp, dc cr st) 5 times, dc in last st, turn (15 dc cr sts, 14 dc fp, 2 dc).

Row 13: Ch 3, dc cr st, (dc bp, dc cr st) 5 times, *dc bp next 2 fp tog skipping dc cr st in between*, dc cr st; repeat between **, dc cr st, (dc bp, dc cr st) 5 times, dc in last st, turn (13 dc cr sts, 12 dc bp, 2 dc).

Row 14: Ch 3, dc cr st, (dc fp, dc cr st) 5 times, dc fp next 2 bp tog skipping dc cr st in between, dc cr st, (dc fp, dc cr st) 5 times, dc in last st, turn (12 dc cr sts, 11 dc fp, 2 dc).

Row 15: For **center back seam,** fold row 14 in half right sides tog; matching sts and working through both thicknesses, sl st in each st across, fasten off.

For **bottom edging,** working in ends of rows, join with sc in row 8, sc in same row, 2 sc in each of next 7 rows, sc in next 10 rows, 2 sc in each of next 8 rows, fasten off.

For **tie,** weave 40" length of ribbon through spaces between last 2 sts of each row across bottom of Bonnet leaving ends long.

BOOTIE (make 2)

NOTE: Ch-3 at beginning of each row or rnd counts as first dc fp or dc bp.

Rnd 1: Starting at toe, ch 4, sl st in first ch to form ring, ch 3, 23 dc in ring, join with sl st in top of ch-3, **turn** (24 dc).

Rnd 2: Ch 3, dc cr st, (dc bp, dc cr st) around, join, **turn** (8 dc cr sts, 8 dc bp).

Rnd 3: Ch 3, dc cr st, (dc fp, dc cr st) around, join, **turn.**

Rnds 4-6: Repeat rnds 2 and 3 alternately, ending with rnd 2.

Row 7: Working in rows, ch 3, dc cr st, (dc fp, dc cr st) across, dc in same st as first ch-3, **do not** join, turn.

Row 8: Ch 3, dc cr st, (dc bp, dc cr st) across to last st, dc in last st, turn.

Row 9: Ch 3, dc cr st, (dc fp, dc cr st) across to last st, dc in last st, turn.

Rows 10-12: Repeat rows 8 and 9 alternately, ending with row 8.

Row 13: For **center back seam,** fold last row in half right sides tog, working through both thicknesses, sl st in each st across, fasten off.

Ankle

Rnd 1: Join with sl st in center back seam, ch 3, 2 dc in end of each row around with 2 dc in same st on rnd 6 as first and last st on row 7 at center front, join with sl st in top of ch-3, **turn** (27 dc).

Rnd 2: Ch 3, dc cr st, (dc bp, dc cr st) around, join, **turn.**

NOTE: For **beginning popcorn (beg pc),** ch 3, 3 dc in same st, drop lp from hook, insert hook in top of ch-3, draw dropped lp through.

Rnd 3: Beg pc, dc cr st, (pc, dc cr st) around, join with sl st in top of beg pc, **turn.**

Rnd 4: Ch 3, dc cr st, (dc in next st, dc cr st) around, join with sl st in top of ch-3, **turn.**

Rnd 5: Ch 3, dc cr st, (dc fp, dc cr st) around, join, **do not** turn.

Rnd 6: Beg pc, ch 3, sc in each of next 2 sts, ch 3, (pc, ch 3, sc in each of next 2 sts, ch 3) around, join with sl st in top of beg pc, fasten off.

Weave 16" length of ribbon through 2-dc groups on rnd 1 of Ankle, tie in bow at center front. ❖

GENTLE COUNTRY DAYS

THE OLD FRONT PORCH

Old rockers squeak and the swings begin to sway
As we gather on the porch in the evening of the day.

We reminisce of old times and dream of things to come,
Of places we'll be going or maybe just come from.

Listening to the bird calls as the fireflies start to play
And seeping in the pleasure of these gentle country days.

Watching little ripples as they form upon the lake.
Sniffing at the apple pie just put on to bake.

What could be better than friends and family gathered near.
Listening to old stories that bring laughter or a tear.

No matter how far life leads me to adventure and new ways,
I'll always love this old front porch and the gentle country days.

Delectable diagonals in subtle shades of purple, green and rose add an interesting effect to this electrifying afghan. Fuzzy worsted-weight yarn lends a soft, warm glow to this appealing design.

FUZZY LOG CABIN AFGHAN

DESIGNED BY KATHERINE ENG

SIZE
45¼" x 70".

MATERIALS
Fuzzy worsted-weight yarn — 25 oz. purple, 21 oz. dk. green, 11 oz. lt. green and 9 oz. rose; tapestry needle; G crochet hook or size needed to obtain gauge.

GAUGE
Rnds 1-3 of Block = 2" across. Each Block is 8¼" square.

BLOCK (make 40)
Rnd 1: With purple, ch 4, sl st in first ch to form ring, ch 1, 8 sc in ring, join with sl st in first sc (8 sc).

Rnd 2: Ch 1, sc in first st, (sc, ch 2, sc) in next st, *sc in next st, (sc, ch 2, sc) in next st; repeat from * around, join (12 sc, 4 ch-2 sps).

Rnd 3: Ch 1, sc in each st around with (sc, ch 2, sc) in each ch-2 sp, join, fasten off (20 sc, 4 ch-2 sps).

Row 4: Working in rows, join lt. green with sc in any ch-2 sp, sc in each st across to next ch-2 sp, (sc, ch 2, sc) in next ch-2 sp, sc in each st across to next ch-2 sp, sc in next ch-2 sp leaving remaining sts unworked, turn (14 sc, 1 ch-2 sp).

Row 5: Ch 1, sc in each st across with (sc, ch 2, sc) in corner ch-2 sp, turn, fasten off (16 sc, 1 ch-2 sp).

Row 6: Working on opposite side of Block, join purple with sc in end of last row, sc in end of next row, sc in next worked ch-2 sp, sc in each st across to next ch-2 sp, (sc, ch 2, sc) in next ch-2 sp, sc in each st across to next worked ch-2 sp, sc in next ch-2 sp, sc in end of each of next 2 rows, turn.

Row 7: Repeat row 5.

Rows 8-23: Working in color sequence of rose, dk. green, lt. green and purple, repeat rows 6 and 7 alternately.

Rnd 24: Working around outer edge, with right side facing you, join dk. green with sc in 2nd sc after any corner ch-2 sp, ch 1, skip next st, *(sc in next st, ch 1, skip next st) across to next corner

ch-2 sp or corner sc, (sc, ch 3, sc) in next corner ch-2 sp or corner sc, ch 1, skip next st or end of next row; repeat from * around, join with sl st in first sc, **do not** turn, fasten off (56 sc, 52 ch-1 sps, 4 ch-3 sps).

Working in **back lps**, using dk. green, sew Blocks together in five rows of eight Blocks each according to Assembly Diagram.

ASSEMBLY DIAGRAM

BORDER
Rnd 1: Working around entire outer edge of Blocks, join dk. green with sc in first sc after any corner ch-3 sp, sc in each ch-1 sp, in each sc, in each ch sp on each side of seams and hdc in each seam around with (sc, ch 3, sc) in each corner ch-3 sp, join with sl st in first sc (149 sc across each short end, 239 sc across each long side, 4 corner ch-3 sps).

Rnd 2: Ch 1, sc in first st, ch 1, skip next st, *(sc in next st, ch 1, skip next st) across to next ch-3 sp, (sc, ch 3, sc) in next ch-3 sp, ch 1, skip next st; repeat from * around, join, fasten off.

Rnd 3: Join purple with sl st in first sc after any

Continued on page 112

Add color and texture to your holiday scene with this festive runner. Its lasting beauty will make it a regular feature in your Christmas decor.

HOLIDAY TWEED RUNNER

DESIGNED BY KATHERINE ENG

SIZE
13¼" x 39¾".

MATERIALS
Worsted-weight yarn — 6 oz. red; 30 yds. ⅛" satin ribbon; G crochet hook or size needed to obtain gauge.

GAUGE
4 dc sts = 1"; 3 dc rows and 2 sc rows = 2".

TABLE RUNNER
NOTE: Front of row 1 is wrong side of work.

Row 1: With red yarn, ch 176, sc in 2nd ch from hook, *(ch 1, skip next ch, sc in next ch) 2 times, ch 5, skip next 5 chs, sc in next ch; repeat from * across to last 4 chs, (ch 1, skip next ch, sc in next ch) 2 times, turn (54 sc, 36 ch-1 sps, 17 ch-5 sps).

Row 2: Ch 3, dc in next 4 ch-1 sps and sts, (ch 3, sl st in next ch-5 sp, ch 3, dc in next 5 sts and ch-1 sps) across, turn (90 dc, 34 ch-3 sps).

Row 3: Ch 1, sc in same st, (ch 1, skip next st, sc in next st) 2 times, *ch 5, skip next 2 ch-3 sps, sc in next st, (ch 1, skip next st, sc in next st) 2 times; repeat from * across, turn.

Rows 4-33: Repeat rows 2 and 3 alternately.

NOTES: For **beginning shell (beg shell)**, ch 3, (dc, ch 2, 2 dc) in same st.

For **shell**, (2 dc, ch 2, 2 dc) in next st or ch sp.

Rnd 34: Working around outer edge, beg shell in first st, [ch 1, sc in next st, ch 1, *dc in next st, ch 1, shell in next ch-5 sp, ch 1, dc in next st, ch 1, sc in next st, ch 1; repeat from * across to last st, shell in last st; working in ends of rows, [ch 1, skip next dc row, sc in next row, ch 1, skip next row, (shell in next row, ch 1, skip next row, sc in next row, ch 1, skip next row) across to last row,

skip last row]; working in starting ch on opposite side of row 1, shell in first ch, ch 1, skip next ch, sc in next ch, ch 1, skip next ch, (dc in next ch, ch 1, shell in next ch-5 sp, ch 1, dc in next ch, ch 1, skip next ch, sc in next ch, ch 1, skip next ch) across to last ch, shell in last ch; repeat between [ ], join with sl st in top of ch-3, fasten off.

Rnd 35: Join ribbon with sc in first ch-1 sp, [(ch 1, sc in next ch-1 sp) 2 times, ch 2, (sc, ch 2, sc) in ch sp of next shell, ch 2, sc in next ch-1 sp, *(ch 1, sc in next ch-1 sp) 3 times, ch 2, (sc, ch 2, sc) in ch sp of next shell, ch 2, sc in next ch-1 sp; repeat from * across to last 2 ch-1 sps before next corner shell, (ch 1, sc in next ch-1 sp) 2 times, ch 3, (sc, ch 3, sc) in ch sp of next corner shell, ch 3, sc in next ch-1 sp, ch 1, sc in next ch-1 sp, ◊ch 2, (sc, ch 2, sc) in ch sp of next shell, ch 2, sc in next ch-1 sp, ch 1, sc in next ch-1 sp; repeat from ◊ across to next corner shell, ch 3, (sc, ch 3, sc) in ch sp of next corner shell, ch 3], sc in next ch-1 sp; repeat between [ ], join with sl st in first sc, fasten off.

Rnd 36: Join red yarn with sc in any corner ch-3 sp, (ch 3, sc, ch 5, sc, ch 3, sc) in same sp, [ch 2, sc in next ch-3 sp, ch 1, (sc, ch 3, sc) in next ch-1 sp, *ch 1, skip next ch-1 sp, sc in next ch-2 sp, ch 2, (sc, ch 3, sc) in next ch-2 sp, ch 2, sc in next ch-2 sp, ch 1, skip next ch-1 sp, (sc, ch 3, sc) in next ch-1 sp; repeat from * across to last ch-3 sp before next corner, ch 1, sc in next ch-3 sp, ch 2, (sc, ch 3, sc, ch 5, sc, ch 3, sc) in next corner ch-3 sp, ch 2, sc in next ch-3 sp, ch 1, (sc, ch 3, sc) in next ch-1 sp, ◊ch 3, skip next ch-2 sp, (sc, ch 3, sc) in next ch-2 sp, ch 3, skip next ch-2 sp, (sc, ch 3, sc) in next ch-1 sp; repeat from ◊ across to last ch-3 sp before next corner, ch 1, sc in next ch-3 sp, ch 2], (sc, ch 3, sc, ch 5, sc, ch 3, sc) in next corner ch-3 sp; repeat between [ ], join, fasten off.❖

Keep your little loved one warm and comfy on those cold winter days wearing this cleverly designed gingham-look pullover. Made with worsted-weight yarn, it's easy to care for and attractive, too.

⇜ GINGHAM PULLOVER ⇝

DESIGNED BY MELISSA LEAPMAN FOR MONSANTO'S DESIGNS FOR AMERICA PROGRAM

SIZE
Instructions given fit girl's size 4. Changes for sizes 5 and 6 are in [ ].

MATERIALS
Worsted-weight acrylic yarn — 9 [11, 13] oz. lt. rose, 6 [7, 8] oz. each dk. rose and off-white; tapestry needle; H crochet hook or size needed to obtain gauge.

GAUGE
7 sc = 2"; 4 sc rows = 1".

BACK
NOTES: Wind each color into 5 balls each.

When changing colors (see page 159), always drop yarn to same side of work. **Do not** carry dropped color across to next section of same color. Use a separate ball of yarn for each color section.

Work graph from left to right on odd rows and from right to left on even rows.

Each square on graph equals one sc.

Row 1: With lt. rose, ch 51, sc in 2nd ch from hook, sc in each of next 3 chs changing to dk. rose in last st made, (sc in next 5 chs changing to lt. rose in last st made, sc in next 5 chs changing to dk. rose in last st made) across to last 5 chs, sc in last 5 chs, turn (50 sc).

Rows 2-10: Changing colors according to Body Graph on page 113, ch 1, sc in each st across, turn.

NOTE: Color pattern is established in rows 1-10.

Rows 11-45 [11-50, 11-52]: Ch 1, work in pattern across, turn.

Row 46 [51, 53]: For **armhole shaping,** sl st in first 5 sts, ch 1, work in pattern across leaving last 5 sts unworked, turn (40).

Rows 47-70 [52-75, 54-80]: Ch 1, work in pattern across, turn. At end of last row, fasten off.

FRONT
Rows 1-46 [1-51, 1-53]: Repeat same rows of Back.

Rows 47-50 [52-55, 54-60]: Ch 1, work in pattern across, turn.

Row 51 [56, 61]: For **first front,** ch 1, work in pattern across first 10 sts leaving remaining sts unworked, turn (10).

Rows 52-70 [57-75, 62-80]: Ch 1, work in pattern across, turn. At end of last row, fasten off.

Row 51 [56, 61]: For **neck,** skip next 20 sts on row 50 [55, 60]; for **second front,** using color needed to continue pattern, join with sc in next st, work in pattern across last 10 sts, turn (10).

Rows 52-70 [57-75, 62-80]: Ch 1, work in pattern across, turn. At end of last row, fasten off.

Sew shoulder seams.

Sew rows 9-50 [9-50, 9-52] together on each side of Body for side seams.

SLEEVE (make 2)
Cuff
Row 1: With lt. rose, ch 26, dc in 4th ch from hook, dc in each ch across, turn (24 dc).

NOTES: For **front post stitch (fp-**see page 159), yo, insert hook from front to back around post of next st, complete as dc.

For **back post stitch (bp),** yo, insert hook from back to front around post of next st, complete as dc.

Rows 2-5: Ch 2, fp around next st, (bp around next st, fp around next st) across, turn. At end of last row, fasten off.

Arm
Row 1: For **row 1 of Sleeve Graph,** join dk. rose with sc in first st on Cuff, sc in next st changing to lt. rose, (sc in next 5 sts changing to dk. rose in last st made, sc in next 5 sts changing to lt. rose in last st made) across to last 2 sts, sc in each of last 2 sts, turn (24 sc).

Row 2: Changing colors according to next row on Sleeve Graph, ch 1, 2 sc in first st, sc in each st across with 2 sc in last st, turn (26 sc).

Row 3: Changing colors according to next row on Sleeve Graph, ch 1, sc in each st across, turn.

Rows 4-7: Repeat rows 2 and 3 alternately, ending with 30 sc in last row.

Rows 8-9: Repeat row 3.

Row 10: Repeat row 2 (32).

Rows 11-34 [11-34, 11-42]: Repeat rows 7-10 consecutively, ending with 44 sc [44 sc, 48 sc] in last row.

Continued on page 113

Who could resist these adorable sock-lined booties? The sleepy lamb motif will certainly please Baby, and knowing little feet are extra warm will keep Mom smiling, too.

Lamb Booties

Designed by Sue Penrod

Captivating Crochet

SIZE
Fits 4"-4½" sole.

MATERIALS
Sport yarn — 2 oz. white, 1 oz. black and small amount pink; 1 pair of purchased socks with 4"-4½" sole; tapestry needle; E crochet hook or size needed to obtain gauge.

GAUGE
5 sc = 1"; 5 sc rows = 1".

BOOTIE (make 2)

NOTE: Do not join rnds unless otherwise stated. Mark first st of each rnd.

Rnd 1: Starting at sole, with black, ch 21, sc in 2nd ch from hook, sc in each ch across; working on opposite side of starting ch, sc in each ch across (40 sc).

Rnd 2: (2 sc in next st, sc in next 18 sts, 2 sc in next st) 2 times (44).

Rnd 3: (2 sc in next st, sc in next 20 sts, 2 sc in next st) 2 times (48).

Rnd 4: (2 sc in next st, sc in next 22 sts, 2 sc in next st) 2 times (52).

Rnds 5-6: Sc in each st around. At end of last rnd, join with sl st in first sc, **turn,** fasten off.

NOTE: For loop stitch (lp st), wrap yarn clockwise around one finger, insert hook in next st and through lp on finger, draw lp through st, yo, draw through both lps on hook.

Rnd 7: Join white with sl st in first st, ch 1, lp st in same st, lp st in each st around.

Rnds 8-9: Lp st in each st around. At end of last rnd, join with sl st in first lp st, **turn.**

Rnd 10: Ch 1, sc in each of first 2 sts, changing to black in last st made; (for **ear,** sl st in **front lp** of next st, ch 6, dc in 3rd ch from hook, dc in each of next 3 chs, sl st in same st on last rnd as last sl st changing to white), sc in next 46 sts changing to black in last st made; repeat between ( ), sc in each of last 2 sts.

Rnd 11: Sc in each of first 2 sts; working in front of ear, sc in **back lp** of next st on rnd 9, sc in next 46 sts, sc in **back lp** of next st on rnd 9, sc in each of last 2 sts.

Rnd 12: Sc in first 12 sts; for **ankle opening,** skip next 28 sts; sc in last 12 sts (24).

Rnds 13-14: Sc in each st around.

Rnd 15: (Sc in next st, skip next st, sc in next st) around changing to black in last st made (16).

Rnd 16: Sc in each st around.

Rnd 17: (Sc in next st, skip next st) around (8).

Rnd 18: (Sl st in next st, skip next st) around, join with sl st in first sl st, fasten off (4).

FINISHING

1: With black, using Fly Stitch (see illustration), embroider eyes below ears over rnds 13 and 14.

FLY STITCH

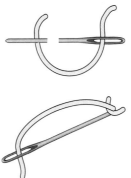

2: With pink, using Satin Stitch (see page 159), embroider nose below eyes over rnd 17.

3: Matching shaping, insert sock inside Bootie. Cut top of cuff down to 2½". Fold raw edge of cuff down. Easing to fit, sew ankle opening of Bootie to raw edge of cuff.❖

Capture the spirit of country charm with these striped pot holders adorned with a pretty sunflower and a pesky blackbird. They'll fill your kitchen with the feeling of down-home hospitality.

COUNTRY POT HOLDERS

DESIGNED BY MICHELE WILCOX

SIZE
Each Pot Holder is 7" x 7¼".

MATERIALS
Worsted-weight yarn — 2 oz. each lt. green, dk. green and off-white, small amount black, brown and gold; tapestry needle; F crochet hook or size needed to obtain gauge.

GAUGE
9 sc sts = 2"; 9 sc rows = 2".

POTHOLDER SIDE (make 4)
Row 1: With off-white, ch 31, sc in 2nd ch from hook, sc in each ch across, turn (30 sc).

NOTE: Work remaining rows in **back lps** only, unless otherwise stated.

Row 2: Ch 1, sc in each st across, turn, fasten off.

Row 3: Join lt. green with sc in first st, sc in each st across, turn.

Row 4: Repeat row 2.

Rows 5-6: With off-white, repeat rows 3 and 4.

Rows 7-28: Repeat rows 3-6 consecutively, ending with row 4. At end of last row, **do not** turn, fasten off.

Rnd 29: Working around outer edge, join dk. green with sc in any st, sc in each st around with 3 sc in each corner st, join with sl st in first sc.

Rnd 30: Working this rnd in **both lps,** ch 1, sc in each st around with 3 sc in each center corner st, join, fasten off.

Hold two Sides wrong sides together with stripes running up and down, matching sts; join dk. green with sl st in center top st, sl st in each st around; for **hanger,** ch 10, join with sl st in first sc, fasten off.

Repeat with other two Sides.

SUNFLOWER
NOTE: Do not join rnds unless otherwise stated. Mark first st of each rnd.

Rnd 1: With brown, ch 2, 6 sc in 2nd ch from hook (6 sc).

Rnd 2: 2 sc in each st around (12).

Rnd 3: (Sc in next st, 2 sc in next st) around (18).

Rnd 4: (Sc in each of next 2 sts, 2 sc in next st) around (24).

Rnd 5: (Sc in each of next 3 sts, 2 sc in next st) around, join with sl st in first sc, fasten off (30).

Rnd 6: Join gold with sl st in any st, (*ch 5, hdc in 3rd ch from hook, dc in each of next 2 chs, skip next 2 sts on rnd 5*, sl st in next st) 9 times; repeat between **, join, fasten off.

Stem
With dk. green, ch 12, sl st in 2nd ch from hook, sl st in each ch across, fasten off.

Leaf (make 2)
Rnd 1: With dk. green, ch 6, sc in 2nd ch from hook, hdc in next ch, dc in each of next 2 chs, (3 dc, ch 2, 3 dc) in last ch; working on opposite side of starting ch, dc in each of next 2 chs, hdc in next ch, sc in last ch, join with sl st in first sc (14 sts).

Rnd 2: Ch 1, sc in first st, 2 hdc in next st, 2 dc in each of next 2 sts, dc in each of next 2 sts, 2 dc in next st, (3 dc, ch 2, 3 dc) in next ch-2 sp, 2 dc in next st, dc in each of next 2 sts, 2 dc in each of next 2 sts, 2 hdc in next st, sc in last st, join, fasten off.

Tack Sunflower, Stem and Leaves to one side of one Pot Holder as shown in photo.

BLACKBIRD
Head
Rnds 1-4: With black, repeat same rnds of Sunflower. At end of last rnd, join with sl st in first sc, fasten off.

With lt. green, using French Knot (see page 159), embroider eye on rnd 3 of Head.

Body
Rnds 1-5: With black, repeat same rnds of Sunflower. At end of last rnd, join with sl st in first sc, fasten off.

Tail
Row 1: With black, ch 9, sc in 2nd ch from hook, sc in each ch across, turn (8 sc).

Row 2: Ch 1, sc in first 7 sts leaving last st unworked, turn (7).

Continued on page 112

CAPTIVATING CROCHET

COUNTRY POT HOLDERS

Continued from page 110

Row 3: Ch 1, sc first 2 sts tog, sc in each st across, turn (6).

Row 4: Ch 1, sc in each st across with 2 sc in last st, ch 2, turn (7 sc, 2 ch).

Row 5: Sc in 2nd ch from hook, sc in each st across, fasten off.

Wing

Rnd 1: With black, ch 6, sc in 2nd ch from hook, sc in each of next 3 chs, 3 sc in last ch; working on opposite side of starting ch, sc in each of next 3 chs, 2 sc in last ch, join with sl st in first sc (12 sc).

Rnd 2: Ch 1, 2 sc in first st, sc in each of next 3 sts, 2 sc in each of next 3 sts, sc in each of next 3 sts, 2 sc in each of last 2 sts, join (18).

Rnd 3: Ch 1, sc in first st, 2 sc in next st, sc in next 4 sts, 2 sc in each of next 3 sts, ch 2, sc in 2nd ch from hook, sc in next 5 sts, sl st in next st leaving remaining sts unworked, fasten off.

Leg

With gold, ch 11, sl st in 2nd ch from hook, sl st in each of next 2 chs, (ch 4, sl st in 2nd ch from hook, sl st in each of next 2 chs) 2 times, sl st in remaining 7 chs of first ch-11, fasten off.

Beak

With gold, (ch 3, sl st in 2nd ch from hook, sl st in last ch) 2 times, fasten off.

Sew Head, Body, Tail, Wing, Leg and Beak to remaining Pot Holder as shown.❖

FUZZY LOG CABIN AFGHAN

Continued from page 102

corner ch-3 sp, ch 3, dc in each ch-1 sp and in each st around with (2 dc, ch 3, 2 dc) in each corner ch-3 sp, join with sl st in top of ch-3 (155 dc across each short end, 245 dc across each long side, 4 corner ch-3 sps).

NOTE: For **corner shell,** (3 dc, ch 3, 3 dc) in next corner ch-2 sp.

For **shell,** (2 dc, ch 3, 2 dc) in next st.

Rnd 4: Ch 1, sc in first st, ◊[skip next 2 sts, *shell in next st, skip next 2 sts, sc in next st, skip next 2 sts; repeat from * across to next corner ch-3 sp, ch 1, corner shell in next corner ch-3 sp, ch 1, skip next 2 sts], sc in next st; repeat from ◊ 2 more times; repeat between [ ], join with sl st in first sc.

Rnd 5: Ch 1, sc in first st, ◊[ch 3, *(sc, ch 3, sc) in ch-2 sp of next shell, ch 3, sc in next sc, ch 3; repeat from * across to next corner shell, sc in 2nd dc of next corner shell, ch 3, skip next dc, (sc, ch 3, sc, ch 5, sc, ch 3, sc) in ch-3 sp of same shell, ch 3, skip next dc, sc in next dc, ch 3], sc in next sc; repeat from ◊ 2 more times; repeat between [ ], join, fasten off.❖

CAPTIVATING CROCHET

GINGHAM PULLOVER

Continued from page 106

Row 35 [Rows 35-40, 43-45]: Repeat row 3. At end of last row, fasten off.

Matching center of last row on Sleeve to shoulder seam, sew Sleeve to armhole opening.

Sew Sleeve seams.

COLLAR

Row 1: Working in ends of rows and sts across neck opening, join lt. rose with sc in first row on right front, sc in each row across, 3 sc in shoulder seam, sc in each st across back neck, 3 sc in shoulder seam, sc in each row across, turn.

Rows 2-12: Ch 1, sc in each st across with 3 sc in center sc of each 3-sc group at shoulders, turn. At end of last row, fasten off.

Easing to fit, sew one end of Collar to **back lps** of first 10 sts on front neck and other end of Collar to **back lps** of last 10 sts on front neck.

BOTTOM TRIM

Working around bottom opening in ends of rows and in starting ch on opposite side of row 1 on Front and Back, join lt. rose with sc in row 8 on either side, sc in each row and in each ch around with 3 sc in each corner, join with sl st in first sc, fasten off.❖

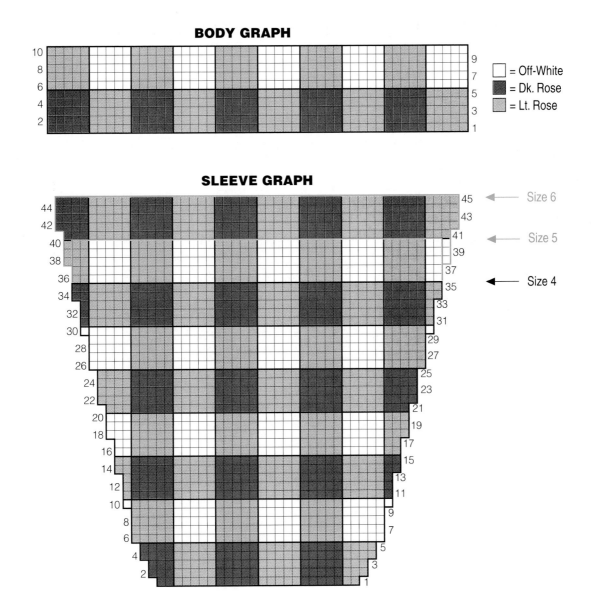

BODY GRAPH

☐ = Off-White
■ = Dk. Rose
▦ = Lt. Rose

SLEEVE GRAPH

Size 6
Size 5
Size 4

You'll take first prize with this afghan in alluring shades of blue created with an interestingly textured pattern. Lacy and airy in appearance, it's still warm enough to keep a cool wind's chill at bay.

COUNTRY EYELET

DESIGNED BY JENNIFER CHRISTIANSEN MCCLAIN

SIZE
47" x 68½".

MATERIALS
Worsted-weight yarn — 14 oz. lt. blue, 13 oz. dk. blue and 6 oz. off-white; G crochet hook or size needed to obtain gauge.

GAUGE
Row 1 of Strip No. 1 = 1" wide; 4 dc rows = 3".

STRIP NO. 1
NOTE: Ch-3 at beginning of each row counts as first dc.

Row 1: With off-white, ch 6, dc in 4th ch from hook, dc in each of last 2 chs, turn (4 dc).

Rows 2-87: Ch 3, dc in each st across, turn. At end of last row, **do not** turn, fasten off.

Rnd 88: Working around outer edge, in ends of rows and in sts, join lt. blue with sc in top of last dc made on last row, *ch 2; working in **front** of last dc, sc around 3rd dc on same row, ch 2, (sc around last dc on next row, ch 2; working in **front** of last dc, sc around 3rd dc on next row, ch 2) across to next corner; working across short end, sc in first st, ch 2, dc in sp between center 2 dc, ch 2*, sc in last st; repeat between **, join with sl st in first sc (178 sc, 180 ch-2 sps, 2 dc).

Rnd 89: Sl st in first ch-2 sp, ch 3, dc in same sp, ch 1, (2 dc in next ch-2 sp, ch 1) around with (2 dc, ch 1) 2 times in each ch-2 sp across each short end, join with sl st in top of ch-3, fasten off.

Rnd 90: Join dk. blue with sc in first st, sc in next st;

working behind next ch-1 sp, dc in next unworked sc on rnd before last, (sc in each of next 2 sts; working behind next ch-1 sp, dc in next unworked sc on rnd before last) 87 times, sc in next st, 2 sc in next st; working behind next ch-1 sp, dc in next ch-2 sp on rnd before last between 2-dc groups, 2 sc in each of next 2 sts; working behind next ch-1 sp, dc in next unworked dc on rnd before last, 2 sc in each of next 2 sts; working behind next ch-1 sp, dc in next ch 2 sp on rnd before last between 2-dc groups, 2 sc in next st, sc in next st; working behind next ch-1 sp, dc in next unworked sc on rnd before last, sc in each of next 2 sts; repeat between **, join.

Rnd 91: Ch 1, sc in each sc around skipping each dc, join, fasten off.

Rnd 92: Join lt. blue with sl st in first st, *(ch 3, skip next st, sl st in next st) across to center of next short end, ch 3, sl st in next st; repeat from *, ch 3, skip next st, (sl st in next st, ch 3, skip next st) around, join with sl st in first sl st, fasten off.

STRIPS NO. 2-11
Rows/Rnds: 1-91: Repeat same rows/rnds of Strip No. 1.

Rnd 92: Join lt. blue with sl st in first st (ch 3, skip next st, sl st in next st) across to center of next short end, ch 3, sl st in next st, (ch 3, skip next st, sl st in next st) 3 times; holding long edges of last Strip and this Strip tog, (ch 1, sl st in corresponding ch sp on last Strip, ch 1, skip next st on this Strip, sl st in next st) 89 times, (ch 3, skip next st, sl st in next st) 3 times, ch 3, (sl st in next st, ch 3, skip next st) around, join with sl st in first sl st, fasten off.❖

GRACIOUS LIVING

❦

HOME

Whether large or small, expensive or not,
It takes heart to make a home.
A place you always yearn to be, wherever you may roam.

I used to wake on Saturday to the smell of fresh cut grass
And listen to the sounds of Spring as the day would slowly pass.

All the kids would quickly gather on a silky summer night
And we sometimes caught the fireflies to marvel at their light.

The fall was full of bonfires and raking leaves from noon to night.
And dressing up on Halloween to make others run in fright.

Christmas was a magic time, we kids all camped out in one room
Hoping we'd see Santa in the silver of the moon.

All the memories of my childhood still live in me today.
They fill my heart with gladness as I travel on my way.

PINWHEEL & CROCUS DOILY

DESIGNED BY JEAN CARPENTER

SIZE
12½" across. This project may ruffle until blocked.

MATERIALS
Size 10 bedspread cotton — 350 yds. cream; spray starch; No. 7 steel crochet hook or size needed to obtain gauge.

GAUGE
Rnds 1-3 = 1¾" across.

DOILY

Rnd 1: Ch 8, sl st in first ch to form ring, ch 1, 16 sc in ring, join with sl st in first sc (16 sc).

Rnd 2: Ch 3, 2 dc in same st, ch 1, skip next st, (3 dc in next st, ch 1, skip next st) around, join with sl st in top of ch-3 (24 dc, 8 ch-1 sps).

Rnd 3: Ch 3, dc in each of next 2 sts, ch 3, skip next ch-1 sp, (dc in each of next 3 sts, ch 3, skip next ch-1 sp) around, join.

Rnd 4: Ch 3, dc in each of next 2 sts, ch 5, skip next ch-3 sp, (dc in each of next 3 sts, ch 5, skip next ch-3 sp) around, join.

NOTE: For **cluster (cl),** *yo, insert hook in next st, yo, draw lp through, yo, draw through 2 lps on hook; repeat from * one time in same st, yo, draw through all 3 lps on hook.

Rnd 5: Ch 2, dc in next st, tr in next st, ch 3, cl in 3rd ch of next ch-5, ch 3, *hdc in next st, dc in next st, tr in next st, ch 3, cl in 3rd ch of next ch-5, ch 3; repeat from * around, join with sl st in top of ch-2.

Rnd 6: Ch 2, dc in next dc, tr in next tr, ch 4, cl in top of next cl, ch 4, *hdc in next hdc, dc in next dc, tr in next tr, ch 4, cl in top of next cl, ch 4; repeat from * around, join.

Rnd 7: Ch 2, dc in next dc, tr in next tr, ch 5, cl in next cl, ch 5, *hdc in next hdc, dc in next dc, tr in next tr, ch 5, cl in next cl, ch 5; repeat from * around, join.

Rnd 8: Ch 2, *[dc in next dc, tr in next tr, ch 3, (2 dc, ch 2, cl, ch 2, 2 dc) in next cl, ch 3], hdc in next hdc; repeat from * 6 more times; repeat between [ ], join.

Rnd 9: Ch 2, *[dc in next dc, tr in next tr, ch 3, dc in each of next 2 dc, ch 3, cl in next cl, ch 3, dc in each of next 2 dc, ch 3], hdc in next hdc; repeat from * 6 more times; repeat between [ ], join.

Rnd 10: Ch 2, *[dc in next dc, tr in next tr, ch 4, dc next 2 dc tog, ch 5, cl in next cl, ch 5, dc next 2 dc tog, ch 4], hdc in next hdc; repeat from * 6 more times; repeat between [ ], join.

Rnd 11: Ch 2, *[dc in next dc, tr in next tr, ch 7, skip next dc, (cl, ch 3, cl, ch 3, cl) in next cl, ch 7, skip next dc], hdc in next hdc; repeat from * 6 more times; repeat between [ ], join.

Rnd 12: Ch 2, *[dc in next dc, tr in next tr, ch 6, cl in next cl, (ch 5, cl in next cl) 2 times, ch 6], hdc in next hdc; repeat from * 6 more times; repeat between [ ], join.

Rnd 13: Ch 2, *[dc in next dc, tr in next tr, ch 5, (2 dc, ch 3, cl) in next cl, ch 7, cl in next cl, ch 5, 5 dc in next cl, ch 5], hdc in next hdc; repeat from * 6 more times; repeat between [ ], join (64 dc, 16 cls, 8 tr, 8 hdc).

Rnd 14: Ch 2, *[dc in next dc, tr in next tr, ch 7, dc next 2 dc tog, ch 1, 5 dc in next cl, ch 5, cl in next cl, ch 5, 2 dc in next dc, dc in each of next 3 dc, 2 dc in next dc, ch 5], hdc in next hdc; repeat from * 6 more times; repeat between [ ], join.

NOTE: For **decrease (dec),** yo, insert hook in same dc as last st worked, yo, draw lp through, yo, draw through 2 lps on hook, *yo, insert hook in next dc, yo, draw lp through, yo, draw through 2 lps on hook; repeat from * one time, yo, draw through all 4 lps on hook.

Rnd 15: Ch 2, *[dc in next dc, tr in next tr, ch 9, skip next dc, 2 dc in next dc, dc in each of next 3 dc, 2 dc in next dc, ch 5, 7 dc in next cl, ch 5, dc next 3 dc tog, (ch 5, dec) 2 times, ch 7], hdc in next hdc; repeat from * 6 more times; repeat between [ ], join.

Rnd 16: Ch 2, *[dc in next dc, tr in next tr, ch 9, dc next 3 dc tog, (ch 5, dec) 2 times, ch 5, 2 dc in next dc, dc in next 5 dc, 2 dc in next dc, ch 7, sc in next ch-5 sp, ch 5, sc in next ch-5 sp, ch 7], hdc in next hdc; repeat from * 6 more times; repeat between [ ], join.

Rnd 17: Ch 2, *[dc in next dc, tr in next tr, ch 5, sc in next ch-9 lp, ch 5, (sc in next ch-5 lp, ch 5) 3 times, dc next 3 dc tog, (ch 5, dc next 3 sts tog) 2

Continued on page 134

Sweet and fragile as a rose is this delicately designed and beautifully embossed baby dress. Trimmed with satin ribbon and rose appliqués, it even has a matching corsage and booties.

≈ BABY DRESS & BOOTIES ≈

DESIGNED BY SUE CHILDRESS

SIZES
Infant's 0-3 mos. or 3-6 mos.

GAUGE
For size **0-3 mos.,** with B hook, 7 dc = 1"; 8 dc rnds = 3". For size **3-6 mos.,** with C hook, 13 dc = 2"; 3 dc rnds = 1".

MATERIALS
Size 5 crochet cotton — 450 or 550 yds. pink, 300 or 375 yds. white and small amount aqua; 1 yd. pink ⅛" satin ribbon; 4 pearl 8-mm buttons; four ⅞" flower apppliqués; 13 white double-headed stamens; 12" pink 1¼"-wide irridescent ribbon; one large safety pin; floral wire; floral tape; wire clippers; tapestry needle; crochet hook stated above or hook needed to obtain gauge for size.

DRESS
Bodice
Row 1: Starting at neck, with pink, ch 90, sc in 2nd ch from hook, sc in next ch, 2 sc in next ch, (sc in each of next 3 chs, 2 sc in next ch) across to last 2 chs, sc in each of last 2 chs, turn (111 sc).

NOTE: Ch-2 at beginning of row counts as first hdc; ch-3 at beinning of row counts as first dc.

Row 2: Ch 2, hdc in each st across, turn.

Row 3: Ch 3, dc in next 4 sts, 2 dc in next st, (dc in next 4 sts, 2 dc in next st) across, turn (133 dc).

Row 4: Ch 3, dc in each st across, turn.

NOTE: For **cluster shell (cl-shell),** *yo, insert hook in next st, yo, draw lp through, yo, draw through 2 lps on hook, (yo, insert hook in same st, yo, draw lp through, yo, draw through 2 lps on hook) 2 times, yo, draw through all 4 lps on hook, ch 1; repeat from * 2 more times.

Row 5: Ch 3, dc in same st, skip next 2 sts, cl-shell in next st, skip next 2 sts, *dc in next 9 sts, skip next 2 sts, cl-shell in next st, skip next 2 sts; repeat from * across to last st, 2 dc in last st, turn (85 dc, 10 cl-shells).

Row 6: Ch 3, dc in same st, cl-shell in center cl of next cl-shell, skip next dc, *(3 dc in next st, skip next st) 4 times, cl-shell in center cl of next cl-shell; repeat from * across to last 2 dc, skip next dc, 2 dc in last

dc, turn (36 3-dc groups, 10 cl-shells, 4 dc).

NOTES: For **small shell (sm-shell),** (3 dc, ch 2, 3 dc) in next st.

For **large shell (lg-shell),** (5 dc, ch 2, 5 dc) in ch sp of next sm-shell.

Row 7: Ch 3, dc in same st, skip next st, cl-shell in center cl of next cl-shell, (3 dc in center dc of next 3-dc group) 4 times, cl-shell in center cl of next cl-shell, *(sm-shell in center dc of next 3-dc group) 4 times, cl-shell in center cl of next cl-shell*; repeat between **, [(3 dc in center dc of next 3-dc group) 4 times, cl-shell in center cl of next cl-shell]; repeat between [ ] 2 more times; repeat between ** 2 more times; repeat between [ ] one more time, skip next dc, 2 dc in last dc, turn (20 3-dc groups, 16 sm-shells, 10 cl-shells, 4 dc).

Row 8: Ch 3, dc in same st, skip next st, cl-shell in center cl of next cl-shell, (3 dc in center dc of next 3-dc group) 4 times, cl-shell in center cl of next cl-shell, *(lg-shell in next sm-shell) 4 times, cl-shell in center cl of next cl-shell*; repeat between **, [(3 dc in center dc of next 3-dc groups) 4 times, cl-shell in center cl of next cl-shell]; repeat between [ ] 2 more times; repeat between ** 2 more times; repeat between [ ] one more time, skip next dc, 2 dc in last dc, turn.

Row 9: Ch 3, dc in same st, skip next st, cl-shell in center cl of next cl-shell, *(3 dc in center dc of next 3-dc group) 4 times, cl-shell in center cl of next cl-shell*; for **first armhole opening,** ch 4, skip next 9 shells; cl-shell in center cl of next cl-shell; repeat between ** 3 more times; for **second armhole opening,** ch 4, skip next 9 shells; cl-shell in center cl of next cl-shell; repeat between ** one more time, skip next st, 2 dc in last st, turn (20 3-dc groups, 8 cl-shells, 4 dc).

Row 10: Ch 3, dc in next st, skip next ch-1 sp, *3 dc in each of next 2 ch-1 sps on cl-shell, (3 dc in center dc of next 3-dc group) 4 times, skip next ch-1 sp*, [3 dc in each of next 2 ch-1 sps on cl-shell, skip next ch, (3 dc in next ch, skip next ch) 2 times]; repeat between ** 3 more times; repeat between [ ]; repeat between ** one more time, 3 dc in each of next 2 ch-1 sps on cl shell, dc in each of last 2 dc, turn (124 dc).

Row 11: Ch 3, dc in each st across, **do not** turn or fasten off.

Continued on page 124

These beautiful potpourri balls, fashioned from bedspread cotton and embossed with beads and flowers, will be treasured family heirlooms handed down from generation to generation.

POTPOURRI BALLS

DESIGNED BY JO ANN MAXWELL

SIZE

3½" x 3½" excluding decorations.

MATERIALS FOR PINK BALL

Size 10 bedspread cotton — 75 yds. cream; ½ yd. pink netting fabric; 14 or 15 dried rosebuds; 21" lt. teal ⅛" satin ribbon; 60" white 6-mm strung pearl beads; metallic gold dried baby's breath flowers; potpourri; pink sewing thread; craft glue or hot glue gun; small round white balloon; liquid fabric stiffener; No. 5 steel crochet hook or size needed to obtain gauge.

MATERIALS FOR GREEN BALL

Size 10 bedspread cotton — 75 yds. cream; ½ yd. green netting fabric; 24" metallic gold 4-mm strung beads; metallic gold dried baby's breath flowers; potpourri; green sewing thread; craft glue or hot glue gun; small round white balloon; liquid fabric stiffener; No. 5 steel crochet hook or size needed to obtain gauge.

GAUGE

Rnd 1 = 1" across.

PINK POTPOURRI BALL

Rnd 1: Ch 4, sl st in first ch to form ring, ch 3, 15 dc in ring, join with sl st in top of ch-3 (16 dc).

Rnd 2: Ch 6, (tr in next st, ch 2) around, join with sl st in 4th ch of ch-6 (16 tr, 16 ch-2 sps).

NOTES: For **beginning cluster (beg cl)**, ch 4, *yo 2 times, insert hook in same st, yo, draw lp through, (yo, draw through 2 lps on hook) 2 times; repeat from * 2 more times, yo, draw through all 4 lps on hook.

For **cluster (cl)**, *yo 2 times, insert hook in st, yo, draw lp through, (yo, draw through 2 lps on hook) 2 times; repeat from * 3 more times in same st, yo, draw through all 5 lps on hook.

For ⅜" **love knot (⅜"-lk**, see page 159), draw up ⅜"-long lp on hook, yo, draw lp through, sc in back strand of long lp.

Rnd 3: Beg cl, ⅜"-lk, (cl in next st, ⅜"-lk) around, join with sl st in top of beg cl (16 cls, 16 ⅜"-lks).

Rnd 4: Ch 1, sc in same st, (ch 5, skip next lk, sc in top of next cl) around; to **join,** ch 2, dc in first sc.

NOTE: For ½"-**love knot (½"-lk),** draw up ½"-long lp on hook, yo, draw lp through, sc in back strand of long lp.

Rnd 5: Beg cl around joining dc, ½"-lk, (cl in next ch-5 sp, ½"-lk) around, join with sl st in top of beg cl.

Rnds 6-8: Repeat rnds 4 and 3 alternately, ending with rnd 4.

Rnd 9: Ch 1, sc around joining dc, (ch 5, sc in next ch-5 sp) around; to **join,** ch 2, dc in first sc.

Rnd 10: Ch 1, sc around joining dc, ch 1, (sc in next ch-5 sp, ch 1) around, join with sl st in first sc, fasten off.

FINISHING

1: Carefully insert end of balloon inside Ball through opening on last rnd, Inflate balloon until crocheted piece is stretched taut; knot end of balloon to secure.

2: Apply fabric stiffener to Ball according to manufacturer's instructions; shape and let dry. Burst and remove balloon when completely dry.

3: Cut one 10" circle from netting. With sewing needle and thread, run a gathering stitch around outer edge of net circle. Place netting inside Ball and fill with potpourri. Pull gathering stitches to close, secure.

4: Cut a 4" x 12" piece of netting and fold in half lengthwise so that it measures 2" x 12". Sew short ends together to form a circle. With sewing needle and thread, run a gathering stitch around raw edges. Pull gathering stitches to tighten, secure. Glue to top of Ball.

5: Glue dried roses and baby's breath over netting. Roll 10" piece of strung beads into a ball and glue to middle of rosebuds. Cut ribbon into seven 3" pieces. Fold each piece in half, glue loops around rosebud bouquet as desired.

6: Roll another 10" piece of strung beads into a ball and glue to bottom of crocheted Ball over rnd 1.

7: For **bottom trim,** cut one 6½" piece of strung beads. Glue ends to love knots of rnd 3 on each side of Ball. Cut one 10" piece of strung beads. Glue ends to clusters of rnd 5 on each side of Ball.

8: For **hanger,** cut 22" piece of strung beads.

Continued on next page

POTPOURRI BALLS

Continued from page 123

Insert one end through 2 ch-5 sps on rnd 6 just above 10" bottom trim, pull pearl strand through until ends are even. Glue ends to ch-5 sps on rnd 6 on opposite side of Ball.

GREEN POTPOURRI BALL

Rnd 1: Ch 4, sl st in first ch to form ring, ch 3, 15 dc in ring, join with sl st in top of ch-3 (16 dc).

Rnd 2: Ch 7, (tr in next st, ch 3) around, join with sl st in 4th ch of ch-7 (16 tr, 16 ch-3 sps).

Rnd 3: Sl st in next ch, ch 3, dc in each of next 2 chs, ch 3, skip next tr, (dc in each of next 3 chs, ch 3, skip next tr) around, join with sl st in top of ch-3.

Rnds 4-8: Sl st in each of next 2 sts, sl st in first ch of next ch-3, ch 3, dc in each of next 2 chs, ch 3, (dc in each of next 3 chs, ch 3) around, join.

Rnd 9: Sl st in each of next 2 sts, sl st in next ch, ch 3, dc in each of next 2 chs, ch 2, (dc in each of next 3 chs, ch 2) around, join.

Rnd 10: Sl st in next st, ch 1, sc in same st, skip next st, sc in next ch-2 sp, (sc in center st of next 3-dc group, sc in next ch-2 sp) around, join with sl st in first sc, fasten off.

FINISHING

1-4: Repeat same steps of Pink Potpourri Ball's Finishing.

5: Glue approximately ⅓ cup of the larger pieces from potpourri to net on top of Ball. Glue small nut or pine cone to center of rnd 1 on bottom of Ball.

6: For **bottom trim,** cut 4½" piece of strung beads. Glue ends to spaces between 3-dc groups of rnd 3 on each side of Ball.

7: For **hanger,** cut 13" piece of strung beads. Insert one end around 3-dc group of rnd 6 on same side as one end of Bottom trim, pull beads through until ends are even. Tie a loose knot in strands 5¼" from side of Ball. Glue ends to 3-dc group of rnd 6 on opposite side of Ball.❖

BABY DRESS & BOOTIES

Continued from page 120

Neck & Back Plackets Trim

Row 1: Working in ends of rows on back opening, ch 1, 3 sc in each of first 9 rows, 2 sc in next row, sc in last row; working in starting ch on opposite side of row 1 on Bodice, sc in each ch across; working on other back, sc in first row, 2 sc in next row, 3 sc in each of last 9 rows, turn (149 sc).

Rnd 2: Ch 1, sc in first 30 sts, 2 sc in next st, sc in next 87 sts, 2 sc in next st; for **buttonhole,** ch 2, skip next 2 sts; (sc in next 7 sts, buttonhole) 3 times, sc in last st, join with sl st in first st on this rnd to close bottom of back opening, **do not** turn or fasten off.

Skirt

Rnd 1: Working in ends of rows on Back Plackets and in sts on Bodice, ch 3, 2 dc in first row, skip next row, dc in next st, 2 dc in each of next 122 sts, 2 dc in last row, skip first ch-3, join with sl st in next dc (249 dc).

Rnd 2: Ch 4, dc in same st, skip next 2 sts, *(dc, ch 1, dc) in next st, skip next 2 sts; repeat from * around, join with sl st in 3rd ch of ch-4 (83 ch-1 sps).

Rnd 3: Sl st in next ch sp, ch 3, 2 dc in same sp, 3 dc in each ch sp around, join (83 3-dc groups).

Rnds 4-5: Sl st in next st, ch 3, 2 dc in same st, 3 dc in center st of each 3-dc group around, join. At end of last rnd, fasten off.

Rnd 6: Join white with sl st in center st of first 3-dc group, ch 3, 2 dc in same st, 3 dc in center st of each 3-dc group around, join.

Rnds 7-12: Repeat rnd 4. At end of last rnd, fasten off.

Rnd 13: Join pink with sc in center st of first 3-dc group, ch 3, sc in sp between last 3-dc group and next 3-dc group, ch 3, (sc in center st of next 3-dc group, ch 3, sc in sp between last 3-dc group and next 3-dc group) around, join with sl st in first sc.

Rnd 14: Sl st in next ch sp, ch 3, 4 dc in same sp,

(2 sc in each of next 2 ch sps, 5 dc in next ch sp) around to last 3 ch sps, 2 sc in next ch sp, sc in each of last 2 ch sps, join with sl st in top of ch-3, fasten off.

Finishing

1: Attach appliqués evenly spaced around Skirt over rnds 8 and 9.

2: Sew buttons to Back Placket opposite buttonholes.

3: Cut 16" piece of ⅛" ribbon. Tie into bow around one st on row 2 of left front Bodice.

CORSAGE
Small Flower (make one each white and aqua)
Ch 4, sl st in first ch to form ring, ch 3, (6 dc, ch 3, sl st) in ring, fasten off.

Large Flower
Rnd 1: With pink, ch 4, 9 dc in 4th ch from hook, join with sl st in top of ch-3 (10 dc).

Rnd 2: Ch 1, 3 sc in each st around, join with sl st in first sc (30 sc).

Rnd 3: Ch 1, (sc, hdc) in each st around, join, fasten off.

Finishing

1: Insert 1" at one end of floral wire through center of white Small Flower, fold over and twist tightly. Cut wire to 4". Repeat with aqua Small Flower, cutting wire to 3½".

2: Fold 8 stamens in half; insert folded end through center of Large Flower. Wrap floral wire tightly around center bottom of Flower and around stamens. Cut wire to 3".

3: Wrap floral tape around wire of each Flower, covering completely. Holding all Flowers together as shown in photo, wrap floral tape around all stems. Twist end into a small circle as shown.

4: Tie 1¼" ribbon into a bow around bottom of stem.

5: Pin corsage to right front Bodice.

BOOTIE (make 2)
Instep
Rnd 1: With pink, ch 6, sl st in first ch to form ring, ch 1, 18 sc in ring, join with sl st in first sc (18 sc).

Rnd 2: Ch 1, sc in first st, ch 3, skip next 2 sts, (sc in next st, ch 3, skip next 2 sts) around, join (6 sc, 6 ch-3 sps).

Rnd 3: Ch 1, sc in first st, 5 dc in next ch sp, (sc in next st, 5 dc in next ch sp) around, join, fasten off (30 dc, 6 sc).

Sole
Rnd 1: With pink, ch 18, dc in 3rd ch from hook,

dc in next 14 chs, 5 dc in last ch; working on opposite side of ch, dc in next 12 chs, 2 dc in each of next 2 chs, skip last ch, 2 dc in 2nd ch of first ch-2, 2 dc in last ch, **do not** join (41 dc).

Rnd 2: 2 dc in each of next 2 sts, dc in next 11 sts, 2 dc in each of next 8 sts, dc in next 13 sts, (2 dc in next st, dc in next st) 2 times, hdc in next st, sc in last st, **do not** join (52 sts).

Rnd 3: Hdc in each st around, join with sl st in first hdc.

NOTE: For **back post stitch (bp),** yo, insert hook from back to front around post of next st, yo, draw lp through, (yo, draw through 2 lps on hook) 2 times.

Rnd 4: Ch 3, bp around same st, bp around each st around, join with sl st in top of ch-3 (53 sts).

Rnd 5: Ch 3, dc in each st around, join.

Rnd 6: Ch 1, sc in first st, (ch 3, skip next st, sc in next st) 6 times; to join Instep and Sole, holding wrong sides together, ch 3, sc in center dc of any 5-dc group on Instep, ch 3, skip next st on Sole, sc in next st, (ch 3, sc in next sc on Instep, ch 3, skip next st on Sole, sc in next st, ch 3, sc in center dc of next 5-dc group on Instep, ch 3, skip next st on Sole, sc in next st) 5 times, ch 3, skip next st, (sc in next st, ch 3, skip next st) 9 times, join with sl st in first sc.

Rnd 7: Ch 4, dc in next sc, (ch 1, dc in next sc) 5 times, ch 1, dc in first joining sc on Instep, ch 1, dc in next unworked dc, ch 1, dc in next sc, ch 1, skip next dc, dc in next dc, ch 1, dc in next joining sc, ch 1, (dc in next sc, ch 1) 10 times, join with sl st in 3rd ch of ch-4 (22 ch-1 sps).

Rnd 8: Sl st in next ch sp, ch 1, sc in same sp, 3 dc in next ch sp, (sc in next ch sp, 3 dc in next ch sp) around, join with sl st in first sc, fasten off.

Cut remaining ⅛" ribbon in half. Starting at center front, weave each piece through rnd 7 on each Bootie. Tie ends into a bow.❖

SOFT & LACY TURBAN

DESIGNED BY ELIZABETH OWENS

SIZE
Lady's one size fits all.

MATERIALS
Fuzzy baby yarn — 2 oz. blue; 24 white 5-mm pearls; white sewing thread; bobby pin or stitch marker; beading needle; F crochet hook or size needed to obtain gauge.

GAUGE
4 sc sts = 1"; 4 sc **back lp** rows = 1".

TURBAN
Row 1: Ch 150, sc in 2nd ch from hook, sc in each ch across, turn (149 sc).

NOTE: Work remaining rows in **back lps** unless otherwise stated.

Row 2: Ch 1, sc in first st, (ch 1, skip next st, sc in next st) across, turn.

Rows 3-6: Ch 1, sc in first st, (ch 1, skip next ch-1 sp, sc in next st) across, turn.

NOTES: For **beginning cluster (beg cl)**, ch 2, *yo, insert hook in same st, yo, draw lp through, yo, draw through 2 lps on hook; repeat from *, yo, draw through all 3 lps on hook.

For **cluster (cl)**, *yo, insert hook in next st, yo, draw lp through, yo, draw through 2 lps on hook; repeat from * 2 more times in same st, yo, draw through all 4 lps on hook.

Each ch-1 between sc sts on row 6 counts as a st.

Rnd 7: Ch 1, sc in first st, hdc in next st, dc in next st, *beg cl in top of dc just made, skip next 2 sts, cl in next st, beg cl in top of cl just made, skip next 2 sts, dc in next st; repeat from * across to last 2 sts, hdc in next st, sc in last st, turn.

Row 8: Ch 1, sc in first st, hdc in next st, dc in next st, *ch 2, skip next cl, cl in top of next cl, ch 2, dc in next dc; repeat from * across to last 2 sts, hdc in next st, sc in last st, turn.

Row 9: Ch 1, sc in each st across with 2 sc in each ch-2 sp, turn (149 sc).

Row 10: Repeat row 2.

Rows 11-15: Repeat row 3. At end of last row, fasten off.

FINISHING
NOTE: Mark center stitch of row 15.

1: To **form turban**, overlap ends according to Diagram No. 1, working through both thicknesses in **back lps** only, sl st 20 sts together on edges indicated by arrows.

2: Working on ends of Turban, join with sc in end of row 1, evenly space 17 more sc across to opposite end, turn; holding center 18 sts of Turban and ends together according to Diagram No. 2, working through both thickness in **front lps**, sl st in each st across, fasten off.

3: Sew 12 sts on each side of back seam together. Tack overlap together at center front.

4: With beading needle and sewing thread, sew one pearl to center of each cluster flower around Turban.❖

TURBAN DIAGRAM

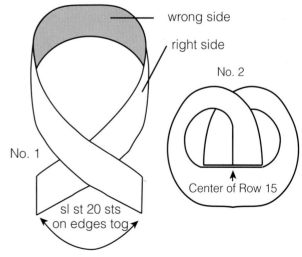

CAPTIVATING CROCHET

Rose bedspread cotton over burgundy fabric lends romantic appeal to this pretty pillow enhanced with an edging of frothy lace. It will be a valuable complement to your decor.

⮾ PUFF STITCH PILLOW ⮾

DESIGNED BY FRANCES HUGHES

SIZE
13" across not including ruffle.

MATERIALS
Size 10 bedspread cotton — 282 yds. rose; ½ yd. burgundy fabric; burgundy sewing thread; polyester fiberfill; sewing needle; No. 7 steel crochet hook or size needed to obtain gauge.

GAUGE
Rnds 1-3 of Pillow Side = 2¾" across.

PILLOW SIDE (make 2)

Rnd 1: Ch 4, sl st in first ch to form ring, ch 3, 17 dc in ring, join with sl st in top of ch-3 (18 dc).

Rnd 2: Ch 4, (dc in next st, ch 1) around, join with sl st in 3rd ch of ch-4 (18 dc, 18 ch-1 sps).

Rnd 3: Ch 3, 2 dc in same st, ch 2, (dc in next st, ch 2) 2 times, *3 dc in next st, ch 2, (dc in next st, ch 2) 2 times; repeat from * around, join with sl st in top of ch-3 (30 dc, 18 ch-2 sps).

NOTE: For **puff stitch (puff st),** yo, insert hook in next ch sp, yo, draw up long lp, (yo, insert hook in same sp, yo, draw up long lp) 3 times, yo, draw through all 9 lps on hook.

Rnd 4: Ch 3, dc in same st, 2 dc in each of next 2 sts, (*ch 2, dc in next ch-2 sp, ch 2, puff st in next ch-2 sp, ch 2, dc in next ch-2 sp, ch 2*, 2 dc in each of next 3 sts) 5 times; repeat between **, join.

Rnd 5: Ch 3, dc in next 5 sts, *[ch 2, dc in next ch-2 sp, ch 2, (puff st in next ch-2 sp, ch 2) 2 times, dc in next ch-2 sp, ch 2], dc in next 6 sts; repeat from * 4 more times; repeat between [ ], join.

Rnd 6: Ch 3, dc in next 5 sts, *[ch 2, dc in next ch-2 sp, ch 2, (puff st in next ch-2 sp, ch 2) 3 times, dc in next ch-2 sp, ch 2], dc in next 6 sts; repeat from * 4 more times; repeat between [ ], join.

Rnd 7: Sl st in next st, ch 3, dc in each of next 3 sts, *[ch 2, skip next st, dc in next ch-2 sp, ch 2, (puff st in next ch-2 sp, ch 2) 4 times, dc in next ch-2 sp, ch 2, skip next st], dc in each of next 2 sts; repeat from * 4 more times; repeat between [ ], join.

Rnd 8: Sl st in next st, ch 3, dc in next st, *[ch 2, skip next st, dc in next ch-2 sp, ch 2, (puff st in next ch-2 sp, ch 2) 5 times, dc in next ch-2 sp, ch 2, skip next st], dc in each of next 2 sts; repeat from * 4 more times; repeat between [ ], join.

Rnd 9: Sl st in sp between first 2 sts, ch 5, *[dc in next ch-2 sp, ch 2, (puff st in next ch-2 sp, ch 2) 6 times, dc in next ch-2 sp, ch 2], dc in sp between next 2 sts, ch 2; repeat from * 4 more times; repeat between [ ], join with sl st in 3rd ch of ch-5.

Rnd 10: Sl st in first ch-2 sp, ch 6, (puff st in next ch-2 sp, ch 3) 7 times, *(dc in next ch-2 sp, ch 3) 2 times, (puff st in next ch-2 sp, ch 3) 7 times; repeat from * 4 more times, dc in last ch-2 sp, ch 3, join with sl st in 3rd ch of ch-6.

Rnd 11: Sl st in first ch-3 sp, ch 3, puff st in same sp, ch 3, (puff st in next ch-3 sp, ch 3) 7 times, *dc in next ch-3 sp, ch 3, (puff st in next ch-3 sp, ch 3) 8 times; repeat from * 4 more times, dc in last ch-3 sp, ch 3, join with sl st in top of first puff st.

Rnds 12-13: Sl st in first ch-3 sp, ch 3, puff st in same sp, ch 3, (puff st in next ch-3 sp, ch 3) around, join.

Rnd 14: Sl st in each of next 2 chs, ch 1, sc in same ch sp, (ch 5, sc in next ch-3 sp) around; to **join,** ch 2, dc in first sc (54 ch-5 sps).

Rnd 15: Ch 1, sc around joining dc, ch 5, (sc in next ch-5 sp, ch 5) around, join with sl st in first sc, fasten off.

For **pillow,** cut two 14" circles from fabric. With right sides held together, allowing ⅝" for seam, sew fabric circles together leaving 4" open for stuffing. Clip curves, turn right side out, press. Stuff firmly, sew opening closed.

RUFFLE

Rnd 1: To **join,** holding Pillow Sides wrong sides together, matching sts, working through both thicknesses, join with sc in any ch-5 sp, 4 sc in same sp, 5 sc in each ch-5 sp around inserting pillow before closing, join with sl st in first sc (270 sc).

Rnd 2: Ch 3, *(2 dc in next st, 5 dc in next st, 2 dc in next st, dc in next st, skip next 2 sts, sc in

Continued on page 134

Crochet this delicate, stunning angel for a lasting family heirloom to be enjoyed
for years and years of holiday magic.

 AMBER ANGEL

DESIGNED BY JO ANN MAXWELL

SIZE
16" tall x 9" across bottom x 11½" across wings.

MATERIALS
Size 10 bedspread cotton — 350 yds. ecru; 9 gold 7 mm x 21 mm faceted acrylic pendant beads; 9 gold 4-mm filagree bell caps with loops; 9 each of 4-, 5- and 8-mm ivory pearl beads; 16 gold 4.5-mm acrylic rhinestones; 2 yds. gold metallic cord; 1 yd. off-white ¼" picot satin ribbon; 1½ yds. dk. olive green ⅛" satin ribbon; 5 gold/orange silk dried roses (about 1" wide) with stems; dried baby's breath flowers with gold glitter; small piece of hosiery fabric; blonde curly doll hair; 2" Styrofoam® egg; 3 small round white balloons; ½ sheet of white poster board; plastic drinking straw; plastic wrap; mixing bowl measuring about 5-6" across bottom, 9" across top and 4-5" deep; fabric stiffener; Styrofoam® or blocking board; rust-proof pins; invisible thread; cellophane tape; beading needle; craft glue or hot glue gun; tapestry needle; No. 5 steel crochet hook or size needed to obtain gauge.

GAUGE
8 sts = 1"; dc = ⅜" tall; triple treble crochet = ⅞" tall.

HEAD & BODY
Rnd 1: Beginning at top of Head, ch 5, (dc, ch 1) 17 times in 4th ch from hook, join with sl st in 3rd ch of ch-4 (18 dc, 18 ch-1 sps).

Rnds 2-4: Sl st in next ch sp, ch 5, (dc, ch 2) in each ch sp around, join with sl st in 3rd ch of ch-5.

Rnd 5: Sl st in next ch sp, ch 4, (dc, ch 1) in each ch sp around, join with sl st in 3rd ch of ch-4.

Rnd 6: Sl st in next ch sp, ch 2, hdc in each ch sp around, join with sl st in top of ch-2 (18 hdc).

Rnd 7: For **Body**, ch 5, (dc, ch 2) in each hdc around, join with sl st in 3rd ch of ch-5 (18 dc, 18 ch-2 sps).

Rnds 8-12: Repeat rnd 2.

Rnd 13: Ch 3, dc in next ch sp, (dc in next dc, dc in next ch sp) around, join with sl st in top of ch-3 (36 dc).

NOTE: For **picot**, ch 3, sl st in top of last st made.

Rnd 14: Ch 5, tr in next st, picot, ch 1, (tr in next st, ch 1, tr in next st, picot, ch 1) around, join with sl st in 4th ch of ch-5.

Rnd 15: Ch 1, sc in first st, ch 5, skip next picot, (sc in next tr, ch 5, skip next picot) around, join with sl st in first sc (18 ch-5 sps).

Rnd 16: Sc in first ch of first ch-5, (2 sc in next ch, sc in next ch) 2 times, *sl st in next sc, sc in next ch, (2 sc in next ch, sc in next ch) 2 times; repeat from * around, join with sl st in joining sl st of last rnd (18 7-sc groups).

NOTES: For **small love knot (small lk)**, using ⅛" loop, work according to illustration on page 159.

For **medium love knot (med lk)**, using ⅜" loop, work same as small love knot.

For **medium double love knot (med d-lk)**, using ⅜" loop, work according to illustration on page 159.

Rnd 17: Working this rnd in **back lps** only, sl st in next 4 sc, ch 3, dc in same st, small lk, (2 dc in center sc of next 7-sc group, small lk) around, join with sl st in top of ch-3 (36 dc, 18 small lk).

Rnd 18: Ch 3, dc in next dc, ch 5, skip next lk, (dc in each of next 2 dc, ch 5, skip next lk) around, join (36 dc, 18 ch-5 lps).

NOTE: For **triple treble crochet (ttr)**, see page 158.

Rnd 19: Sl st in next st, sl st in each of first 2 chs on next ch-5, ch 8, ttr in next ch, ch 1, ttr in next ch, ch 2, skip next 2 chs and 2 dc, *ttr in 2nd ch of next ch-5, (ch 1, ttr) in each of next 2 chs, ch 2; repeat from * around, join with sl st in 7th ch of ch-8 (54 ttr, 36 ch-1 sps, 18 ch-2 sps).

Rnd 20: Ch 3, dc in next ch-1 sp, dc in next st, picot, dc in next ch-1 sp, dc in next st, ch 2, sc in next ch-2 sp, ch 2, (dc in next st, dc in next ch-1 sp, dc in next st, picot, dc in next ch-1 sp, dc in next st, ch 2, sc in next ch-2 sp, ch 2) around, join with sl st in top of ch-3 (36 ch-2 sps, 18 5-dc/picot groups, 18 sc).

Rnd 21: Ch 1, sc in first st, ch 5, sc in last dc of same 5-dc group, ch 3, (sc in first st of next 5-dc group, ch 5, sc in last st of same 5-dc group, ch 3) around, join with sl st in first sc (18 ch-5 lps, 18 ch-3 sps).

Continued on page 132

AMBER ANGEL

Continued from page 130

Continued from page 130

Rnd 22: Sl st in next ch, ch 5, dc in next ch, (ch 2, dc) in each of next 3 chs (first scallop made), skip next sc, sc in next ch-3 sp, dc in first ch of next ch-5 lp, ch 1, med d-lk, dc in last ch of same ch-5 lp, sc in next ch-3 sp; for **scallop,** *dc in first ch of next ch-5 lp, (ch 2, dc) in next 4 chs; sc in next ch-3 sp, dc in first ch of next ch-5 lp, ch 1, med d-lk, dc in last ch of same ch-5 lp, sc in next ch-3 sp; repeat from * around, join with sl st in 3rd ch of beginning ch-5 (9 5-dc scallops, 9 med d-lks).

Rnd 23: Sl st in next 6 chs and sts, ch 1, sc in same st, ch 7, sc in center of next d-lk, ch 7, (sc in center dc of next scallop, ch 7, sc in center of next d-lk, ch 7) around, join with sl st in first sc (18 ch-7 lps).

Rnd 24: (*Sc in next ch, 2 sc in each of next 2 chs, sc in next ch, 2 sc in each of next 2 chs, sc in last ch*, sl st in next sc) 17 times; repeat between **, join with sl st in joining sl st of last rnd (18 11-sc groups).

Rnd 25: Working this rnd in **back lps** only, sl st in next 5 sc, ch 8, ttr in next sc, ch 1, ttr in next sc, ch 4, *ttr in 5th sc of next 11-sc group, (ch 1, ttr) in each of next 2 sc, ch 4; around, join with sl st in 7th ch of ch-8 (54 ttr, 36 ch-1 sps, 18 ch-4 sps).

Rnd 26: Ch 3, *[(dc in next ch-1 sp, dc in next st) 2 times, ch 2, sc in next ch-4 sp, ch 2], dc in next st; repeat from * 16 more times; repeat between [ ], join with sl st in top of ch-3 (36 ch-2 sps, 18 5-dc groups, 18 sc).

Rnd 27: Ch 3, dc in same st, ch 3, skip next 3 dc, 2 dc in next st, ch 1, med lk, (skip next 2 ch-2 sps and sc, 2 dc in next dc, ch 3, skip next 3 dc, 2 dc in next dc, ch 1, med lk) around, join (72 dc, 18 lks, 18 ch-3 sps).

NOTE: For **shell,** (2 dc, ch 2, 2 dc) in next ch.

Rnd 28: Sl st in next st, sl st in each of next 2 chs, ch 3, (dc, ch 2, 2 dc) in same ch, ch 5; (skipping sts between, shell in center ch of next ch-3, ch 5) around, join (18 shells, 18 ch-5 sps).

Rnd 29: Sl st in next st, sl st in next ch sp, ch 1, sc in same sp, *[dc in first ch of next ch-5, (ch 2, dc) in next 4 chs], sc in ch-2 sp of next shell; repeat from * around to last ch-5; repeat between [ ], join with sl st in first sc (18 5-dc scallops).

Rnd 30: Sl st in next 7 chs and sts, ch 1, sc in same st, ch 9, (sc in center st of next scallop, ch 9) around, join (18 ch-9 lps).

Rnd 31: *[Sc in next ch, (2 sc in next ch, sc in next ch) 4 times], sl st in next sc; repeat from * 16 more times; repeat between [ ], join with sl st in joining sl st of last rnd (18 13-sc groups).

Rnd 32: Working this rnd in **back lps** only, sl st in next 6 sts, ch 8, ttr in next sc, ch 1, ttr in next sc, ch 7, *ttr in 6th sc of next 13-sc group, (ch 1, ttr) in each of next 2 sc, ch 7; repeat from * around, join with sl st in 7th ch of ch-8 (54 ttr, 18 ch-7 sps).

Rnd 33: Ch 3, (*dc in next ch-1 sp, dc in next st, picot, dc in next ch-1 sp, dc in next st, ch 4, sc in next ch-7 sp*, ch 4, dc in next st) 17 times; repeat between **; to **join,** ch 2, dc in top of ch-3 (36 ch-4 sps, 18 5-dc/picot groups, 18 sc).

Rnd 34: Ch 1, sc around joining dc; skipping dc groups and picots, ch 7, sc in next ch-4 sp, ch 1, med d-lk, (sc in next ch-4 sp, ch 7, sc in next ch-4 sp, ch 1, med d-lk) around, join with sl st in first sc (18 ch-7 sps, 18 d-lks).

Rnd 35: Sl st in next 4 chs, ch 1, sc in same ch sp, ch 7, sc in center of next d-lk, ch 7, (sc in next ch-7 sp, ch 7, sc in center of next d-lk, ch 7) around, join (36 ch-7 sps).

Rnd 36: Sl st in next ch, ch 5, dc in next ch, (ch 2, dc) in next 5 chs, sc in next ch-7 sp, *dc in first ch of next ch-7, (ch 2, dc) in next 6 chs, sc in next ch-7 sp; repeat from * around, join with sl st in 3rd ch of ch-5, fasten off.

WINGS

Row 1: Beginning at center back, ch 4, 18 dc in 4th ch from hook, turn (19 dc).

Row 2: Ch 5, tr in next st, (ch 2, tr in next st) 16 times, ch 1, tr in last st, turn (19 tr, 16 ch-2 sps, 2 ch-1 sps).

Row 3: Ch 7, (sc in next tr, ch 4) across to last st, dc in last st, turn (18 ch-4 sps, 17 sc, 2 dc).

Row 4: Ch 8, (sc, ch 5) in each ch-4 sp across, dc in 3rd ch of ch-7, turn.

Row 5: Ch 3, dc in next ch, (ch 2, dc) in next 4 chs, *ch 1, sc in next ch-5 sp, ch 1, dc in first ch of next ch-5, (ch 2, dc) in next 4 chs; repeat from * 7 more times, ch 1, sc in next ch-5 sp, ch 1, dc in first ch of last ch-8, (ch 2, dc) in next 4 chs, dc in next ch leaving last 2 chs unworked, turn (10 5-dc scallops, 9 sc, 2 dc).

Row 6: Ch 8, skip next 6 dc and chs, sc in next dc, ch 9, (sc in center dc of next scallop, ch 9) 8 times, sc in center dc of last scallop, ch 5, dc in top of last ch-3, turn (9 ch-9 lps, 1 ch-5 lp, 1 ch-8 lp).

Row 7: Ch 1, sc in first st, *(sc in next ch, 2 sc in next ch) 2 times*, sc in last ch, sl st in next sc, (sc in each of next 2 chs, 2 sc in next ch, sc in each of next 3 chs, 2 sc in next ch, sc in each of last 2 chs, sl st in next sc) across to last ch-8; repeat between **, sc in each of next 2 chs leaving last 2 chs unworked, **do not** turn, fasten off.

Row 8: Working this row in **back lps** only, join with sl st in first sc, ch 10, skip next 2 sc, *ttr in next sc, (ch 1, ttr in next sc) 2 times*, ch 6, skip next 4 sc and sl st; repeat between **, [ch 6, skip next st; repeat between **, (ch 6, skip next 6 sc and sl st; repeat between **) 2 times]; repeat between [ ] 3 more times, ch 6, skip next st; repeat between **, ch 6, skip next 4 sc and sl st; repeat between **, ch 3, ttr in last sc, turn (16 3-ttr groups, 15 ch-6 sps, 1 ch-3 sp, 1 ch-10 sp).

Row 9: Ch 5, sc in first ch-3 sp, ch 2, (*dc in next ttr, dc in next ch-1 sp, dc in next ttr, picot, dc in next ch-1 sp, dc in next ttr*, ch 3, sc in next ch-6 sp, ch 3) 15 times; repeat between **, ch 2, sc in last ch-10 sp, ch 2, dc in 7th ch of ch-10, turn.

Row 10: Ch 3, med d-lk, (sc in next dc; skipping sts and picot between, ch 6, sc in last dc of same 5-dc group, ch 1, med d-lk) 16 times, dc in 3rd ch of last ch-5, turn.

Row 11: Ch 10, sc in center of first d-lk, ch 7, (sc in next ch-6 sp, ch 7, sc in center of next d-lk, ch 7) across, dc in top of ch-3, turn (34 ch-7 sps).

Row 12: Ch 3, dc in first ch of first ch-7, *(ch 2, dc) in next 6 chs, ch 1, sc in next ch-7 sp, ch 1, dc in first ch of next ch-7*; repeat between ** 6 more times, (ch 2, dc) in next 6 chs, ch 1, sc in next ch-7 sp, (ch 7, sc in next ch-7 sp) 3 times, ch 1, dc in first ch of next ch-7; repeat between ** 6 more times, (ch 2, dc) in next 6 chs, ch 1, sc in next ch-7 sp, ch 1, dc in first ch of last ch-10, (ch 2, dc) in next 6 chs, dc in next ch leaving last 2 chs unworked, fasten off.

SLEEVE (make 2)

NOTE: For **double treble crochet (dtr),** see page 158.

Rnd 1: Ch 5, sl st in first ch to form ring, ch 8, (dtr in ring, picot, ch 1, dtr in ring, ch 2) 7 times, dtr in ring, picot, ch 1, join with sl st in 6th ch of ch-8 (16 dtr, 8 picots).

Rnd 2: Ch 1, sc in same st, ch 5, skip next picot, (sc in next dtr, ch 5, skip next picot) around, join with sl st in first sc (8 ch-5 lps).

Rnd 3: *[Sc in first ch of next ch-5, (2 sc in next ch, sc in next ch) 2 times], sl st in next sc; repeat from * 6 more times; repeat between [ ], join with sl st in joining sl st of last rnd (8 7-sc groups).

Rnd 4: Working this rnd in **back lps** only, sl st in next 4 sc, ch 1, sc in same st, (*ch 5, sc in center st of next 7-sc group, med lk*, sc in center st of next 7-sc group) 3 times; repeat between **, join with sl st in first sc (4 ch-5 sps, 4 lks).

Rnd 5: Sl st in each of first 3 chs on next ch-5, ch 1, sc in same ch sp, ch 4, skip next lk, (sc in next ch-5 sp, ch 4, skip next lk) around, join (4 ch-4 sps).

Rnd 6: Sl st in each of first 2 chs on first ch-4, ch 3, dc in next ch, (skip first ch on next ch-4, dc in each of next 2 chs) around, join with sl st in top of ch-3 (8 dc).

Rnds 7-13: Ch 3, dc in each dc around, join. At end of last rnd, fasten off.

FINISHING

1: For **body form,** make a cone from poster board about 10" tall with an 8" opening at the bottom and a 1½" opening at the top. Staple or glue together to secure. Place bowl upside down on a flat surface and place cone on top of bowl. Place skirt portion of Head & Body over form to check fit. Adjust cone as needed, then cover entire form completely with plastic wrap. (Remember, crocheted piece will stretch when wet.) Tape to secure. Place form on plastic-covered blocking board.

2: For **bodice form,** stretch hosiery fabric over foam egg and tie with thread at bottom (small end) to secure. Cover with plastic wrap, twisting excess together at bottom.

3: Soak Head & Body in fabric stiffener according to manufacturer's instructions. (Use a paint brush or cotton ball to re-moisten crocheted piece while shaping, if needed.)

4: To **shape head,** using blunt end of crochet hook, carefully insert one balloon through any ch sp on head; inflate balloon until stitches are stretched slightly. Tie end of balloon securely.

5: Insert bodice form into bodice (large end up) through opening at top of skirt. Shape bodice around form.

6: Place skirt over cone, stretching to shape. Pin center st of each bottom scallop to blocking board. Let dry completely.

7: For **Wings,** soak crocheted piece in fabric stiffener and pin to blocking board, shaping into a three-quarter circle. Let dry completely.

8: For **Sleeves,** cut plastic straw in half; soak Sleeves in fabric stiffener. To **shape each sleeve,** insert one balloon through any ch sp on top portion; inflate balloon until stitches are stretched slightly. Insert half of straw through bottom portion of sleeve, being careful not to puncture balloon. Shape and let dry completely.

9: Puncture balloon in Head and gently pull out. Remove Head & Body from cone and carefully pull bodice form out through bottom (you may need needle-nose pliers for this procedure). Puncture balloons in Sleeves and remove; remove straws. Un-pin Wings from board.

Continued on next page

AMBER ANGEL

Continued from page 133

10: Glue Sleeves to rnds 8 and 9 on each side of Body with arms in front as shown in photo. Glue Wings to center back with tips pointing up and bottom edge over rnd 20.

11: For **each skirt ornament,** glue bell cap to top of one pendant bead. Thread one 8-mm, one 5-mm and one 4-mm pearl bead onto an 8" length of invisible thread; run thread through bell cap, then back through beads. Tie thread securely to sl st at center top of space between 3-ttr groups on rnd 32 as shown, pulling 8-mm bead up close to stitches. Clip excess thread leaving ¼" ends. Glue ends on inside to secure (use only a very small amount of glue). Repeat in every other space around skirt.

12: Glue one rhinestone to sc worked in center of each d-lk on rnd 23 as shown.

13: Arrange curly hair around top and sides of head as shown; tack with small amount of glue to secure. Glue remaining rhinestones to hair at ran-dom around "face." For **halo,** cut a 7" length of gold cord; glue ends together and tack to top of hair with small amount of glue.

14: For **bouquet,** twist stems of silk roses together, shaping as shown. Trim excess stems and glue to secure. Tie off-white ribbon in a bow around center of stems, making 2" loops and leaving long ends for streamers.

15: From gold cord, cut two 6", one 5" and two 3" lengths. From green ribbon, cut one 5", one 4", two 3" and one 2" length. Folding each length of ribbon or cord in half to form loop, glue loops to stems between roses as shown. Tie remaining lengths of cord and ribbon around stems for streamers.

16: Arrange and glue baby's breath around bouquet; glue bouquet between arms of Sleeves as shown. Trim ends of streamers about 1" longer than end of skirt. Knot ends of gold cord to prevent fraying. ❖

PINWHEEL & CROCUS DOILY

Continued from page 119

times, ch 5, sc in next ch-7 lp, ch 5, sc in next ch-5 lp, ch 5, sc in next ch-7 lp, ch 5], hdc in next hdc; repeat from * 6 more times; repeat between [ ], join (88 ch-5 lps).

Rnds 18-20: Ch 2, *[dc in next dc, tr in next tr, (ch 5, sc in next ch-5 lp) 11 times, ch 1], hdc in next hdc; repeat from * 6 more times; repeat between [ ], join (88 ch-5 lps, 8 ch-1 sps).

NOTE: For **picot,** ch 3, sl st in 3rd ch from hook.

Rnd 21: Ch 2, dc next 2 sts tog, picot, ch 3, (sc in next ch-5 lp, picot, ch 3) 11 times, skip next ch-1 sp, *dc next 3 sts tog, picot, ch 3, (sc in next ch-5 lp, picot, ch 3) 11 times, skip next ch-1 sp; repeat from * around, join, fasten off.

Starch and block Doily, shaping in a clockwise direction for pinwheel shape. ❖

PUFF STITCH PILLOW

Continued from page 129

next st, skip next 2 sts), dc in next st; repeat from * around to last 9 sts; repeat between ( ), join with sl st in top of first ch-3.

Rnd 3: Ch 1, (sc, hdc) in first st, 2 dc in each of next 9 sts, (hdc, sc) in next st, skip next st, *(sc, hdc) in next st, 2 dc in each of next 9 sts, (hdc, sc) in next st, skip next st; repeat from * around, join with sl st in first sc.

Rnd 4: Ch 1, sc in first st, ch 3, (sc in next st, ch 3) around, join, fasten off. ❖

GOLD BOW

DESIGNED BY MICHELE WILCOX

SIZE
10" x 14".

MATERIALS
Worsted-weight yarn — 8 oz. white; 1½ yds. metallic gold wire-edged ribbon; polyester fiberfill; tapestry needle; G crochet hook or size needed to obtain gauge.

GAUGE
2 pattern sts (see Row 1 of Pillow Side) = 1½"; 2 pattern st rows = 1".

PILLOW SIDE (make 2)

Row 1: Ch 44, (sc, hdc, dc) in 2nd ch from hook, skip next 2 chs, *(sc, hdc, dc) in next ch, skip next 2 chs; repeat from * across to last ch, sc in last ch, turn (14 pattern sts, one sc).

Rows 2-34: Ch 1, (sc, hdc, dc) in same st, skip next dc, skip next hdc, *(sc, hdc, dc) in next sc, skip next dc, skip next hdc; repeat from * across to last sc, sc in last sc, turn. At end of last row, fasten off.

Sew Pillow Sides together, stuffing before closing. Tie ribbon in bow around Pillow as shown in photo.❖

This generously-sized afghan with its classic lines and interesting texture will be a favorite around your home. Curl up beneath its folds for a quick nap or just to read your favorite book.

VARIEGATED OPEN STRIPES

DESIGNED BY ELEANOR ALBANO-MILES

SIZE
55" x 63½".

MATERIALS
Fuzzy bulky-weight yarn — 30 oz. plum variegated and 15 oz. cream; J crochet hook or size needed to obtain gauge.

GAUGE
3 sc sts = 1"; 2 sc rows and 1 dc row = 1¼".

AFGHAN

Row 1: With variegated, ch 158, sc in 2nd ch from hook, sc in each ch across, turn (157 sc). Front of row 1 is right side of work.

Row 2: Ch 3, dc in each st across, turn.

Row 3: Ch 1, sc in each st across, turn, fasten off.

Row 4: Join cream with sc in first st, (ch 7, skip next 5 sts, sc in next st) across, turn (27 sc, 26 ch-7 lps).

Row 5: Ch 1, sc in same st, (ch 7, skip next ch-7 lp, sc in next sc) across, turn, fasten off.

NOTE: Ch-5 at beginning of next row counts as first (dc, ch 2).

Row 6: Join variegated with sl st in first st, (ch 5, sc around both ch-7 lps of last 2 rows) across to last st, ch 2, dc in last st, turn.

Row 7: Ch 1, sc in each st, 2 sc in each ch-2 sp and 5 sc in each ch-5 sp across to last ch-5, 2 sc in last ch-5 sp, sc in 3rd ch of same ch-5, turn (157 sc).

Rows 8-153: Repeat rows 2-7 consecutively, ending with row 3.

EDGING

Row 1: For **first side,** working in ends of rows, join variegated with sc in first row, sc in each row across, turn (153 sc).

Row 2: Ch 1, sc in each st across, fasten off.

For **2nd side,** working on opposite side of afghan and joining in last row, work same as first side.

BORDER

Rnd 1: Working in sts and in ends of rows around entire outer edge, with wrong side facing you, join cream with sc in any st, ch 3, skip next st or row, (sc in next st or row, ch 3, skip next st or row) around, join with sl st in first sc, **turn.**

Rnd 2: Ch 1, sc in same st, ch 3, skip next ch-3 sp, (sc in next st, ch 3, skip next ch-3 sp) around, join, fasten off.❖

SENTIMENTAL JOURNEY

LIFE'S ROAD

Reflections of yesterday sometimes stir my heart.
Memories of old times, of all the lives I've been a part.

As the seasons march along and my dark hair turns to gray,
I seek all the beauty around me and enjoy life from day to day.

There's wonder all around us, all we have to do is see.
From the blooming of a flower to the buzzing of the bees.

The road through life is an adventure, made to explore and enjoy.
Whether your a dainty little girl or a rough and ready boy.

Hold your friends and family near if you travel down hard roads.
They're the loved ones you depend on to help you share the loads.

My life has been a treasure, filled with laughter and with tears.
Blessed with joyful memories as I've wandered through the years.

Display your good taste in decorating with the ever popular spiderweb design.
This beautiful antimacassar set fills your home with the ambiance of gracious living.

ANTIMACASSAR SET

DESIGNED BY LUELLA L. CARTWRIGHT

SIZE
Each Small Doily is 11½" x 12½". Large Doily
is 12½" x 20½".

MATERIALS FOR ONE SET
Size 30 crochet cotton — 950 yds. white; No. 6
steel crochet hook or size needed
to obtain gauge.

GAUGE
11 dc sts = 1"; 4 dc rows = 1".

SMALL DOILY

NOTES: For **mesh,** ch 2, skip next 2 chs or sts, dc in next ch or st.

For **beginning mesh (beg mesh),** ch 5, skip next 2 chs, dc in next ch or st.

For **block,** 2 dc in next ch sp, dc in next dc, **or,** dc in each of next 3 sts.

This project may ruffle until blocked.

Row 1: Ch 140, dc in 8th ch from hook (first mesh made), mesh across, turn (45 mesh).

Row 2: Beg mesh, mesh 13 times, block, mesh 5 times, block 2 times, mesh, block 2 times, mesh 5 times, block, mesh 14 times, turn.

Row 3: Beg mesh, mesh 11 times, block 2 times, mesh 8 times, block, mesh 8 times, block 2 times, mesh 12 times, turn.

Row 4: Beg mesh, mesh 9 times, block 2 times, mesh 8 times, block 2 times, mesh, block 2 times, mesh 8 times, block 2 times, mesh 10 times, turn.

Row 5: Beg mesh, mesh 4 times, block 5 times, mesh 12 times, block, mesh 12 times, block 5 times, mesh 5 times, turn.

Row 6: Beg mesh, mesh 3 times, block, mesh 16 times, block, ch 17, skip next 2 dc, dc in next dc, block, mesh 16 times, block, mesh 4 times, turn.

Row 7: Beg mesh, mesh 3 times, block, mesh 15 times, block, ch 9, sc in next ch lp, ch 9, skip next 3 dc, dc in next dc, block, mesh 15 times, block, mesh 4 times, turn.

Row 8: Beg mesh, mesh 3 times, block, mesh 14 times, block, ch 8, sc in next ch lp, sc in next sc, sc in next ch lp, ch 8, skip next 3 dc, dc in next dc, block, mesh 14 times, block, mesh 4 times, turn.

Row 9: Beg mesh, mesh 3 times, block, mesh 13 times, block, ch 8, sc in next ch lp, sc in each of next 3 sc, sc in next ch lp, ch 8, skip next 3 dc, dc in next dc, block, mesh 13 times, block, mesh 4 times, turn.

Row 10: Beg mesh, mesh 3 times, block, mesh 5 times, block 5 times, mesh 2 times, block, ch 8, sc in next ch lp, sc in next 5 sc, sc in next ch lp, ch 8, skip next 3 dc, dc in next dc, block, mesh 2 times, block 5 times, mesh 5 times, block, mesh 4 times, turn.

Row 11: Beg mesh, mesh 2 times, block, mesh 5 times, block, mesh 6 times, block, ch 10, sc in next ch lp, sc in next 7 sc, sc in next ch lp, ch 10, skip next 3 dc, dc in next dc, block, mesh 6 times, block, mesh 5 times, block, mesh 3 times, turn.

Row 12: Beg mesh, mesh 2 times, block, (mesh 5 times, block) 2 times, ch 17, skip next 2 dc, dc in next dc, 3 dc in next ch lp, ch 8, skip next sc, sc in next 7 sc, ch 8, skip next sc, 3 dc in next ch lp, dc in next dc, ch 17, skip next 2 dc, dc in next dc, block, (mesh 5 times, block) 2 times, mesh 3 times, turn.

Row 13: Beg mesh, mesh, block, mesh 6 times, block, mesh 4 times, block, (ch 9, skip next block, sc in next ch lp, ch 9, skip next block, dc in next dc), 3 dc in next ch lp, ch 8, skip next sc, sc in next 5 sc, ch 8, skip next sc, 3 dc in next ch lp, dc in next dc; repeat between ( ), block, mesh 4 times, block, mesh 6 times, block, mesh 2 times, turn.

Row 14: Beg mesh, mesh, block, mesh 6 times, block, mesh 3 times, block, (ch 8, sc in next ch lp, sc in next sc, sc in next ch lp, ch 8, skip next 3 dc, dc in next dc), 3 dc in next ch lp, ch 8, skip next sc, sc in each of next 3 sc, ch 8, skip next sc, 3 dc in next ch lp, dc in next dc; repeat between ( ), block, mesh 3 times, block, mesh 6 times, block, mesh 2 times, turn.

Row 15: Beg mesh, block, mesh 7 times, block, mesh 2 times, block, (ch 8, sc in next ch lp, sc in each of next 3 sc, sc in next ch lp, ch 8, skip next 3 dc, dc in next dc), 3 dc in next ch lp, ch 9, skip next sc, sc in next sc, ch 9, skip next sc, 3 dc in next ch lp, dc in next dc; repeat between ( ), block, mesh 2 times, block, mesh 7 times, block, mesh, turn.

Row 16: Beg mesh, mesh 10 times, block, (ch 8, sc in next ch lp, sc in next 5 sc, sc in next ch lp, ch 8, skip next 3 dc, dc in next dc), 3 dc in next ch lp, ch 2, skip next sc, 3 dc in next ch lp, dc in next dc; repeat between ( ), block, mesh 11 times, turn.

Row 17: Beg mesh, mesh 9 times, block, (ch 10, sc

Continued on page 154

CAPTIVATING CROCHET

Captivating Crochet

Clusters and chain loops are artfully combined to create this lacy white bonnet and booties made with size 10 crochet cotton. This duet is perfect for baby's first excursions.

BONNET & BOOTIES

DESIGNED BY NANCY CASE

SIZE
Bonnet fits 0-3 mos. and Booties fit 3" sole. Changes for 3-6 mos. and 3½" sole are obtained by acheiving gauge given below.

MATERIALS
Size 10 bedspread cotton — 500 yds. for 0-3 mos. and 550 yds. for 3-6 mos.; 2 yds. of ¼" satin ribbon; No. 8 or No. 7 steel crochet hook or size needed to obtain gauge.

GAUGE
For **0-3 mos. and 3" sole,** using No. 8 steel hook, 8 dc sts = 1"; 4 dc rows = 1".
For **3-6 mos. and 3½" sole,** using No. 7 steel hook, 7 dc sts = 1"; 3 dc rows = 1".

BOOTIE (make 2)
Sole
Rnd 1: Ch 21; for **toe,** 7 dc in 4th ch from hook; dc in next 16 chs; for **heel,** 6 dc in end ch; working on opposite side of starting ch, dc in next 16 chs, join with sl st in top of ch-3 (46 dc).

Rnd 2: Ch 3, 2 dc in same st, 3 dc in each of next 6 sts, dc in next 17 sts, 3 dc in each of next 5 sts, dc in last 17 sts, join (70).

Rnd 3: Ch 1, sc in same st, ch 3, skip next st, (sc in next st, ch 3, skip next st) around, join with sl st in first sc (70 ch-3 sps).

NOTES: For **beginning cluster (beg cl),** ch 3, (yo, insert hook in same sp, yo, draw lp through, yo, draw through 2 lps on hook) 4 times, yo, draw through all 5 lps on hook.

For **cluster (cl),** yo, insert hook in next ch sp, yo, draw lp through, yo, draw through 2 lps on hook, (yo, insert hook in same sp, yo, draw lp through, yo, draw through 2 lps on hook) 4 times, yo, draw through all 6 lps on hook.

Rnds 4-5: Sl st in first ch sp, beg cl, ch 1, (cl in next ch sp, ch 1) around, join with sl st in top of beg cl, ending with 35 cls and 35 ch-1 sps in last rnd. At end of last rnd, fasten off.

Row 6: Working in rows, skip first 12 ch-1 sps, join with sl st in next ch-1 sp, beg cl, (ch 1, cl in next ch sp) 17 times leaving remaining ch sps unworked, turn, fasten off (18 cls, 17 ch-1 sps).

Instep
Rnd 1: Ch 5, sl st in first ch to form ring, beg cl, ch 3, (cl in ring, ch 3) 4 times, join with sl st in top of beg cl (5 cls, 5 ch-3 sps).

Rnd 2: (Beg cl, ch 3, cl) in first st, ch 3, sc in next ch-3 sp, ch 3, *(cl, ch 3, cl) in next st, ch 3, sc in next ch-3 sp, ch 3; repeat from * around, join (15 ch-3 sps, 10 cls).

Rnd 3: Ch 1, sc in first st, *[ch 3, sc in next ch-3 sp, ch 3, sc in top of next cl, ch 3, (sc in next ch-3 sp, ch 3) 2 times], sc in top of next cl; repeat from * 3 more times; repeat between [ ] one more time, join with sl st in first sc (25 sc, 25 ch-3 sps).

Row 4: Working in rows, sl st in next ch-3 sp; to **join,** hold wrong side of Instep and right side of rnd 5 on Sole together, with Instep facing you; working in unworked ch sps of rnd 5, matching ch sps and working through both thicknesses, ch 1, 2 sc in same sp, 2 sc in each of next 16 ch sps leaving remaining sts unworked, fasten off.

Ankle
NOTE: Ch-6 at beginning of next rnd counts as first dc and ch-3 sp.

Rnd 1: With right side of row 6 on Sole facing you, join with sl st in ch-1 sp at center back of Bootie, ch 6, (dc in next ch-1 sp, ch 3) around to last ch-1 sp before Instep, dc next ch-1 sp on Sole and next ch-3 sp on Instep tog, ch 3, (dc in next ch-3 sp, ch 3) 6 times, dc next ch-3 sp on Instep and next ch-1 sp on Sole tog, ch 3, (dc in next ch-1 sp, ch 3) around, join with sl st in 3rd ch of ch-6 (23 ch-3 sps).

Rnd 2: Sl st in first ch-3 sp, beg cl, ch 3, cl in same sp, ch 3, *(cl, ch 3, cl) in next ch-3 sp, ch 3; repeat from * around, join with sl st in top of beg cl (46 cls, 46 ch-3 sps).

Rnd 3: Sl st in first ch-3 sp, beg cl, ch 3, cl in same sp, ch 3, sc in next ch-3 sp, ch 3, *(cl, ch 3, cl) in next ch-3 sp, ch 3, sc in next ch-3 sp, ch 3; repeat from * around, join.

Rnds 4-5: Sl st in first ch-3 sp, ch 1, sc in same sp, ch 3, (sc in next ch-3 sp, ch 3) around, join with sl st in first sc. At end of last rnd, fasten off.

Starting at front, weave 18" piece of ribbon through ch sps on rnd 1 of Ankle. Pull ends even and tie into a bow.

Continued on page 153

Keep the Fall afternoon chill off with this lacy shawl. Sure to be a favorite addition to your wardrobe, you'll want to make several in an array of colors.

WHITE SHAWL

DESIGNED BY JOSIE RABIER

SIZE
22½" x 71".

MATERIALS
Fuzzy 3-ply sport yarn — 12 oz. white; H crochet hook or size needed to obtain gauge.

GAUGE
3 shells and 2 sc = 5¼"; 2 shell rows and 1 sc row = 2½".

SHAWL
NOTES: For **shell,** 7 tr in next ch or st.

For **V-stitch (V-st),** (dc, ch 1, dc) in next st.

Ch-3 at beginning of row counts as first dc. Ch-4 at beginning of row counts as first tr.

Row 1: Ch 90, sc in 2nd ch from hook, (skip next 3 chs, shell in next ch, skip next 3 chs, sc in next ch) across, turn (12 sc, 11 shells).

Row 2: Ch 3, dc in same st, ch 3, sc in 4th tr of next shell, ch 3, (V-st in next sc, ch 3, sc in 4th tr of next shell, ch 3) across to last sc, 2 dc in last sc, turn (11 sc, 10 V-sts, 4 dc).

Row 3: Ch 4, 3 tr in same st, skip next dc, sc in next sc, (shell in ch-1 sp of next V-st, sc in next sc) across to last 2 dc, skip next dc, 4 tr in last dc, turn (11 sc, 10 shells, 8 tr).

Row 4: Ch 1, sc in same st, ch 3, skip next 3 tr, V-st in next sc, ch 3, (sc in 4th tr of next shell, ch 3, V-st in next sc, ch 3) across to last 4 tr, skip next 3 tr, sc in last tr, turn (12 sc, 11 V-sts).

Row 5: Ch 1, sc in same st, (shell in next V-st, sc in next sc) across, turn.

Rows 6-93: Repeat rows 2-5 consecutively.

Row 94: Ch 1, skip first sc, sl st in next 4 tr of next shell, ch 1, sc in same st, (ch 3, V-st in next sc, ch 3, sc in 4th tr of next shell) across to last sc, skip last sc, turn (11 sc, 10 V-sts).

Row 95: Ch 1, sc in same st, (shell in next V-st, sc in next sc) across, turn.

Rows 96-113: Repeat rows 94 and 95 alternately, ending with 2 sc and one shell in last row. At end of last row, fasten off.

Row 114: Working in starting ch on opposite side of row 1, with wrong side facing you, join with sl st in first ch, ch 3, dc in same ch, ch 3, skip next 3 chs, sc in next ch, ch 3, skip next 3 chs, (V-st in next ch, ch 3, skip next 3 chs, sc in next ch, ch 3, skip next 3 chs) across to last ch, 2 dc in last ch, turn (11 sc, 10 V-sts, 4 dc).

Rows 115-116: Repeat rows 3 and 4.

Rows 117-135: Repeat rows 95 and 94 alternately, ending with row 95 and 2 sc and one shell. At end of last row, **do not** turn or fasten off.

EDGING
NOTE: For **beginning popcorn (beg pc),** ch 3, 4 dc in same st, drop lp from hook, insert hook in top of ch-3, draw dropped lp through, ch 1.

For **popcorn (pc),** 5 dc in next st, drop lp from hook, insert hook in first dc of 5-dc group, draw dropped lp through, ch 1.

When working in ends of rows, work around post or side of end st.

Rnd 1: Working in ends of rows and in sts around outer edge, beg pc, *(ch 3, skip next tr of shell on next row, sc in next tr, ch 3, pc in next row) 10 times, ch 3, (sc in next row, ch 3, pc in next row, ch 3) 3 times, (sc in next row, ch 3, pc in next row, ch 3, sc in next row, ch 3, skip next row, pc in next row, ch 3, sc in next row, ch 3, pc in next row, ch 3, skip next row) 11 times, skip next tr, (sc in next tr, ch 3, pc in next row, ch 3, skip next tr of shell on next row) 10 times; working in shell on point, sc in next tr, ch 3, skip next tr, (pc, ch 3, pc) in center tr of same shell, ch 3, skip next tr, sc in next tr, ch 3, skip next tr*, pc in next row; repeat between **, join with sl st in top of beg pc.

Rnd 2: Ch 1, sc in same st, *ch 5, (tr in next sc, ch 5, sc in next pc, ch 5) around to ch-3 sp between 2 pc on corner, tr in same corner ch-3 sp, ch 5*, sc in next pc; repeat between **, join with sl st in first sc.

Rnd 3: Sl st in each of next 3 chs, ch 3, pc in next tr, (ch 3, sl st in 3rd ch of each of next 2 ch-5 sps, ch 3, pc in next tr) around to last ch-5 sp, sl st in 3rd ch of last ch-5 sp, join with sl st in 3rd sl st, fasten off. ❖

Make this lovely heart and key for a secret pal or special friend to symbolize the lasting warmth of a dear friendship.

⚘ KEYHOLE HEART & KEY ⚘

DESIGNED BY JO ANN MAXWELL

SIZE
Heart is 5" x 5" without hanger. Key is 4" long.

MATERIALS
Size 10 bedspread cotton — 50 yds. cream; 25 yds. metallic gold thread; 5 pink ⅜" satin ribbon roses; 8" lt. teal ⅛" satin ribbon; small amount dried baby's breath flowers; 8 pink 3-mm pearl beads; 12" piece of metallic gold cord; 2" jewelry tassel; invisible thread; craft glue or hot glue gun; liquid fabric stiffener; rustproof pins; plastic wrap; Styrofoam® or blocking board; No. 5 steel crochet hook or size needed to obtain gauge.

GAUGE
Rnds 1-2 = 1½" x 1¾".

HEART

Rnd 1: With cream, ch 22, sl st in first ch to form ring, ch 1, 3 sc in same ch, 2 sc in each of next 4 chs, sc in next 4 chs, ch 2, sc in next 5 chs, ch 2, sc in next 4 chs, 2 sc in each of last 4 chs, join with sl st in first sc (32 sc, 2 ch-2 sps).

Rnd 2: Sl st in next st, ch 1, sc in same st, ch 3, skip next 2 sts, sc in next st, (ch 5, skip next 2 sts, sc in next st) 3 times, ch 3, skip next st, sc in next ch-2 sp, ch 3, skip next st, sc in next st; for **point**, ch 5, skip next st, sc in next st; ch 3, skip next st, sc in next ch-2 sp, ch 3, skip next st, sc in next st, (ch 5, skip next 2 sts, sc in next st) 3 times, ch 3, skip last 2 sts, join (7 ch-5 lps, 6 ch-3 sps).

NOTE: For **double treble crochet (dtr)** (see page 158).

Rnd 3: Ch 3, (dc, ch 3, dc) in next ch-3 sp, *ch 3, tr in 2nd ch of next ch-5 sp, ch 3, tr in 3rd ch of same sp, ch 3, dtr in 2nd ch of next ch-5 sp, ch 3, dtr in 3rd ch of same sp, ch 3, tr in 2nd ch of next ch-5 sp, ch 3, tr in 3rd ch of same sp, ch 3*, dc in next ch-3 sp, ch 3, hdc in next ch-3 sp, ch 3, (dc, ch 3, dc) in 3rd ch of next ch-5 sp, ch 3, hdc in next ch-3 sp, ch 3, dc in next ch-3 sp; repeat between **, (dc, ch 3, dc) in last ch-3 sp, ch 3, join with sl st in bottom of first ch-3 (23 ch-3 sps, 22 sts).

Rnd 4: Ch 3, skip first ch-3 sp, sc in next st, ch 1, skip next ch-3 sp, (dc, ch 2, dc) in next st, *ch 1, sc in next ch-3 sp, ch 1, (dc, ch 2, dc) in next st*; repeat between ** 5 more times, ch 1, skip next ch-3 sp, sc in next st, ch 1, skip next ch-3 sp, (dc, ch 2, dc) in next st, ch 1, skip next ch-3 sp, sc in next st, ch 1, (dc, ch 3, dc) in next ch-3 sp, ch 1, sc in next st, ch 1, skip next ch-3 sp, (dc, ch 2, dc) in next st, ch 1, skip next ch-3 sp, sc in next st, ch 1, skip next ch-3 sp, (dc, ch 2, dc) in next st; repeat between ** 6 more times, ch 1, skip next ch-3 sp, sc in last st, ch 3, skip last ch-3 sp, join as before, fasten off (16 ch-2 sps, 3 ch-3 sps).

Rnd 5: Join metallic thread with sl st in joining sl st of last rnd, ch 3, sc in next sc, ch 3, (5 sc in next ch-2 sp, ch 3) 8 times, 6 sc in next ch-3 sp, ch 3; repeat between ( ) 8 more times, sc in last sc, ch 3, join with sl st in first sl st, fasten off (88 sc, 20 ch-3 sps).

Rnd 6: Working this rnd in **back lps**, join cream with sl st in joining sl st of last rnd, ch 2, sc in next ch-3 sp, *hdc in next st, (ch 2, hdc in next st) 4 times*; repeat between ** 7 more times, (hdc in next st, ch 2) 2 times, (dc in next st, ch 2) 2 times, hdc in next st, ch 2, hdc in next st; repeat between ** 8 more times, ch 2, sc in next ch-3 sp, ch 2, join with sl st in first sl st, fasten off.

Rnd 7: Working in starting ch on opposite side of rnd 1, join metallic thread with sl st in any ch, sl st in each ch around, join with sl st in first sl st, fasten off.

KEY
Large Heart

Rnd 1: With cream, ch 34, sl st in first ch to form ring, fasten off (34 chs).

Rnd 2: Join metallic thread with sc in first ch, sc in next ch, 2 sc in each of next 10 chs, sc in next 5 chs; for **point**, (2 sc, ch 2, 2 sc) in next ch, sc in next 5 chs, 2 sc in each of next 10 chs, sc in last ch, join with sl st in first sc, fasten off.

Small Heart

Rnd 1: With cream, ch 16, sl st in first ch to form ring, fasten off (16 chs).

Rnd 2: Join metallic thread with sc in first ch, 2 sc in each of next 4 chs, sc in each of next 3 chs; for **point**, (2 sc, ch 2, 2 sc) in next ch; sc in each of next 3 chs, 2 sc in each of last 4 chs, join with sl st in first sc, fasten off.

For **stem**, with cream, ch 22, hdc in 3rd ch from hook, hdc in each ch across, fasten off.

FINISHING

1: Apply fabric stiffener to Heart and Key pieces according to manufacturer's instructions.

2: Pin all pieces flat to plastic-covered blocking board. Shape center of Heart in the shape of a keyhole and Key Hearts as shown in photo. Let dry completely.

3: Tie 6" piece of gold cord into a bow. Glue to center top of Heart. Glue 3 roses and small amount of baby's breath to Heart below bow. Cut four 1" pieces of ribbon; fold each piece in half and glue behind roses as desired.

4: Glue one rose and small amount of baby's breath to rnd 4 at bottom point. Cut two 1" pieces of ribbon. Fold each piece in half and glue behind rose on each side.

5: With invisible thread, tie tassel to bottom point of Heart.

6: For **hanger**, fold 6" piece of gold cord in half. Glue ends to back of Heart.

7: For **key**, glue bottom point of Large Heart to one end of Stem. Glue top of Small Heart to bottom side of Stem on opposite side as shown in photo. Glue 3 pearl beads to center top of each Heart; glue one pearl bead to bottom point of each Heart. Glue one rose to top of Large Heart above beads. Cut two 1" pieces of ribbon. Fold each piece in half and glue behind rose on each side.❖

*Bring bright sunshine into your home when you make this eye-catching afghan
of large perky sunflowers strewn on a bed of green.*

SUMMER FLOWERS

DESIGNED BY SANDRA SMITH

SIZE
52" x 70".

MATERIALS
Worsted-weight yarn — 21 oz. green, 18 oz. orange, 8 oz. each rust and brown; tapestry needle; size 50 broomstitck lace pin; size G crochet hook or size needed to obtain gauge.

GAUGE
4 sts = 1"; Rnds 1-2 of Motif = 2¼" across.

FIRST ROW
First Sunflower Motif
Rnd 1: With rust, ch 2, 12 sc in 2nd ch from hook, join with sl st in first sc (12 sc).

Rnd 2: Ch 3, dc in same st, 2 dc in each st around, join with sl st in top of ch-3 (24 dc).

Rnd 3: Ch 7, skip next 2 sts, (dc in next st, ch 4, skip next 2 sts) around, join with sl st in 3rd ch of ch-7, fasten off (8 dc, 8 ch-4 sps).

Rnd 4: Join brown with sc in any dc, sc in same dc; (*working in front of next ch-4 lp, 2 tr in each of next 2 skipped sts on rnd before last*, 2 sc in next dc on last rnd) 7 times; repeat between **, join with sl st in first sc, fasten off (32 tr, 16 sc).

Rnd 5: For **petals,** with orange, *ch 2; working in **back lps,** sl st in next 4 sts on rnd 4, pull up long lp on hook, place on pin (see illustration No. 1 on page 155); working from left to right in **back lps** of sl sts just made, skip first st, (pull up lp in next st to the right, place on pin) 3 times, (pull up lp in next ch of ch-2, place on pin) 2 times; insert hook through all 6 lps on pin (see illustration No. 2), slide off pin allowing lps to twist, yo, draw through all 6 lps, ch 1, 8 sc in 6-lp group; repeat from * 11 more times, sl st in worked st at end of last petal, fasten off (12 petals).

Sew end of first and last petals together to match others.

Rnd 6: Working this rnd in **back lps** only, join green with sl st in 4th sc of any petal, ch 6, (sl st in 4th sc of next petal, ch 6) around, join with sl st in first sl st (12 ch-6 lps).

NOTE: For **picot,** ch 2, sl st in 2nd ch from hook.

Rnd 7: (5 sc, picot, 5 sc) in next ch-6 lp, *sl st in next sl st, (5 sc, picot, 5 sc) in next ch-6 lp; repeat from * around, join with sl st in first sl st, fasten off.

Second Sunflower Motif
Rnds 1-6: Repeat same rnds of First Sunflower Motif.

NOTE: For **joining picot,** ch 1, sl st in designated picot on adjacent Motif, ch 1, sl st in first ch-1 made.

Rnd 7: (5 sc, picot, 5 sc) in next ch-6 lp, *sl st in next sl st, (5 sc, picot, 5 sc) in next ch-6 lp; repeat from * 9 more times; joining to side of last Sunflower Motif made (see Assembly Diagram on page 155), (5 sc, joining picot, 5 sc) in each of next 2 ch-6 lps, join with sl st in first sl st, fasten off.

Repeat Second Sunflower Motif 4 more times for a total of 6 Motifs.

SECOND ROW
First Sunflower Motif
Joining to bottom of First Motif on last Row, work same as First Row's Second Sunflower Motif.

Second Sunflower Motif
Rnds 1-6: Repeat same rnds of First Row's First Sunflower Motif.

Rnd 7: (5 sc, picot, 5 sc) in next ch-6 lp, *sl st in next sl st, (5 sc, picot, 5 sc) in next ch-6 lp; repeat from * 6 more times; joining to bottom of corresponding Motif on last Row, (5 sc, joining picot, 5 sc) in each of next 2 ch-6 lps, (5 sc, picot, 5 sc) in next ch-6 lp; joining to side of last Motif made on this Row, (5 sc, joining picot, 5 sc) in each of last 2 ch-6 lps, join with sl st in first sl st, fasten off.

Repeat Second Sunflower Motif 4 more times for a total of 6 Motifs.

Repeat Second Row 6 more times for a total of 8 Rows.

FILLER MOTIF
Rnds 1-2: With green, repeat same rnds of First Row's First Sunflower Motif.

Rnd 3: For **leaves,** *[pull lp up on hook and place over broomstick pin; working from left to right in **back lps** only, (insert hook in next st to the

Continued on page 155

CAPTIVATING CROCHET

*Decorate your home with the lasting grace of a time gone by with these
lovely ornaments fashioned from fine crochet cotton.*

VICTORIAN ORNAMENTS

DESIGNED BY JO ANN MAXWELL

SIZES
Teacup is 1¾" tall. Slipper is 4" long. Bottom Half of Bowl is 3" across; Top Half is 2" across.

MATERIALS FOR TEACUP
Size 10 bedspread cotton — 50 yds. cream; small amount metallic gold thread; ¾" purchased flower appliqué; 3" x 6" piece of pink net fabric with sparkles; 1½" Styrofoam® ball; 3" Styrofoam® ball; blocking board; liquid fabric stiffener; plastic wrap; rustproof pins; craft glue or hot glue gun; No. 5 steel crochet hook or size needed to obtain gauge.

MATERIALS FOR ONE SLIPPER
Size 10 bedspread cotton — 35 yds. cream; small amount metallic gold thread; 2 burgundy ¾" silk flowers with leaves; 20" pink ⅛" satin ribbon; Darice™ plastic shoe form; liquid fabric stiffener; plastic wrap; rustproof pins; craft glue or hot glue gun; No. 5 steel crochet hook or size needed to obtain gauge.

MATERIALS FOR BOWL
Size 10 bedspread cotton — 50 yds. cream; small amount metallic gold thread; 15 or 16 dried rosebuds; metallic gold dried baby's breath flowers; 23" pink 3-mm strung beads; 30" lt. teal ⅛" satin ribbon; 9" pink ⅛" satin ribbon; 6" x 10" piece of pink net fabric; pink sewing thread; 2" Styrofoam® ball; 3" Styrofoam® ball; liquid fabric stiffener; plastic wrap; rustproof pins; craft glue or hot glue gun; sewing needle; No. 5 steel crochet hook or size needed to obtain gauge.

GAUGE
7 sts = 1"; 4 dc rows = 1".

TEACUP
Saucer
Rnd 1: Starting at center, with cream, ch 4, sl st in first ch to form ring, ch 4, 23 tr in ring, join with sl st in top of ch-4 (24 tr).

Rnd 2: Working this rnd in **front lps**, ch 3, dc in same st, 2 dc in each st around, join with sl st in top of ch-3 (48 dc).

Rnd 3: Ch 3, dc in each of next 2 sts, 2 dc in next st, (dc in each of next 3 sts, 2 dc in next st) around, join (60).

Rnd 4: Working this rnd in **back lps,** ch 1, sc in each st around, join with sl st in first sc.

Rnd 5: Ch 4, skip next 2 sts, (sl st in next st, ch 4, skip next 2 sts) around, join with sl st in first ch of first ch-4, fasten off.

For **base,** working in **back lps** of rnd 1, join cream with sc in first st, 2 sc in next st, (sc in next st, 2 sc in next st) around, join with sl st in first sc, fasten off.

Cup
Rnd 1: Starting at bottom, with cream, ch 4, sl st in first ch to form ring, ch 3, 19 dc in ring, join with sl st in top of ch-3 (20 dc).

Rnd 2: Working this rnd in **back lps**, ch 3, dc in same st, 2 dc in each st around, join (40).

Rnds 3-4: Ch 3, dc in each st around, join.

Rnd 5: Working this rnd in **back lps**, ch 1, sc in each st around, join with sl st in first sc, fasten off.

For **base,** working in **front lps** of rnd 1, join cream with sl st in first st, ch 3, dc in same st, 2 dc in each st around, join, fasten off.

Handle
With cream, ch 30, sl st in 2nd ch from hook, sl st in each ch across, fasten off.

Finishing
1: Apply fabric stiffener to Saucer, Cup and Handle according to manufacturer's instructions.

2: Cover foam balls and blocking board with plastic wrap. Pin and shape Saucer over 3" foam ball. Shape Cup over 1½" foam ball. Twist ends of Handle as shown in photo and pin to blocking board. Let all pieces dry completely.

3: Glue Cup inside Saucer, placing 3" square of net between. Glue remaining net inside Cup and glue Handle to one side of Cup. Glue appliqué to center front.

4: For **hanger,** fold 8" piece of metallic thread in half; glue ends inside Cup near handle, glue fold to opposite side of Cup.

SLIPPER (make 2)
Rnd 1: Starting at bottom of heel, with cream, ch 2, 12 sc in 2nd ch from hook, join with sl st in first sc (12 sc).

Rnd 2: Working this rnd in **back lps**, ch 3, dc in each st around, join with sl st in top of ch-3 (12 dc).

Rnd 3: Ch 3, dc in each st around, join.

Rnd 4: Ch 3, dc in each of next 3 sts, 2 dc in each of next 4 sts, dc in last 4 sts; for **sole,** ch 20, hdc in 4th ch from hook, hdc in next 16 chs, join (17 hdc, 16 dc).

Rnd 5: Sl st in next st, ch 3, dc in each of next 2 sts, 2 dc in each of next 8 sts, dc in each of next 3 sts, skip next st; working in chs on opposite side of sole, dc in next 17 chs, 5 dc in end ch-3 sp, dc in next 17 sts, join with sl st in top of ch-3 (61 dc).

Continued on next page

Continued from page 151

Rnds 6-8: Ch 3, dc in each st around, join.

Rnd 9: Ch 3, dc in next 32 sts, (dc next 2 sts tog) 9 times, dc in each st around, join, fasten off (52).

Rnd 10: Join metallic thread with sc in first st, sc in each st around, join with sl st in first sc, fasten off.

Finishing

1: Apply fabric stiffener to Slipper according to manufacturer's instructions.

2: Cover shoe form with plastic wrap. Shape Slipper over form. Let dry completely.

3: Fold 7" piece of metallic thread in half. Lace across top of Slipper through sc sts on rnd 10 as shown in photo; glue to secure. Trim ends if necessary. Glue 2 silk Flowers to outside edge of Slipper over ends of laces.

4: Cut 6" piece of ribbon, tie into a bow. Glue bow to rnd 10 on back of Slipper. Insert one end of remaining ribbon through a stitch on rnd 8 at center back of Slipper, knot end to secure. Repeat with opposite end of ribbon in other Slipper.

BOWL
Bottom Half

Rnd 1: With cream, ch 5, sl st in first ch to form ring, ch 3, 23 dc in ring, join with sl st in top of ch-3 (24 dc).

NOTE: For **triple treble crochet (tr tr),** see page 158.

Rnd 2: Ch 9, (ttr in next st, ch 3) around, join with sl st in 6th ch of ch-9 (24 ttr, 24 ch-3 sps).

Rnd 3: Ch 1, sc in same st, ch 3, skip next ch-3 sp, (sc in next st, ch 3, skip next ch-3 sp) around, join with sl st in first sc, fasten off.

Top Half

Rnd 1: Ch 4, sl st in first ch to form ring, ch 9, (ttr in ring, ch 3) 15 times, join with sl st in 6th ch of ch-9 (16 ttr, 16 ch-3 sps).

Rnd 2: Repeat rnd 3 of Bottom Half.

Finishing

1: Apply fabric stiffener to both pieces according to manufacturer's instructions.

2: Cut both foam balls in half, cover one piece of each ball with plastic wrap. Shape Bottom Half over 3" piece; shape Top Half over 2" piece. Let dry completely.

3: Cut net into 2 pieces each 3" x 10". For **each ruffle,** fold net in half lengthwise so that it measures 1½" x 10". Sew short ends together to form a circle. With sewing needle and thread, run a gathering stitch around raw edges. Pull gathering sts to tighten, secure. Glue one ruffle to Top Half; glue remaining ruffle inside Bottom Half as shown in photo.

4: For **bouquet,** glue several rosebuds and small amount of baby's breath over ruffle on Top Half. Glue seven 1½" pieces of strung beads around bouquet as desired. Cut five 3" pieces of lt. teal ribbon. Fold each piece in half, glue ends around bouquet as desired.

5: Repeat Step 4 in Bottom Half.

6: Fold 9" pink ribbon in half, glue fold to rnd 1 on inside of Top Half. Thread ends through ch-3 sp of rnd 2 on each side. Glue each end of ribbon to top of one tr tr on inside of Bottom Half on each side.

7: For **hanger,** glue ends of a 5½" piece of metallic thread to each side of bouquet on Top Half.❖

BONNET & BOOTIES

Continued from page 143

BONNET

NOTE: For cluster instructions, see Note after rnd 3 of Bootie on page 143.

Rnd 1: Starting at center back, ch 5, sl st in first ch to form ring, beg cl, ch 3, (cl in ring, ch 3) 4 times, join with sl st in top of beg cl (5 cls, 5 ch-3 sps).

Rnd 2: (Beg cl, ch 3, cl) in first st, ch 3, sc in next ch-3 sp, ch 3, *(cl, ch 3, cl) in top of next cl, ch 3, sc in next ch-3 sp, ch 3; repeat from * around, join (15 ch-3 sps, 10 cls).

Rnd 3: Sl st in next ch-3 sp, ch 1, sc in same sp, ch 3, (sc in next ch-3 sp, ch 3) around, join with sl st in first sc (15 ch-3 sps).

Rnd 4: Sl st in next ch-3 sp, ch 1, sc in same sp, ch 3, (cl, ch 3, cl) in next ch-3 sp, ch 3, *(sc in next ch-3 sp, ch 3) 2 times, (cl, ch 3, cl) in next ch-3 sp, ch 3; repeat from * around to last ch-3 sp, sc in last ch-3 sp, ch 3, join (20 ch-3 sps).

Rnd 5: Sl st in next ch-3 sp, ch 1, sc in same sp, ch 3, (cl, ch 3, cl) in next ch-3 sp, ch 3, *sc in next ch-3 sp, ch 3, (cl, ch 3, cl) in next ch-3 sp, ch 3; repeat from * around, join (30 ch-3 sps).

Rnd 6: Repeat rnd 4 (40 ch-3 sps).

Rnd 7: Sl st in each of next 3 chs, sl st in top of next cl, sl st in each of next 2 chs, ch 1, sc in same ch sp, *[ch 3, skip next ch-3 sp, (cl, ch 3, cl) in next ch-3 sp, ch 3, skip next ch-3 sp], sc in next ch-3 sp; repeat from * around to last 3 ch-3 sps; repeat between [ ], join (30 ch-3 sps).

Rnd 8: Repeat rnd 4 (40 ch-3 sps).

Rnd 9: Sl st in each of next 3 chs, sl st in top of next cl, sl st in next ch-3 sp, beg cl, ch 3, cl in same ch sp, ch 2, skip next ch-3 sp, *(cl, ch 3, cl) in next ch-3 sp, ch 2, skip next ch-3 sp; repeat from * around, join with sl st in top of beg cl (20 ch-3 sps, 20 ch-2 sps).

Rnd 10: Sl st in next ch-3 sp, beg cl, ch 3, cl in same ch sp, ch 3, skip next ch-2 sp, *(cl, ch 3, cl) in next ch-3 sp, ch 3, skip next ch-2 sp; repeat from * around, join (40 ch-3 sps).

Row 11: Working in rows, ch 3, cl in next ch-3 sp, (ch 1, cl in next ch-3 sp) 32 times, dc in next ch-3 sp leaving remaining ch-3 sps unworked, **turn**.

Row 12: Beg cl around dc just made, (ch 1, cl in next ch-1 or ch-3 sp) across, turn (34 cls, 33 ch-1 sps).

Row 13: Ch 3, cl in next ch-1 sp, (ch 1, cl in next ch-1 sp) across to last cl, dc in top of last cl, turn.

Rows 14-18: Repeat rows 12 and 13 alternately, ending with row 12.

NOTE: Ch-6 at beginning of next row counts as first dc and ch-3 sp.

Row 19: Ch 6, dc in next ch-1 sp, (ch 3, dc in next ch-1 sp) across, turn.

Row 20: Sl st in next ch-3 sp, beg cl, ch 3, cl in same sp, *ch 2, (cl, ch 3, cl) in next ch-3 sp; repeat from * across, turn.

Row 21: Sl st in next ch-3 sp, beg cl, ch 3, cl in same sp, *ch 3, sc in next ch-2 sp, ch 3, (cl, ch 3, cl) in next ch-3 sp; repeat from * across, turn.

Rows 22-25: Sl st in first ch-3 sp, ch 1, sc in same sp, (ch 3, sc in next ch-3 sp) across, turn. At end of last row, fasten off.

Weave remaining ribbon through ch-3 sps of row 19. Leave ends long to tie in bow under neck.❖

ANTIMACASSAR SET

Continued from page 140

in next ch lp, sc in next 7 sc, sc in next ch lp, ch 10, skip next 3 dc, dc in next dc), 2 dc in next ch-2 sp, dc in next dc; repeat between ( ) , block, mesh 10 times, turn.

Row 18: Beg mesh, mesh 8 times, block, ch 17, skip next 2 dc, dc in next dc, *3 dc in next ch lp, ch 8, skip next sc, sc in next 7 sc, ch 8, skip next sc, 3 dc in next ch lp, dc in next dc, ch 17, skip next 2 dc, dc in next dc; repeat from *, block, mesh 9 times, turn.

Row 19: Beg mesh, mesh 7 times, block, *(ch 9, sc in next ch lp, ch 9, skip next 3 dc, dc in next dc), 3 dc in next ch lp, ch 8, skip next sc, sc in next 5 sc, ch 8, skip next sc, 3 dc in next ch lp, dc in next dc; repeat from *; repeat between ( ) , block, mesh 8 times, turn.

Row 20: Beg mesh, mesh 6 times, block, *(ch 8, sc in next ch lp, sc in next sc, sc in next ch lp, ch 8, skip next 3 dc, dc in next dc), 3 dc in next ch lp, ch 8, skip next sc, sc in each of next 3 sc, ch 8, skip next sc, 3 dc in next ch lp, dc in next dc; repeat from *; repeat between ( ) , block, mesh 7 times, turn.

Row 21: Beg mesh, block, mesh, block, mesh 2 times, block, *[ch 8, sc in next ch lp, sc in each of next 3 sc, sc in next ch lp, ch 8, skip next 3 dc, dc in next dc], 3 dc in next ch lp, ch 9, skip next sc, sc in next sc, ch 9, skip next sc, 3 dc in next ch lp, dc in next dc; repeat from *; repeat between [ ], block, mesh 2 times, (block, mesh) 2 times, turn.

Row 22: Beg mesh, block, (mesh, block) 2 times, *[ch 8, sc in next ch lp, sc in next 5 sc, sc in next ch lp, ch 8, skip next 3 dc, dc in next dc], 3 dc in next ch lp, ch 2, skip next sc, 3 dc in next ch lp, dc in next dc; repeat from *; repeat between [ ], (block, mesh) 3 times, turn.

Row 23: Beg mesh, (mesh, block) 2 times, *ch 10, sc in next ch lp, sc in next 7 sc, sc in next ch lp, ch 10, skip next 3 dc, dc in next dc, block; repeat from * 2 more times, mesh, block, mesh 2 times, turn.

Row 24: Beg mesh, (block, mesh) 2 times, *[3 dc in next ch lp, ch 8, skip next sc, sc in next 7 sc, ch 8, skip next sc, 3 dc in next ch lp, dc in next dc], ch 17, skip next 2 dc, dc in next dc; repeat from *; repeat between [ ], mesh, (block, mesh) 2 times, turn.

Row 25: Beg mesh, block, mesh, block, mesh 2 times, *[3 dc in next ch lp, ch 8, skip next sc, sc in next 5 sc, ch 8, skip next sc, 3 dc in next ch lp, dc in next dc], ch 9, sc in next ch lp, ch 9, skip next 3 dc, dc in next dc; repeat from *; repeat between [ ], mesh 2 times, (block, mesh) 2 times, turn.

Row 26: Beg mesh, mesh 6 times, *(3 dc in next ch lp, ch 8, skip next sc, sc in each of next 3 sc, ch 8, skip next sc, 3 dc in next ch lp, dc in next dc), ch 8, sc

in next ch lp, sc in next sc, sc in next ch lp, ch 8, skip next 3 dc, dc in next dc; repeat from *; repeat between ( ) , mesh 7 times, turn.

Row 27: Beg mesh, mesh 7 times, *(3 dc in next ch lp, ch 9, skip next sc, sc in next sc, ch 9, skip next sc, 3 dc in next ch lp, dc in next dc), ch 8, sc in next ch lp, sc in each of next 3 sc, sc in next ch lp, ch 8, skip next 3 dc, dc in next dc; repeat from *; repeat between ( ) , mesh 8 times, turn.

Row 28: Beg mesh, mesh 8 times, *(3 dc in next ch lp, ch 2, skip next sc, 3 dc in next ch lp, dc in next dc), ch 8, sc in next ch lp, sc in next 5 sc, sc in next ch lp, ch 8, skip next 3 dc, dc in next dc; repeat from *; repeat between ( ) , mesh 9 times, turn.

Row 29: Beg mesh, mesh 9 times, (block, ch 10, sc in next ch lp, sc in next 7 sc, sc in next ch lp, ch 10, skip next 3 dc, dc in next dc) 2 times, block, mesh 10 times, turn.

Row 30: Beg mesh, mesh 10 times, (3 dc in next ch lp, ch 8, skip next sc, sc in next 7 sc, ch 8, skip next sc, 3 dc in next ch lp, dc in next dc), ch 17, skip next 2 dc, dc in next dc; repeat between ( ) , mesh 11 times, turn.

Row 31: Beg mesh, block, mesh 7 times, block, mesh 2 times, (3 dc in next ch lp, ch 8, skip next sc, sc in next 5 sc, ch 8, skip next sc, 3 dc in next ch lp, dc in next dc), ch 9, sc in next sc, ch 9, skip next 3 dc, dc in next dc; repeat between ( ) , mesh 2 times, block, mesh 7 times, block, mesh, turn.

Row 32: Beg mesh, mesh, block, mesh 6 times, block, mesh 3 times, (3 dc in next ch lp, ch 8, skip next sc, sc in each of next 3 sc, ch 8, skip next sc, 3 dc in next ch lp, dc in next dc), ch 8, sc in next ch lp, sc in next sc, sc in next ch lp, ch 8, skip next 3 dc, dc in next dc; repeat between ( ) , mesh 3 times, block, mesh 6 times, block, mesh 2 times, turn.

Row 33: Beg mesh, mesh, block, mesh 6 times, block, mesh 4 times, (3 dc in next ch lp, ch 9, skip next sc, sc in next sc, ch 9, skip next sc, 3 dc in next ch lp, dc in next dc), ch 8, sc in next ch lp, sc in each of next 3 sc, sc in next ch lp, ch 8, skip next 3 dc, dc in next dc; repeat between ( ) , mesh 4 times, block, mesh 6 times, block, mesh 2 times, turn.

Row 34: Beg mesh, mesh 2 times, block, mesh 5 times, block, mesh 5 times, *3 dc in next ch lp, ch 2, skip next sc, 3 dc in next ch lp, dc in next dc*, ch 8, sc in next ch lp, sc in next 5 sc, sc in next ch lp, ch 8, skip next 3 dc, dc in next dc; repeat between **, (mesh 5 times, block) 2 times, mesh 3 times, turn.

Row 35: Beg mesh, mesh 2 times, block, mesh 5 times, block, mesh 6 times, block, ch 10, sc in next ch lp, sc in next 7 sc, sc in next ch lp, ch 10, skip next 3 dc, dc in next dc, block, mesh 6 times, block, mesh 5 times, block, mesh 3 times, turn.

Row 36: Beg mesh, mesh 3 times, block, mesh 5 times, block 5 times, mesh 2 times, 3 dc in next ch lp, ch 8, skip next sc, sc in next 7 sc, ch 8, skip next sc, 3 dc in next ch lp, dc in next dc, mesh 2 times, block 5 times, mesh 5 times, block, mesh 4 times, turn.

Row 37: Beg mesh, mesh 3 times, block, mesh 13 times, 3 dc in next ch lp, ch 8, skip next sc, sc in next 5 sc, ch 8, skip next sc, 3 dc in next ch lp, dc in next dc, mesh 13 times, block, mesh 4 times, turn.

Row 38: Beg mesh, mesh 3 times, block, mesh 14 times, 3 dc in next ch lp, ch 8, skip next sc, sc in each of next 3 sc, ch 8, skip next sc, 3 dc in next ch lp, dc in next dc, mesh 14 times, block, mesh 4 times, turn.

Row 39: Beg mesh, mesh 3 times, block, mesh 15 times, 3 dc in next ch lp, ch 9, skip next sc, sc in next sc, ch 9, skip next sc, 3 dc in next ch lp, dc in next dc, mesh 15 times, block, mesh 4 times, turn.

Row 40: Beg mesh, mesh 3 times, block, mesh 16 times, 3 dc in next ch lp, ch 2, skip next sc, 3 dc in next ch lp, dc in next dc, mesh 16 times, block, mesh 4 times, turn.

Rows 41-44: Repeat rows 5, 4, 3 and 2.

Row 45: Beg mesh, mesh across, **do not** turn.

Rnd 46: Working around outer edge, ch 1, (2 sc in end of next row or in next ch-2 sp, ch 1) around with (2 sc, ch 1, 2 sc, ch 1, 2 sc, ch 1) in each corner, join with sl st in first sc, fasten off.

LARGE DOILY

Rows 1-40: Repeat same rows of Small Doily.

Rows 41-76: Repeat rows 5-40 of Small Doily.

Rows 77-80: Repeat rows 5, 4, 3 and 2 of Small Doily.

Row 81: Beg mesh, mesh across, **do not** turn.

Rnd 82: Working around outer edge, ch 1, (2 sc in end of next row or in next ch-2 sp, ch 1) around with (2 sc, ch 1, 2 sc, ch 1, 2 sc, ch 1) in each corner, join with sl st in first sc, fasten off.❖

SUMMER FLOWERS
Continued from page 148

right, draw up long lp and place on pin) 3 times, insert hook under all 4 lps on pin, slide lps off pin, yo, draw through all 4 lps, ch 1, (5 sc, picot, 5 sc) in 4-lp group, fasten off]; skip next 5 sts on rnd 2, join green with sl st in next st; repeat from * 2 more times; repeat between [ ], ending with 4 leaves.

Rnd 4: Join green with sl st in **back lp** of 2nd sc on any leaf, ch 4, sl st in top of next picot; to **join,** working in open space between first 4 Motifs, *[work joining picot into joined picots between Motifs (see Assembly Diagram), ch 4, skip next 3 sc on same leaf, sl st in **back lp** of next sc, ch 4, sl st in **back lps** of both of next 2 skipped sts on rnd 2 **at same time** (see illustration below), work joining picot in picot of next free loop on Sunflower Motif, ch 4], skip first sc of next leaf on Filler Motif, sl st in **back lp** of next st, ch 4, sl st in next picot; repeat from * 2 more times; repeat between [ ], join with sl st in first sl st, fasten off.

Repeat Filler Motif 34 more times, filling all spaces between Sunflower Motifs.❖

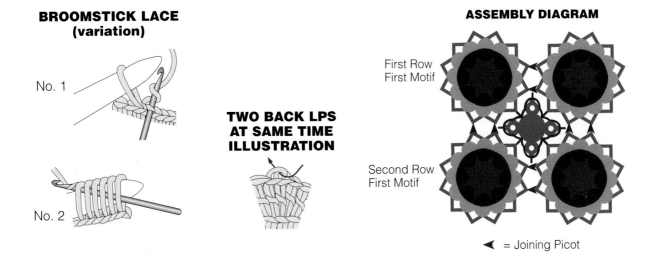

BROOMSTICK LACE
(variation)

No. 1

No. 2

TWO BACK LPS AT SAME TIME ILLUSTRATION

ASSEMBLY DIAGRAM

First Row
First Motif

Second Row
First Motif

◄ = Joining Picot

GETTING STARTED

Yarn & Hooks

Always use the weight of yarn specified in the pattern so you can be assured of achieving the proper gauge. It is best to purchase at least one extra skein of each color needed to allow for differences in tension and dyes.

The hook size stated in the pattern is to be used as a guide. Always work a swatch of the stitch pattern with the suggested hook size. If you find your gauge is smaller or larger than what is specified, choose a different size hook.

Gauge

Gauge is measured by counting the number of rows or stitches per inch. Each of the patterns featured in this book will have a gauge listed. Gauge for some small motifs or flowers is given as an overall measurement. Proper gauge must be attained for the project to come out the size stated, and to prevent ruffling and puckering.

Make a swatch in the stitch indicated in the gauge section of the instructions. Lay the swatch flat and measure the stitches. If you have more stitches per inch than specified in the pattern, your gauge is too tight and you need a larger hook. Fewer stitches per inch indicates a gauge that is too loose. In this case, choose a smaller hook size. Next, check the number of rows. If necessary, adjust your row gauge slightly by pulling the loops down a little tighter on your hook, or by pulling the loops up slightly to extend them.

Once you've attained the proper gauge, you're ready to start your project. Remember to check your gauge periodically to avoid problems later.

Pattern Repeat Symbols

Written crochet instructions typically include symbols such as parentheses, asterisks and brackets. In some patterns a diamond or bullet (dot), may be added.

( ) Parentheses enclose instructions which are to be worked again later or the number of times indicated after the parentheses. For example, "(2 dc in next st, skip next st) 5 times" means to follow the instructions within the parentheses a total of five times. If no number appears after the parentheses, you will be instructed when to repeat further into the pattern. Parentheses may also be used to enclose a group of stitches which should be worked in one space or stitch. For example, "(2 dc, ch 2, 2 dc) in next st" means to work all the stitches within the parentheses in the next stitch.

* Asterisks may be used alone or in pairs, usually in combination with parentheses. If used in pairs, the instructions enclosed within asterisks will be followed by instructions for repeating. These repeat instructions may appear later in the pattern or immediately after the last asterisk. For example, "*Dc in next 4 sts, (2 dc, ch 2, 2 dc) in corner sp*, dc in next 4 sts; repeat between ** 2 more times" means to work through the instructions up to the word "repeat," then repeat only the instructions that are enclosed within the asterisks twice.

If used alone an asterisk marks the beginning of instructions which are to be repeated. Work through the instructions from the beginning, then repeat only the portion after the * up to the word "repeat"; then follow any remaining instructions. If a number of times is given, work through the instructions one time, repeat the number of times stated, then follow the remainder of the instructions.

[ ] Brackets, ◊ diamonds and • bullets are used in the same manner as asterisks. Follow the specific instructions given when repeating.

Finishing

Patterns that require assembly will suggest a tapestry needle in the materials. This should be a #16, #18 or #26 blunt-tipped tapestry needle. When stitching pieces together, be careful to keep the seams flat so pieces do not pucker.

Hiding loose ends is never a fun task, but if done correctly, may mean the difference between an item looking great for years. Always leave 6-8" of yarn when beginning or ending. Thread the loose end into your tapestry needle and carefully weave through the back of several stitches. Then, weave in the opposite direction, going through different strands. Gently pull the end and clip, allowing the end to pull up under the stitches.

If your afghan needs blocking, a light steam pressing works well. Lay your project on a large table or on the floor, depending on the size, shaping and smoothing by hand as much as possible. Adjust your steam iron to the permanent press setting, then hold slightly above the stitches, allowing the steam to penetrate the thread. Do not rest the iron on the item. Gently pull and smooth the stitches into shape, spray lightly with starch, and allow to dry completely.

Stiffening

There are many liquid products on the market made specifically for stiffening doilies and other soft items. For best results, carefully read the manufacturer's instructions on the product you select before beginning.

Forms for shaping can be many things. Styrofoam® shapes and plastic margarine tubs work well for items such as bowls and baskets. Glass or plastic drinking glasses are used for vase-type items. If you cannot find an item with the dimensions given in the pattern to use as a form, any similarly sized item can be shaped by adding layers of plastic wrap. Place the dry crochet pieced over the form to check the fit, remembering that it will stretch when wet.

For shaping flat pieces, corrugated cardboard, Styrofoam® or a cutting board designed for sewing may be used. Be sure to cover all surfaces of forms or blocking board with clear plastic wrap, securing with cellophane tape.

If you have not used fabric stiffener before, you may wish to practice on a small swatch before stiffening the actual item. For proper saturation when using conventional stiffeners, work liquid thoroughly into the crochet piece and let stand for about 15 minutes. Then, squeeze out excess stiffener and blot with paper towels. Continue to blot while shaping to remove as much stiffener as possible. Stretch over form, shape and pin with rust-proof pins; allow to dry, then unpin.

ACKNOWLEDGMENTS

Our sincerest thanks and appreciation goes to the following manufacturers for generously providing their product for use in the following projects:

COATS & CLARK
Floral Pillow............................Red Heart Classic
Peach Headband............................Luster Sheen
Flower Heart Motif....................Knit-Cro-Sheen
Pink & White Afghan......Red Heart Super Saver
Sunflower Afghan............Red Heart Super Saver
Orange Sherbert.....................Baby Red Heart

CARON INTERNATIONAL
Rainbow Baby Set................................Wintuk
Gingham Pullover.....................................Wintuk

SPINRITE
Kitchen Caddy...........................Bernat Berella 4
Country Pot Holders.................Bernat Berella 4
Gold Bow...................................Bernat Berella 4

LION BRAND
Fuzzy Log Cabin Afghan....................Jiffy
Variegated Open Stripes.................Jiffy
Holiday Tweed Runner......................Wool-Ease

Photography Locations & Special Help
Photography locations: James and Mary Barnett, Arp; Harrel and Mataline Broach, Mt. Pleasant; Craig and Jan Jaynes, Kilgore; Gary and Pat Jernigan, Arp; Gladys Large, Overton; Terry and Jill Waggoner, Overton.
Models: Misses Hannah and Savannah Waggoner (cover), Mataline Broach, Betty Jo Bessonett, Mason B. Cook, Gracie Farrow, Pat Jernigan, Tanya Kingsepp, Doris Leak, Gladys Large, Mallory Mazarakes, Tommy Oglesby, Jana Robertson, Clayton Taylor, Jeanne Taylor, Brenda Wendling.

STITCH GUIDE

BASIC STITCHES

Front Loop (A)/Back Loop (B)
(front lp/back lp)

Chain *(ch)*

Yo, draw hook through lp.

Slip Stitch *(sl st)*

Insert hook in st, yo, draw through st and lp on hook.

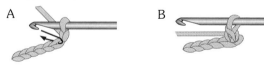

Single Crochet *(sc)*

Insert hook in st (A), yo, draw lp through, yo, draw through both lps on hook (B).

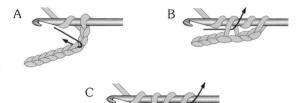

Half Double Crochet *(hdc)*

Yo, insert hook in st (A), yo, draw lp through (B), yo, draw through all 3 lps on hook (C).

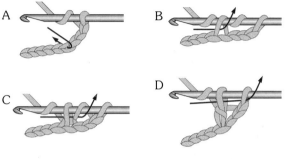

Double Crochet *(dc)*

Yo, insert hook in st (A), yo, draw lp through (B), (yo, draw through 2 lps on hook) 2 times (C and D).

Treble Crochet *(tr)*

Yo 2 times, insert hook in st, yo, draw lp through, (yo, draw through 2 lps on hook) 3 times.

Final Step

Double Treble Crochet *(dtr)*

Yo 3 times, insert hook in st, yo, draw lp through, (yo, draw through 2 lps on hook) 4 times.

Final Step

Standard Stitch Abbreviations

ch(s)	chain(s)
dc	double crochet
dtr	double treble crochet
hdc	half double crochet
lp(s)	loop(s)
rnd(s)	round(s)
sc	single crochet
sl st	slip stitch
sp(s)	space(s)
st(s)	stitch(es)
tog	together
tr	treble crochet
tr tr	triple treble crochet
yo	yarn over

Triple Treble Crochet (ttr)

Yo 4 times, insert hook in st, yo, draw lp through, (yo, draw through 2 lps on hook) 5 times.

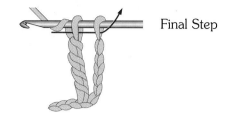

Final Step

SPECIAL STITCHES

Front Post/Back Post Stitches (fp/bp)

Yo, insert hook from front to back (A) or back to front (B) around post of st on indicated row; complete as stated in pattern.

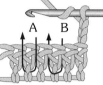

Reverse Single Crochet (reverse sc)

Working from left to right, insert hook in next st to the right (A), yo, draw through st, complete as sc (B).

Love Knot

Completed Love Knot

Satin Stitch

French Knot

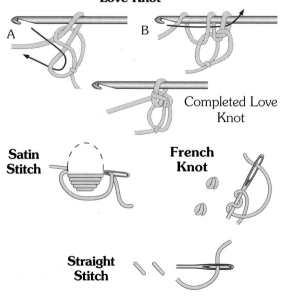

Straight Stitch

CHANGING COLORS

Single Crochet Color Change (sc color change)

Drop first color; yo with 2nd color, draw through last 2 lps of st.

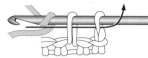

Double Crochet Color Change (dc color change)

Drop first color; yo with 2nd color, draw through last 2 lps of st.

DECREASING

Single Crochet next 2 stitches together (sc next 2 sts tog)

Draw up lp in each of next 2 sts, yo, draw through all 3 lps on hook.

Half Double Crochet next 2 stitches together (hdc next 2 sts tog)

(Yo, insert hook in next st, yo, draw lp through) 2 times, yo, draw through all 5 lps on hook.

Double Crochet next 2 stitches together (dc next 2 sts tog)

(Yo, insert hook in next st, yo, draw lp through, yo, draw through 2 lps on hook) 2 times, yo, draw through all 3 lps on hook.

INDEX